A Guide to the 2002 Revision of the American Psychological Association's Ethics Code

Samuel Knapp, EdD
and
Leon VandeCreek, PhD, ABPP

Professional Resource Press
Sarasota, Florida

Published by
Professional Resource Press
(An imprint of the Professional Resource Exchange, Inc.)
Post Office Box 15560
Sarasota, FL 34277-1560

Printed in the United States of America

This publication is sold with the understanding that the publisher is not engaged in rendering professional services. If legal, psychological, medical, accounting, or other expert advice or assistance is sought or required, the reader should seek the services of a competent professional.

The copy editor for this book was David Anson, the managing editor was Debbie Fink, the production coordinator was Laurie Girsch, and the cover designer was Jami Stinnet.

Library of Congress Cataloging-in-Publication Data

Knapp, Samuel.
    A guide to the 2002 revision of the American Psychological Association's ethics code / Samuel Knapp and Leon VandeCreek.
      p. cm.
    Includes bibliographical references and index.
    ISBN 1-56887-079-5 (alk. paper)
    1. Psychologists--Professional ethics--United States. 2. Psychology--Standards--United States. I. VandeCreek, Leon. II. American Psychological Association. III. Title.

BF76.4 .K63 2003
174'.915--dc21

2002036985

 **DEDICATION**

To Michelle Lynn Dietrich and Valerie Rose Dietrich

Samuel Knapp

To Barbara VandeCreek

Leon VandeCreek

TABLE OF CONTENTS

Chapter 5: Enforceable Ethical Standards *(Continued)*

Chapter 5: Enforceable Ethical Standards *(Continued)*

Chapter 5: Enforceable Ethical Standards *(Continued)*

Chapter 5: Enforceable Ethical Standards *(Continued)*

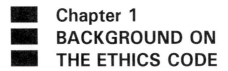

Chapter 1
BACKGROUND ON
THE ETHICS CODE

In August 2002, the American Psychological Association (APA) Council of Representatives voted to adopt a new code of ethics for its members *(Ethical Principles of Psychologists and Code of Conduct)*. This was the 10th ethics code adopted by the American Psychological Association (the previous codes were adopted in 1953, 1959, 1963, 1968, 1977, 1979, 1981, 1990, and 1992).

This book reviews the contents of the 2002 *Ethical Principles of Psychologists and Code of Conduct* (hereafter referred to as the Ethics Code), expands on the meaning of specific standards, and discusses their applicability to the professional lives of psychologists. Before doing so, however, we will review the role of ethics codes in regulating the profession and science of psychology, the process of this Ethics Code revision, and the criteria used in adopting standards.

THE REGULATION OF PSYCHOLOGY

An ethics code is a hallmark of a scientific discipline and a profession. Although conventional speakers may use the term "profession" loosely to refer to any occupation, it traditionally has been restricted to occupations that require its members to (a) have mastered a considerable body of specialized knowledge, (b) use judgment to apply that knowledge (as opposed to using simple algorithms or predetermined formulas), and (c) demonstrate a commitment to public welfare (as articulated in a set of standards such as a code of ethics).

According to this definition, physicians belong to a profession because they must acquire extensive medical training to enter the field, use judgment in the choice of treatment for their patients, and demonstrate commitment to patient welfare. A medical clerk, however, does not need extensive education, applies knowledge in a predetermined and often routine fashion, and would not be considered a professional.

Historically nursing has not been considered a profession because nurses traditionally have acted under the close supervision of physicians and therefore were not permitted to exercise their full professional judgment. However, recent revisions to the nurse practice laws in some states have given advance practice nurses greater autonomy, and it could be argued that they are now professionals.

Psychology is a profession and, as such, has a code of ethics to guide its members. The APA adopted the first code of ethics for psychologists in 1953 or about the time that the movement for licensing psychologists as an independent profession started to gain momentum.

Psychology is also an academic and research discipline that has a body of knowledge based on the scientific method. As practitioners in an academic discipline, psychologists train future psychologists and teach courses as part of a general education requirement for a liberal arts degree or as specialty courses for other disciplines such as teaching, nursing, business, and social work. As a research discipline, psychology conducts research and applies psychological knowledge and methods to problems in business, industry, and government. At one time, academic and research ethics received little attention. However, as more attention has been given to the rights of students and research participants, the discipline has established ethical standards to guide teachers and researchers.

Another essential feature of a profession is that it is self-correcting. It has mechanisms in place that attempt to ensure that only well-qualified persons enter the profession and that members who fail to abide by the standards of the profession will be sanctioned or removed from membership in the profession.

In addition to being guided by an ethics code, psychologists, like all health care professionals, are regulated by many other controls, some of them originating within the profession and others enforced from outside the profession. Some of these controls are established to educate and prevent psychologists from harming their clients/patients and from violating the ethics code and other standards. Other controls function to discipline psychologists after they have violated standards or harmed clients/patients. We describe these means of control as before-the-fact controls (training programs, licensing requirements, and mandatory continuing education) and after-the-fact controls (disciplinary actions by licensing boards and ethics committees, various civil and criminal statutes that allow suits against psychologists, and, if applicable, funding sources and institutional employers).

Before-the-Fact Controls

Before-the-fact controls attempt to regulate the profession before any misconduct or harm to the public has occurred. Before-the-fact controls are preferred because they have the potential to prevent harm.

Training programs select candidates who have adequate academic credentials and make progress in graduate school, including acceptable performance in practica and internships. Presumably the training programs screen out applicants who do not demonstrate the skills to become competent psychologists. Johnson and Campbell (2002) note that two of the essential ingredients for being an effective psychologist are character (virtue) and fitness (psychological soundness).

Licensing boards also establish minimum standards. For entry into the profession, applicants must demonstrate that they have successfully completed a course of academic training; shown acceptable moral character; and passed examinations on the content of psychology (all states and provinces now require the Examination for Professional Practice of Psychology), on state jurisprudence (sometimes), and an oral examination (sometimes). Furthermore, most state boards of psychology require continuing education as a condition of licensure renewal and many require ethics as part of that continuing education requirement.

After-the-Fact Controls

After-the-fact controls attempt to regulate the profession after misconduct or harm to the public has occurred. Licensing boards may discipline or fine licensees and limit or prohibit them from practicing their profession when the boards determine that the psychologist has violated the regulations or licensing law. Typically licensing boards adopt the APA Ethics Code or a variation of it. Licensing boards only have jurisdiction over psychologists who have a license to practice in that state.

APA and most state psychological associations have adopted the APA Ethics Code as binding on its members. The ethics committees of APA and its state affiliates may discipline members who violate that Code. Associations have jurisdiction only over their members. They can issue letters of reprimand or censure, or, if the offense is especially severe, they can suspend or expel a member from their association.

Malpractice refers to the omission or commission of acts conducted in the context of a professional relationship that deviated from acceptable standards of care and directly harmed the client/patient. Behaviors that violate the Ethics Code almost always fall below the minimal standard of care. Unlike complainants in an ethics board or licensing board complaint, however, plaintiffs in a malpractice suit must prove not only that the standard of care was unacceptable but also that the client/patient was harmed. In contrast, in ethics committee or licensing board cases, the complainant only needs to convince the committee or board that the ethics code, licensing law, or board regulation was violated. Harm to the client/patient does not need to be demonstrated. Also, unlike ethics committees and licensing boards, malpractice courts may grant monetary awards against the psychologist if found guilty.

Psychologists could also receive criminal penalties for violating a variety of criminal laws that apply to psychologists, such as the mandatory reporting provisions in child protective service laws, laws against insurance fraud, or, in some states, statutes that criminalize sexual contact between clients/patients and psychotherapists.

Finally, institutions such as hospitals, schools, public mental health centers, and managed care companies oversee the psychologists whom they employ or with whom they have contracts. Often these organizations require adherence to the APA Ethics Code as a condition of employment and may dismiss psychologists for violating it. Consequently, the Ethics Code has influence on psychologists far beyond just the enforcement powers of the APA Ethics Committee.

In a manner similar to their professional colleagues, academic and research psychologists have before-the-fact (training program and institutional review boards) and after-the-fact controls (ethics committee and institutional employers or funding agencies).

The demarcation between the before-the-fact and the after-the-fact controls is not absolute. For example, the mere knowledge of after-the-fact controls can act as a before-the-fact control and deter misconduct.

PURPOSE OF ETHICS CODES

The APA Ethics Code establishes minimum standards for the conduct of psychologists. Like the ethics codes of other professional associations, its content is determined by a mixture of motives including concern for public welfare, protection of the profession, public relations, and a vehicle for educating its members.

The APA Ethics Code represents a "contract" or promise between the profession and society and includes the obligations incumbent upon all the members of the profession. Like the codes of other professional associations, it is based on the "consensus paradigm," meaning that it validates the most recent views of a majority of the APA Council of Representatives about ethical issues. Expressed another way, psychology has established the standards that it expects of itself.

The role of the Ethics Code in protecting the profession should not be overlooked. The desire of psychologists to protect themselves is not necessarily immoral or anticonsumer. The Ethics Code establishes boundaries of acceptable behavior. It benefits neither the profession nor the public when a client/patient, student, or research subject files a frivolous and time-consuming ethics complaint against a psychologist. Self-protection only becomes ethically unjustifiable when it is done at the cost of consumer protection.

Although it is a disciplinary document, the Ethics Code also has an educational function. The fact that the Ethics Code is used to discipline psychologists means that psychologists are more likely to read it and teachers are more likely to teach it.

**Aspirational Ethics, Enforceable Standards,
Guidelines, and Policy Statements**

The 2002 Ethics Code contains the same structure as the 1992 Ethics Code in that it separates the aspirational principles (General Principles) from enforceable standards (Code of Conduct). The aspirational principles encourage psychologists to perform at their highest level of professional skill. In addition, psychologists can use the aspirational principles to help them make decisions in those gray situations where standards of the Code of Conduct require psychologists to apply their judgment. However, psychologists should not be disciplined only because they failed to uphold any one of the aspirational ethics.

Similar to the 1992 Code, the 2002 Code of Conduct portion of the Ethics Code includes the standards under which psychologists may be disciplined. Standards are statements that specifically prohibit certain conduct. They form the basis of the enforcement powers of the APA Ethics Committee. The separation of the Ethics Code into aspirational principles and enforceable standards eliminates the confusion that occurred when they were mixed together (as was the case in the pre-1992 Ethics Codes). The problem at that time was so severe that a North Carolina court ruled that the Code of Ethics of the North Carolina psychology licensing board (based on the APA Code of Conduct) was unconstitutionally vague (*White v. North Carolina*, 1990).

The standards of the Ethics Code are distinct from guidelines which are, from time to time, approved by the APA Council of Representatives and are intended to guide psychologists about proper conduct in certain practice areas (e.g., child custody evaluations, assessment of dementia, services to linguistic or cultural minorities, etc.; a complete list of APA guidelines can be found in Appendix A, p. 191). Guidelines suggest or recommend specific conduct and often provide practical advice on how to apply the Ethics Code. For example, the APA Ethics Code states that psychologists should ordinarily avoid multiple relationships that could harm clients/patients. The APA Guidelines for Child Custody Evaluations in Divorce Procedures applies this standard to child custody evaluations and notes that psychologists should generally avoid conducting therapy with persons with whom they have previously conducted custody evaluations.

The APA Ethics Committee produces policy statements that are designed to give general instructions on the ethical standards that the Committee would apply when dealing with a specific content area such as telehealth or take home psychological tests. Policy statements are not based on an actual case or factual situation but are reasoned comments on an issue that could potentially come to the attention of the Ethics Committee. As of the writing of this book, all of the policies of the Ethics Committee are based on the 1992 Ethics Code. They should be interpreted only in light of the changes made to that Code. A complete listing of Ethics Policy Statements can be found in Appendix B (p. 193). The distinctions between the Ethics Code, APA Guidelines, and Ethics Committee Policy Statements are summarized in Table 1 (below).

Table 1: Aspirational Principles, Standards, Guidelines, and Policies

---

Dimensions	*Aspirational Principles*	*Standards*	*Guidelines*	*Policies*
Source	APA Council of Reps.	APA Council of Reps.	APA Council of Reps.	APA Ethics Committee
Covers	All Psychologists	All Psychologists	Specific Content Areas	Specific Areas
Goal	Inspire and Guide	Discipline	Recommend	Alert
Enforceable	No	Yes	No	No

Limitations of Ethics Codes

Ethics Codes of professions are, by their very nature, incomplete moral codes. "Shared duties form the backbone of professional ethics, but a backbone is not a complete anatomy" (M. Martin, 2000, p. 4). The APA Ethics Code contains standards by which to discipline psychologists but provide little guidance for those who aspire to be the best that they can be. Consequently, the APA Ethics Code should not be viewed as the sum total of all that is known or worth knowing about ethical conduct.

The day-to-day ethical concerns of psychologists involve many more situations than just those identified in the APA Ethics Code. This focus on ethics beyond those found in disciplinary codes has been called positive ethics. The goal of positive ethics is to shift the ethical discussions of psychologists from an almost exclusive focus on wrong doing and disciplinary responses to a more balanced focus that encourages psychologists to aspire to their highest ethical potential and to integrate the ethics from their personal and professional lives (Handelsman, Knapp, & Gottlieb, 2002).

To a certain extent, positive ethics overlaps with aspirational ethics in that both encourage psychologists to perform their professional roles to the best of their abilities, assist them in identifying supererogatory duties (ethical duties that go beyond the minimal floor found in the Ethics Code), and can be used as a guide to ethical decision making. However, positive ethics differs from aspirational ethics in two ways: First, it encourages psychologists to integrate personal and professional ethics. That is, the fundamental principles of ethical conduct that guide their personal lives are the same that guide their professional conduct. Second, positive ethics may lead some to seek an ethical foundation other than the principle-based one found in the aspirational section of the Ethics Code. For example, many North American psychologists base their ethical conduct on religious principles derived from the Judeo-Christian tradition. Others have sought to incorporate recent philosophical traditions or the ethical traditions of other religious systems into their belief systems (Handelsman et al., 2002).

Positive ethics is not opposed to disciplinary codes, but rather sees them as one component of the overall ethical life of psychologists. In other words, disciplinary codes are necessary but not sufficient to function at one's fullest ethical capacity.

APA ETHICS CODE REVISION PROCESS

The revision of the APA Ethics Code took almost 4 years. Although the APA Council of Representatives approved the final document, the Ethics Committee Task Force (ECTF) did most of the background work. Dr. Celia Fisher, Professor of Psychology at Fordham University and well-respected researcher and author on ethics, chaired the Ethics Committee Task Force. The Task Force included representatives from the American Psychological Association Graduate Students (APAGS), the APA Council of Representatives, the APA Board of Directors, the APA Ethics Committee, and other constituencies. The composition of the ECTF represented the ethnic and professional diversity within the discipline. In addition, observers from various APA constituencies attended ECTF meetings and participated in the discussions.

Climate of the Revision Process

The revision process took place in an atmosphere of increasing worry and anxiety among psychologists about the disciplinary process. In addition to its use by the APA Ethics Office, the Ethics Code has also been used by state psychological associations, licensing boards, malpractice courts, and institutional employers to evaluate the conduct of psychologists. Although only a small fraction of psychologists actually face disciplinary action by one of these groups, the fear of being the target of such an action has had a chilling effect on many psychologists.

Psychologists feared that a minor infraction or even the allegation of an infraction could cost them employment, cause them to be dropped from a managed care panel, or otherwise harm them professionally and cause personal embarrassment. Rightly or wrongly, some psychologists viewed the Ethics Code as an antipsychology document that disgruntled students, research subjects, clients/patients, or colleagues could use to intimidate or threaten them for frivolous or technical violations.

In addition, the revision of the Ethics Code took place at the same time that APA was debating the function of its Ethics Committee. Some wanted to remove APA from adjudicating ethics complaints; others wanted to retain that function. Although the functioning of the APA Ethics Office is distinct from the content of the Ethics Code, the convergence of these issues led some psychologists to reexamine the role of ethics for APA.

Sources of Data

The major source of the 2002 Ethics Code was the 1992 Ethics Code. As a general rule the ECTF deferred to the standard in the 1992 Ethics

Code unless there was a compelling reason to change it ("If it ain't broke, don't fix it"). That is, if the experience of psychologists has not revealed a problem with a standard, then the threshold for altering it needed to be high.

The 2002 Ethics Code has the same fundamental structure as the 1992 Ethics Code. It contains an introduction/preamble, the aspirational statements, and the enforceable standards. Many of the enforceable standards in the 1992 Ethics Code were retained verbatim or with little modification.

One way to determine if the wording of the standards in the 1992 Code created problems was to look at the standards under which psychologists were commonly charged by the APA Ethics Office and state and provincial licensing boards. The goal was to determine if the wording in the present standards allowed especially egregious conduct to go unpunished, failed to reflect the intent of the Ethics Code, or placed an unnecessary burden upon psychologists.

Also, the ECTF tried to address ethics issues if evidence showed that psychologists were concerned about them. To that end, the ECTF solicited descriptions of critical incidents in ethics from APA members. This allowed psychologists to identify the situations that provided the ethical tugs for them and captured the essence of what occurs in day-to-day practice.

Thereafter, the ECTF continued to seek input from state and provincial psychological associations, divisions, and individual APA members. The ECTF placed articles in the *APA Monitor* (Clay, 2000; S. Martin, 1999) asking for comments. In addition, the ECTF held open presentations during the APA Conventions in 1999, 2000, and 2001 and gave numerous presentations and held discussions with divisions and other specialty constituencies within APA. Altogether the ECTF received more than 500 comments from APA members, divisions, or other affiliated organizations. Also, the ECTF studied the ethics codes of other psychology organizations (Association of State and Provincial Psychology Boards, Canadian Psychological Association, National Association of School Psychologists) and other mental health professions (social work, psychiatry, counseling, marriage and family therapy, etc.).

In addition, the ECTF reviewed surveys of psychologists concerning the ethical issues that they confront most often in their careers (Fly et al., 1997; Haas, Malouf, & Mayerson, 1986; Jacob-Timm, 1999; Pope, Tabachnick, & Keith-Spiegel, 1987; Pope & Vetter, 1992; Tryon, 2001; Tubbs & Pomerantz, 2001). The ECTF also reviewed the scholarly literature on ethics in psychology. Many members of the ECTF had contributed to that literature.

Furthermore, ECTF members relied on their own experiences as well as those of the APA Ethics Committee and Board of Directors. Finally, the APA Council of Representatives reviewed the document.

Criteria for Changing the Code

For each change considered, the ECTF asked several questions: Would the proposed change significantly improve the value of the Ethics Code? Would it increase its enforceability? Would it enhance fairness? Would the proposed change result in an arbitrary or capricious rule? Would it increase positive personal conduct on the part of psychologists? Should it be a standard or a guideline? Should it be in the aspirational section or the enforceable code? Is it understandable? That is, would the proposed change clarify or obfuscate the obligations of psychologists? Does it meet the needs of a diverse population of psychologists? Does each standard address only one enforceable issue?

The ECTF looked at the standards with reference to institutional racism and other historical or current forms of disempowerment. Specifically, the ECTF tried to identify situations that were characterized by past or present misuse or neglect by psychologists and attempted to view the standard from the perspective of disempowered or disenfranchised group members.

Furthermore, the ECTF tried to ensure that the standards would be consistent with federal laws (such as antitrust laws) and APA's public policy without placing undue burdens on psychologists.

Finally, all the standards were reviewed from the standpoint of general ethical principles (Beneficence and Nonmaleficence; Fidelity and Responsibility; Integrity; Justice; and Respect for People's Rights and Dignity). The goal was to ensure that each standard could be justified from the standpoint of reliance on one or more of these general ethical principles.

Format for the Standards

The ECTF focused on brevity and clarity in writing the standards and used modifiers and obligatory verbs carefully. Also, it was deliberate in its use of definitions and "objective obligations." Understanding these factors may help psychologists to better understand and interpret Standards in the Ethics Code.

Brevity. All things being equal, the ECTF tried to shorten the Ethics Code. Each new standard placed a new burden on psychologists to learn.

In the ideal world, the mandatory obligations of psychologists could be reduced into an easy-to-remember paragraph or list of 10 or 12 statements. Unfortunately, the profession of psychology and the scientific discipline of psychology are too complex to permit such an abbreviated code. Nonetheless, ECTF strived for brevity by writing the standards to apply to psychologists in many different roles, reducing redundancy, and using cross references ("see also" statements) whenever they appeared helpful.

Clarity. The ECTF also tried to reduce unnecessary vagueness. It took the position that psychologists should only be punished on the basis of standards that they could reasonably be expected to understand. The standard should not leave too much to the interpretation of individual psychologists and other bodies such as licensure boards and courts when its intent was not obvious.

Use of Modifiers. Modifiers (such as "reasonably," "appropriately," "potentially," etc.) were used if they allowed professional or scientific judgment on the part of the psychologist or eliminated the injustice or the inequality that would occur if the standard lacked the modifier. These modifiers reflect the recognition that many ethical situations need to be evaluated in light of their unique facts. The ECTF recognized that the standards do not negate the responsibility of psychologists to make some decisions by considering many factors and competing concerns.

For example, Standard 2.05 requires psychologists to "take reasonable steps" to ensure that their supervisees can perform their assigned tasks competently. However, what constitutes a "reasonable step" depends on the circumstances. If clients/patients do not already have an interpreter, then psychologists may identify consulting services for interpreters that are found in most cities. However, it may be difficult, if not impossible, to find interpreters for clients/patients in rural areas or for clients/patients who speak uncommon languages. It would not be a "reasonable step" for psychologists or clients/patients to delay treatment or exhaust themselves in a search for an interpreter that holds little promise of success. In those situations, the psychologist may have to communicate with the client/patient in English, use an untrained interpreter, such as a neighbor or relative, or deny care.

Obligatory Verbs. The word "must" was used carefully. "Must" is an absolute word and conveys that psychologists who fail to act in such a manner are in violation of the Ethics Code. On the other hand, words like "strive," or "seek" only indicate that an effort should be made.

For example, Standard 2.04 states that "Psychologists' work is based upon established scientific and professional knowledge of the discipline." The standard is absolute and leaves no room for discretion on the part of the psychologist.

Definitions. Generally the Ethics Code relies on the plain and ordinary meaning of words. However, the Ethics Code sometimes expands or clarifies the plain and ordinary meaning. Reasonable is defined in the Introduction and Applicability section, sexual harassment is defined in Standard 3.02, multiple relationships in 3.05a, public statements in 5.01a, barter in 6.05, test data in 9.04a, and test materials in 9.11. These definitions are found in Appendix C (pp. 195-196).

Objectivity of Obligations. For the most part, the standards of conduct in the Ethics Code are objective. That is, the obligations of psychologists are unconditional and cannot be modified depending on the circumstances. For example, Standard 3.01 prohibits psychologists from engaging in unfair discrimination. There are no qualifiers for this standard or situations where, based on the judgment of the psychologist, it can be ethically acceptable.

In other situations, psychologists need to use their professional judgment to determine the "reasonable" course of action. For example, Standard 1.03 requires psychologists to resolve, "to the extent feasible," institutional or organizational policies that conflict with the Ethics Code. Such steps depend upon the circumstances, such as the institutional opportunities for redress, the personalities of the decision makers, the potential for harm to clients/patients, or the potential for retaliation for the psychologist. It would be impossible for an ethics code to proscribe the actions to take in all situations. The general standard that psychologists should follow is that of a "reasonable psychologist."

Finally, in a few standards the obligations of psychologists depend upon their knowledge of the problem. For example, psychologists are obligated to take action to correct misrepresentations of their work when they know about it (Standard 1.01), seek resolutions of misconduct by other psychologists when they learn of the harm (Standard 1.04), and seek to assist participants who are harmed by an experiment, when the psychologists learn about it (Standard 8.08c). They do not knowingly engage in behavior that is harassing or demeaning to those with whom they work (3.03). It would not be appropriate for psychologists to be held responsible for ethical problems which were outside their awareness.

ETHICAL ISSUES THAT
ARE NOT IN THE ETHICS CODE

Some critics complained that the Ethics Code ignored many legitimate issues. Some wanted to modify the Code of Conduct so that it would govern the operations of the APA Ethics Office, would sanction the personal behavior of psychologists, address important public policy issues, guide psychologists in specialty or emerging areas, and/or recommend a decision-making model.

Procedures of the APA Ethics Office

Some commentators to the Ethics Code wanted to modify the manner in which the APA Ethics Office conducted its business. However, the functioning of the APA Ethics Office is determined by its Rules and Procedures which specify the steps that must be taken when a complaint is filed, the disciplinary options available to the Ethics Committee, the appeal process, and other details.

The APA Ethics Code is entirely separate from the Rules and Procedures that guide the deliberations of the Ethics Office and the APA Ethics Committee. The Ethics Code deals with the "what" of the adjudication process. The Rules and Procedures deal with the "how" of the adjudication process.

Personal Conduct

The Ethics Code does not regulate the private behavior of psychologists. As stated in the Introduction and Applicability section

> This Ethics Code applies only to psychologists' activities that are part of their scientific, educational, or professional roles as psychologists.... These activities shall be distinguished from the purely private conduct of psychologists, which is not within the purview of the Ethics Code.

One might ask, "Does APA condone extramarital affairs, sexual harassment of restaurant employees, or retail theft?" The answer is that APA does not perceive itself as having the authority to regulate the personal behavior of psychologists.

The distinction between personal and professional behavior is usually clear cut, but sometimes gray. It may not always be clear, for example, when a psychologist who is president of a large university or who participates in a self-help group is acting as a psychologist. In these situations much depends on the context and the manner in which the behavior occurs. The question is whether a reasonable person would construe the actions of the psychologist to be personal or professional. A psychologist at a party who merely makes an offhand comment that "You ought to ditch the bum" would reasonably be construed as making a personal comment. On the other hand, at the same party if the psychologist spoke with the individual alone, asked questions similar to the kinds that would be expected in a typical psychotherapy interview, claimed that she was speaking authoritatively as a psychologist, and said, "You ought to ditch the bum," then the opinion begins to sound more like a professional comment than a personal one.

This does not mean that psychologists should be oblivious to the impact of their personal lives on the public image of psychology. For example, one psychologist had an extramarital affair with a local high school coach which became somewhat of a local scandal. Another psychologist was fined for speeding twice within the same week. Although these acts were entirely within the realm of personal conduct, they could have implications for the psychologist's own professional practice as well as the public perception of psychologists as a whole.

Policy Issues

Some important ethical areas are best addressed through public policy activities as opposed to standards in the Ethics Code. One example is the practice of some psychologists to sell their research expertise on social influence to companies who intend to persuade children to purchase useless or harmful items such as expensive action toys or nutrition poor sugary cereals (Kanner, 2000). This practice raises serious ethical issues but not necessarily those that should be placed in an enforceable section of the Ethics Code.

There is a legitimate social problem of advertisers manipulating children to purchase (or nag their parents into purchasing) useless or harmful products. However, a standard in the Ethics Code forbidding psychologists to participate in child advertising research for exploitative companies might not achieve the desired results.

First, some of the information on child advertising is in the public domain, and many nonpsychologists can educate themselves in the literature and provide much of the same information as psychologists. Forbidding psychologists to disseminate this information will not make it go away and will not eliminate the methodological designs that allow for the creation of new information.

Furthermore, it can be difficult to determine which products are harmful, frivolous, or innocuous. For example, the enforcement of this rule might require the APA Ethics Committee to determine how much sugar a cereal should have before promoting it becomes unethical or how many accessories an action figure should have before it is deemed too aggressive for children. We all drive cars, but would it be an ethical violation for psychologists to use their research skills to encourage consumers to buy a $20,000 car with some safety features as opposed to a $14,000 car with just the basics? Where do we draw the line? How can APA be expected to decide whether the safety features are legitimately worth $6,000 or constitute a marketing technique designed to exploit the fears of consumers?

Finally, there is a problem of setting limits on the logical extension of these rules. Should the Ethics Code go further and place an affirmative duty on professional psychologists to warn parents about the effect of these cereals or action toys? Should psychologists who fail to give such warnings to parents, or who fail to give such warnings with a sufficient emphasis, similarly be disciplined?

APA can address this problem in ways other than disciplining psychologists who violate a standard. It may decide to develop a position paper or resolution warning against the potential abuses and disseminate it to parents or child advocacy groups, comment to the Federal Trade Commission (FTC), appeal to the industries directly, or some combination of all of these strategies.

Policy issues also arise around managed care. Some psychologists wanted to make participation in any capitation agreement or in any utilization review process an ethical violation. Such arguments ignore the fact that some ethical psychologists working within managed care systems are trying to make them more responsive to the needs of clients/patients. Other psychologists are trying to form their own patient-sensitive managed care systems. Furthermore, elements of managed care, such as capitation and utilization review, have long been components of many publicly funded mental health systems. It would not be desirable to make the practice of psychology within public mental health systems inherently unethical. Finally, although capitation and utilization review have been abused by some managed care companies, these practices might not be inherently harmful. Honest and public spirited debates are ongoing as to whether or how they can be part of a compassionate and fair health care system.

Specialty Areas

Finally, some psychologists complained that their particular area of interest did not receive appropriate attention in the Ethics Code. Some marriage and family therapists, for example, complained that few, if any, standards specifically mention marriage and family therapy. However, the ECTF intended to make each standard as generic as possible. Consequently, any standard dealing with counseling or therapy should be applicable to marriage and family therapy as well.

It could be argued that these general standards fail to address many nuances or subtle ethical considerations in marriage and family therapy. That concern is legitimate and points to one limit of the Ethics Code. The standards in the Ethics Code are designed only to address egregious misconduct. Psychologists who wish to perform at a higher level of skill need to supplement their ethics education with sources beyond the Ethics Code.

Similarly, the Ethics Code contains no special section for group therapy, neuropsychology, psychoanalysis, or other specialties of psychology, except for forensic psychology. There are no special sections on telemedicine, internet, or other therapies using electronic technologies. These kinds of electronic interventions present unique problems in that we do not know how they will evolve in future years. An Ethics Code that is too specific may become obsolete in light of technological developments. In the interim psychologists can consult commentaries found in the professional literature.

Decision-Making Models

The Ethics Code does not attempt to serve as a compendium of all possible ethics questions and answers. Rather, it provides aspirational principles and standards for the most common quandaries that arise for psychologists and then exhorts psychologists to exercise judgment in applying the Ethics Codes to other particular situations. The Ethics Code does not prescribe a particular ethical decision-making model for this purpose, unlike the code of ethics of the Canadian Psychological Association, which does. The APA Ethics Code, however, does refer to the need for psychologists to follow a thoughtful process in making decisions about ethical questions, and it identifies the aspirational principles as a source to use for such decision making. For example, the Introduction and Applicability section of the Ethics Code instructs psychologists to "consider other materials and guidelines that have been adopted or endorsed by scientific and professional psychological organizations and the dictates of their own conscience, as well as consult with others within the field."

Psychologists are expected to exercise sound decision-making skills in several predictable situations, such as (a) when working in areas in which the standards use modifiers such as "reasonable," "foreseeable," and so on; (b) when ethical or legal codes are silent about an issue (such as once occurred with the development of the delivery of health care through electronic means or will occur as new modes of transmitting knowledge electronically develop); (c) when organizational or legal demands conflict with the Ethics Code; and (d) when integrating one's own personal ethical positions with those of the Ethics Code.

While the APA Ethics Code does not provide readers with a decision-making model, several authors have recommended models that psychologists can use. Rather than propose yet another model, we summarize here the highlights of four models that have received careful attention in the literature (Canadian Psychological Association, 1991; Haas & Malouf, 2002; Kitchener, 2000; Koocher & Keith-Spiegel, 1998).

We include the specific steps in the four popular models in Table 2 (p. 18). In order to compare these models, we have abbreviated the descriptions of the steps. They generally are far more sophisticated and helpful than is apparent in the table. A careful review of the four models suggests that five steps are common across most of the models. The common five steps are (a) identification of the problem, (b) development of alternatives, (c) evaluation of alternatives, (d) implementation of the best option, and (e) evaluation of the results. Table 2 includes the steps of each model and our estimate of a match with one of the five steps listed here.

The five-step process is helpful, but it is somewhat limited when it comes to the real world of making ethical decisions. The shortcomings of these models are that they do not systematically require psychologists to consider the emotional or situational factors affecting the decision and they presume that psychologists will have time to reflect upon the ethical problem.

Consider Emotional and Situational Factors. We suggest that psychologists supplement these cognitive-based decision-making models by considering the emotional and situational factors that influence their decisions. Any psychologist, given the right set of circumstances, could make an ethical mistake. Two factors that are associated with many ethical mistakes include professional isolation and working during periods of intense personal distress. Ethical decision making can be improved when psychologists engage in self-care activities and become aware of when their emotional needs begin to interfere with sound professional judgment. They can also be alert to situational pressures that might lead them to act contrary to the best standards of the profession. For example, a psychologist was asked by a parent to alter the diagnosis of a child from attention deficit disorder to conduct disorder in order to warrant contin-

---

Table 2: Steps in Ethical Decision-Making Models

Steps in the Kitchener (2000) Model	*Common Five Steps*
1. Think about your response	Identify the problem
2. Review the available information	Develop alternatives
3. Identify possible options	Develop alternatives
4. Consult the Ethics Code	Develop alternatives
5. Assess the foundational ethical principles	Develop alternatives
6. Identify legal concerns	Develop alternatives
7. Reassess options and identify a plan	Evaluate alternatives
8. Implement the plan and document the process	Implement decisions
9. Reflect on the outcome	Evaluate the decision

Steps in the Koocher and Keith-Spiegel (1998) Model	*Common Five Steps*
1. Determine that an ethical problem exists	Identify the problem
2. Consult guidelines	Develop alternatives
3. Consider all sources that may influence decision	Develop alternatives
4. Consult a trusted colleague	Develop alternatives
5. Evaluate rights and responsibilities of affected parties	Develop alternatives
6. Generate alternatives	Develop alternatives
7. Enumerate the consequences	Evaluate alternatives
8. Make the decision	Evaluate alternatives
9. Implement the decision	Implement decision

Steps in the Haas and Malouf (2002) Model	*Common Five Steps*
1. Is there a relevant standard?	Identify the problem
2. Is there reason to deviate from the standard?	Develop alternatives
3. Can a primary ethical dimension be specified?	Develop alternatives
4. Does the course of action satisfy the primary persons?	Evaluate alternatives
5. Is the course of action ethical and able to be implemented?	Evaluate alternatives

Steps in the Canadian Psychological Association (1991) Model	*Common Five Steps*
1. Identify relevant issues and practices	Identify the problem
2. Develop alternate courses of action	Develop alternatives
3. Analyze benefits and risks	Develop alternatives
4. Choose course of action	Evaluate alternatives
5. Implement the decision	Implement decision
6. Evaluate outcome	Evaluate the decision
7. Correct any problems created by the action	Evaluate the decision

---

ued treatment and third-party reimbursement. However, such a change could not be justified clinically; it could not even be considered a judgment call. The psychologist appreciated the financial challenges to the parents and wanted to please them, but she had enough self-awareness to realize that the situational pressures from the parents could not allow her to contradict her clinical judgment and her personal sense of honesty.

Consider the Need for an Immediate Response. Sometimes psychologists will have the opportunity to reflect on the ethical dilemma, consult with others, and generate alternatives. However, many times these ethical dilemmas require an immediate response. For example, during an initial interview with a patient, the psychologist may have to decide, on the spot, whether the threatening comments of the client/patient are sufficient to implement a duty to warn or protect.

The cognitive models of decision making that involve careful delineation of the problem and an opportunity to generate solutions may not work in these situations. The difficulty in thinking through the problem can be exacerbated by worry about the threatening consequences, by the degree of upset of those around the psychologist, and by the fact that the attention of the psychologist is drawn to the immediate task.

One way to improve ethical decision making in crisis situations is to anticipate what kinds of problems might occur in one's areas of practice and then develop a subset of decision-making steps for that situation that permit nearly immediate action. For example, a psychologist conducted many comprehensive child custody evaluations each year. She participated in a biweekly peer consultation group where participants shared their successes and frustrations in this area of practice. Based on her experiences and knowledge, she was able to anticipate most of the ethical problems that could arise when conducting child custody evaluations.

Consider Supererogatory Goals. Supererogatory obligations are those that are freely chosen, in contrast with mandatory obligations that are incumbent upon all psychologists. Supererogatory obligations arise from one's own personal values and beliefs and are reflected, in part, in the aspirational principles of the Ethics Code, in contrast to the mandatory obligations that are found in the standards of the Ethics Code.

Traditional ethical decision-making models do not consider supererogatory goals within their ethical decision-making framework. However, most psychologists, like most other professionals, are guided by a desire to do more than just enough to get by. They may express this desire by providing pro bono or low cost services, by focusing their practices on persons who have traditionally been underserved, by striving to be highly competent with a particular client/patient population, or by increasing the knowledge base of the profession.

Decisions about how to express supererogatory goals are primarily an individual matter, flowing from one's aspirations as a person and as a professional. Psychologists who reflect on the personal meaning of their work should be better able to identify and live up to the standards of the Ethics Code.

For example, a highly competent and successful psychologist experienced the painful loss of a relative from AIDS. He subsequently dedicated a significant portion of his practice to helping low income persons who had the HIV or AIDS virus and regularly volunteered as a speaker to health classes at the local high school. His actions reflected a thoughtful and deliberate decision to express his deepest values.

As can be seen, there is overlap between the strategies for implementing ethical ideals and the strategies for effective ethical decision making. Both require anticipation and self-care.

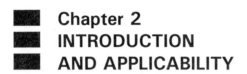

Chapter 2
INTRODUCTION
AND APPLICABILITY

History and Effective Date. This version of the APA Ethics Code was adopted by the American Psychological Association's Council of Representatives during its meeting, August 21, 2002, and is effective beginning June 1, 2003. Inquiries concerning the substance or interpretation of the APA Ethics Code should be addressed to the Director, Office of Ethics, American Psychological Association, 750 First Street, NE, Washington, DC 20002-4242. The Ethics Code and information regarding the Code can be found on the APA web site, http://www.apa.org/ethics. The standards in this Ethics Code will be used to adjudicate complaints brought concerning alleged conduct occurring on or after the effective date. Complaints regarding conduct occurring prior to the effective date will be adjudicated on the basis of the version of the Ethics Code that was in effect at the time the conduct occurred.

The APA has previously published its Ethics Code as follows:

American Psychological Association. (1953). *Ethical Standards of Psychologists.* Washington, DC: Author.

American Psychological Association. (1959). Ethical standards of psychologists. *American Psychologist, 14,* 279-282.

American Psychological Association. (1963). Ethical standards of psychologists. *American Psychologist, 18,* 56-60.

American Psychological Association. (1968). Ethical standards of psychologists. *American Psychologist, 23,* 357-361.

American Psychological Association. (1977, March). Ethical standards of psychologists. *APA Monitor,* pp. 22-23.

American Psychological Association. (1979). *Ethical Standards of Psychologists.* Washington, DC: Author.

American Psychological Association. (1981). Ethical principles of psychologists. *American Psychologist, 36,* 633-638.

American Psychological Association. (1990). Ethical principles of psychologists (Amended June 2, 1989). *American Psychologist, 45,* 390-395.

American Psychological Association. (1992). Ethical principles of psychologists and code of conduct. *American Psychologist, 47,* 1597-1611.

Request copies of the APA *Ethical Principles of Psychologists and Code of Conduct* from the APA Order Department, 750 First Street, NE, Washington, DC 20002-4242 or phone (202) 336-5510.

*INTRODUCTION AND APPLICABILITY**

The American Psychological Association's (APA's) Ethical Principles of Psychologists and Code of Conduct (hereinafter referred to as the Ethics Code) consists of an Introduction, a Preamble, five General Principles (A-E), and specific Ethical Stan-

---

dards. The Introduction discusses the intent, organization, proce-
dural considerations, and scope of application of the Ethics Code.
The Preamble and General Principles are aspirational goals to
guide psychologists toward the highest ideals of psychology. Al-
though the Preamble and General Principles are not themselves
enforceable rules, they should be considered by psychologists in
arriving at an ethical course of action. The Ethical Standards set
forth enforceable rules for conduct as psychologists. Most of the
Ethical Standards are written broadly, in order to apply to psy-
chologists in varied roles, although the application of an Ethical
Standard may vary depending on the context. The Ethical Stand-
ards are not exhaustive. The fact that a given conduct is not specifi-
cally addressed by an Ethical Standard does not mean that it is
necessarily either ethical or unethical.

This Ethics Code applies only to psychologists' activities that
are part of their scientific, educational, or professional roles as
psychologists. Areas covered include but are not limited to the clini-
cal, counseling, and school practice of psychology; research; teach-
ing; supervision of trainees; public service; policy development;
social intervention; development of assessment instruments; con-
ducting assessments; educational counseling; organizational con-
sulting; forensic activities; program design and evaluation; and
administration. This Ethics Code applies to these activities across
a variety of contexts, such as in person, postal, telephone, internet,
and other electronic transmissions. These activities shall be distin-
guished from the purely private conduct of psychologists, which is
not within the purview of the Ethics Code.

Membership in the APA commits members and student affili-
ates to comply with the standards of the APA Ethics Code and to
the rules and procedures used to enforce them. Lack of awareness
or misunderstanding of an Ethical Standard is not itself a defense
to a charge of unethical conduct.

The procedures for filing, investigating, and resolving com-
plaints of unethical conduct are described in the current Rules and
Procedures of the APA Ethics Committee. APA may impose sanc-
tions on its members for violations of the standards of the Ethics
Code, including termination of APA membership, and may notify
other bodies and individuals of its actions. Actions that violate the
standards of the Ethics Code may also lead to the imposition of
sanctions on psychologists or students whether or not they are APA
members by bodies other than APA, including state psychological
associations, other professional groups, psychology boards, other
state or federal agencies, and payors for health services. In addi-
tion, APA may take action against a member after his or her con-
viction of a felony, expulsion or suspension from an affiliated state

psychological association, or suspension or loss of licensure. When the sanction to be imposed by APA is less than expulsion, the 2001 Rules and Procedures do not guarantee an opportunity for an in-person hearing, but generally provide that complaints will be resolved only on the basis of a submitted record.

The Ethics Code is intended to provide guidance for psychologists and standards of professional conduct that can be applied by the APA and by other bodies that choose to adopt them. The Ethics Code is not intended to be a basis of civil liability. Whether a psychologist has violated the Ethics Code standards does not by itself determine whether the psychologist is legally liable in a court action, whether a contract is enforceable, or whether other legal consequences occur.

The modifiers used in some of the standards of this Ethics Code (e.g., reasonably, appropriate, potentially*) are included in the standards when they would (1) allow professional judgment on the part of psychologists, (2) eliminate injustice or inequality that would occur without the modifier, (3) ensure applicability across the broad range of activities conducted by psychologists, or (4) guard against a set of rigid rules that might be quickly outdated. As used in this Ethics Code, the term* reasonable *means the prevailing professional judgment of psychologists engaged in similar activities in similar circumstances, given the knowledge the psychologist had or should have had at the time.*

In the process of making decisions regarding their professional behavior, psychologists must consider this Ethics Code in addition to applicable laws and psychology board regulations. In applying the Ethics Code to their professional work, psychologists may consider other materials and guidelines that have been adopted or endorsed by scientific and professional psychological organizations and the dictates of their own conscience, as well as consult with others within the field. If this Ethics Code establishes a higher standard of conduct than is required by law, psychologists must meet the higher ethical standard. If psychologists' ethical responsibilities conflict with law, regulations, or other governing legal authority, psychologists make known their commitment to this Ethics Code and take steps to resolve the conflict in a responsible manner. If the conflict is unresolvable via such means, psychologists may adhere to the requirements of the law, regulations, or other governing authority in keeping with basic principles of human rights.

The Introduction and Applicability section of the Ethics Code explains that the Code is divided into aspirational principles and enforceable standards, and that the applicability of the Code is restricted to the professional activities of psychologists. It also notes that membership in APA obligates psychologists to adhere to the Code, and that the APA Ethics Office has rules and procedures separate from the Ethics Code.

The reasoning behind the use of modifiers is presented, as is a definition of the modifier *reasonable*. This section also describes the general procedures to follow when laws conflict with the demands of the Ethics Code. Also, as with the earlier Ethics Codes adopted by APA, this section notes that the 2002 Ethics Code would not be applied retroactively. Instead, it is binding upon psychologists only after the effective date determined by the APA Council of Representatives.

Finally, the Introduction section notes that "the Ethics Code is not intended to be a basis of civil liability," nor does the violation of the code necessarily mean that a psychologist "is legally liable in a court action, whether a contract is enforceable, or whether other legal consequences occur." The intent is to dissuade others from using the Ethics Code as an unwarranted weapon against psychologists. That statement is largely symbolic as nothing can stop other bodies from adapting or using the Code as they wish.

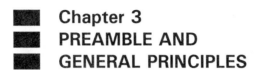 **Chapter 3**
PREAMBLE AND
GENERAL PRINCIPLES

PREAMBLE

Psychologists are committed to increasing scientific and professional knowledge of behavior and people's understanding of themselves and others and to the use of such knowledge to improve the condition of individuals, organizations, and society. Psychologists respect and protect civil and human rights and the central importance of freedom of inquiry and expression in research, teaching, and publication. They strive to help the public in developing informed judgments and choices concerning human behavior. In doing so, they perform many roles, such as researcher, educator, diagnostician, therapist, supervisor, consultant, administrator, social interventionist, and expert witness. This Ethics Code provides a common set of principles and standards upon which psychologists build their professional and scientific work.

This Ethics Code is intended to provide scientific standards to cover most situations encountered by psychologists. It has as its goals the welfare and protection of the individuals and groups with whom psychologists work and the education of members, students, and the public regarding ethical standards of the discipline.

The development of a dynamic set of ethical standards for psychologist's work-related conduct requires a personal commitment and a lifelong effort to act ethically; to encourage ethical behavior by students, supervisees, employees, and colleagues; and to consult with others concerning ethical problems.

GENERAL PRINCIPLES

This section consists of General Principles. General Principles, as opposed to Ethical Standards, are aspirational in nature. Their intent is to guide and inspire psychologists toward the very highest ethical ideals of the profession. General Principles, in contrast to

Ethical Standards, do not represent obligations and should not be the basis for imposing sanctions. Relying upon General Principles for either of these reasons distorts both their meaning and purpose.

Principle A: Beneficence and Nonmaleficence

Psychologists strive to benefit those with whom they work and take care to do no harm. In their professional actions, psychologists seek to safeguard the welfare and rights of those with whom they interact professionally and other affected persons, and the welfare of animal subjects of research. When conflicts occur among psychologists' obligations or concerns, they attempt to resolve these conflicts in a responsible fashion that avoids or minimizes harm. Because psychologists' scientific and professional judgments and actions may affect the lives of others, they are alert to and guard against personal, financial, social, organizational, or political factors that might lead to misuse of their influence. Psychologists strive to be aware of the possible effect of their own physical and mental health on their ability to help those with whom they work.

Principle B: Fidelity and Responsibility

Psychologists establish relationships of trust with those with whom they work. They are aware of their professional and scientific responsibilities to society and to the specific communities in which they work. Psychologists uphold professional standards of conduct, clarify their professional roles and obligations, accept appropriate responsibility for their behavior, and seek to manage conflicts of interest that could lead to exploitation or harm. Psychologists consult with, refer to, or cooperate with other professionals and institutions to the extent needed to serve the best interests of those with whom they work. They are concerned about the ethical compliance of their colleagues' scientific and professional conduct. Psychologists strive to contribute a portion of their professional time for little or no compensation or personal advantage.

Principle C: Integrity

Psychologists seek to promote accuracy, honesty, and truthfulness in the science, teaching, and practice of psychology. In these activities psychologists do not steal, cheat, or engage in fraud, subterfuge, or intentional misrepresentation of fact. Psychologists strive to keep their promises and to avoid unwise or unclear commitments. In situations in which deception may be ethically justifiable to maximize benefits and minimize harm, psychologists have a serious obligation to consider the need for, the possible consequences of, and their responsibility to correct any resulting mistrust or other harmful effects that arise from the use of such techniques.

Principle D: Justice

Psychologists recognize that fairness and justice entitle all persons to access to and benefit from the contributions of psychology and to equal quality in the processes, procedures, and services being conducted by psychologists. Psychologists exercise reasonable judgment and take precautions to ensure that their potential biases, the boundaries of their competence, and the limitations of their expertise do not lead to or condone unjust practices.

Principle E: Respect for People's Rights and Dignity

Psychologists respect the dignity and worth of all people, and the rights of individuals to privacy, confidentiality, and self-determination. Psychologists are aware that special safeguards may be necessary to protect the rights and welfare of persons or communities whose vulnerabilities impair autonomous decision making. Psychologists are aware of and respect cultural, individual, and role differences, including those based on age, gender, gender identity, race, ethnicity, culture, national origin, religion, sexual orientation, disability, language, and socioeconomic status and consider these factors when working with members of such groups. Psychologists try to eliminate the effect on their work of biases based on those factors, and they do not knowingly participate in or condone activities of others based on such prejudices.

The Preamble contains general statements on the importance of using skills to improve human welfare and the necessity to protect human rights, and it encourages psychologists to promote informed judgments by members of the public concerning the use of psychological services. The Preamble also notes that the Ethics Code requires a lifelong commitment by psychologists to (a) act ethically, (b) encourage other psychologists to act ethically, and (c) consult with other psychologists about ethical problems.

The Preamble is followed by five General Principles: Beneficence and Nonmaleficence, Fidelity and Responsibility, Integrity, Justice, and Respect for People's Rights and Dignity. These principles represent the ethical ceiling for psychologists, instead of the ethical floor. That is to say, these aspirational statements encourage psychologists to live up to their fullest potential as psychologists although they cannot be disciplined for failing to do so. They represent idealized, but achievable, goals for psychologists.

Aspirational ideals need not be the dominion of self-righteous fanatics who pursue their ideals without considering the feelings of others or the context of the behavior. Aspirational ideals need not entail expectations of behavior so unrealistic that they appear only as public relations statements that no one believes can be realized. Instead, achievable aspirational ideals can form the foundation for beneficial or compassionate professional or scientific behavior.

One psychologist made substantial contributions to her profession by serving as an officer in her state professional association. Another made an extraordinary effort to provide the best possible treatment for her clients/patients. She developed a well-deserved reputation for effectiveness and compassion. A third psychologist continued to excel at teaching, even though he was tenured and could have easily "coasted" until retirement. None of these psychologists would have been disciplined for failing to achieve excellence in these activities. However, their actions reflect their personal commitment to a lifelong effort to act ethically.

In addition to encouraging psychologists to act to their fullest potential, aspirational ethics also provide psychologists with "decision rules" for their ethical decision making. In a situation where the most ethical decision is not clear, the aspirational principles can help psychologists to clarify how they can best discharge their professional responsibilities.

The General Principles in the Ethics Code are modeled upon the principle-based ethics (or prima facie ethics) that are commonly used in discussions of health care ethics (Beauchamp & Childress, 2001). According to principle-based ethics, psychologists and other moral agents should generally follow these moral principles. However, these principles are not absolute guides to human behavior and may, at times, conflict with each other. In such cases psychologists need to balance the application of these principles to achieve the most favorable result.

Principle-based ethicists do not necessarily agree upon the optimal manner to define or categorize these principles. Beauchamp and Childress (2001) have identified four moral principles which are especially important in the field of biomedical ethics (respect for client/patient autonomy, nonmaleficence, beneficence, justice), and Kitchener (1984, 2000) and Bersoff and Koeppl (1993) have added fidelity as a core moral principle applicable to psychologists. However, the ethics code of the Canadian Psychological Association (CPA) categorized the relevant ethical principles differently (responsible caring, integrity in relationships, responsibility to society, and respect for the dignity of persons). These differences have more to do with wording and emphasis than with substance. A comparison of the different moral principles is shown in Table 3 (p. 29). The 2002 Ethics Code has categorized the General Principles in a manner which is more consistent with that of Beauchamp and Childress.

The choice of principle-based ethics to describe the aspirational goals of psychologists reflects appreciation of one particular philosophical method. However, on a day-to-day basis, many psychologists may find themselves thinking about ethical problems in terms of other philosophi-

Table 3: Comparison of Moral Principles		
APA General Principles	CPA Principles	Beauchamp And Childress
Beneficence and Nonmaleficence	Responsible Caring Responsibility to Society	Beneficence Nonmaleficence
Fidelity and Responsibility	Included Within Respect for the Dignity of Persons	
Integrity	Integrity in Relationships	
Justice	Included Within Respect for the Dignity of Persons	Justice
Respect for People's Rights and Dignity	Respect for the Dignity of Persons	Overlaps With Respect for Client/Patient Autonomy

cal systems such as virtue (character) ethics, utilitarianism, or a deontological (Kantian) framework. For example, a proponent of virtue ethics may think in terms of being benevolent (as opposed to actualizing beneficence and nonmaleficence), faithful (as opposed to actualizing fidelity and responsibility), honest (integrity), and respectful (respect for person's rights and dignity). Although there are important differences in these philosophical systems, the differences should not be overemphasized. The different theories often start in different places but end up in the same location. From a practical standpoint, an understanding of the aspirational principle-based ethics should help most psychologists to better understand and fulfill their ethical ideals.

BENEFICENCE AND NONMALEFICENCE

Although some philosophers separate the notions of beneficence (work to promote the well-being of others) and nonmaleficence (avoid harming others), the Ethics Code considers them together. Beneficence is the moral aspect which is commonly assumed to occur in the helping professions: working to help others. "Morality requires not only that we treat people autonomously and refrain from harming them, but also that we contribute to their welfare" (Beauchamp & Childress, 2001, p. 165). In addition to the primary directive of doing no harm, psychologists have a positive obligation to help clients/patients by selecting and conscientiously implementing appropriate services for them, or they have a positive obligation to society by designing and implementing research programs that can make a meaningful contribution to human welfare. Psychologists strive to "benefit those with whom they work."

For example, the enforceable Standard 2.01a ("Psychologists provide services, teach, and conduct research with populations and in areas only within the boundaries of their competence. . . .") reflects the general principle of beneficence.

"Nonmaleficence asserts an obligation not to inflict harm on others" (Beauchamp & Childress, 2001, p. 113). It can be summarized in the phrase *primum non nocere*, which translates to "above all, do not harm." Psychologists also strive toward nonmaleficence when they "take care to do no harm."

The enforceable Standard 3.04 ("Psychologists take reasonable steps to avoid harming their clients/patients, students, supervisees, research participants, organizational clients, and others with whom they work, and to minimize harm where it is foreseeable and unavoidable") reflects the general principle of nonmaleficence.

Conflicts of Interests

At times the interests of psychologists may conflict with those of their clients/patients, students, or research participants. In those circumstances, psychologists "attempt to resolve these conflicts in a responsible fashion that avoids or minimizes harm" (Principle A). In fact the potential for conflicts of interest is so important that references to conflicts of interest are made in three of the five aspirational principles. Not only should psychologists avoid or minimize harm (nonmaleficence), they should also "seek to manage conflicts of interest that could lead to exploitation or harm" (fidelity; Principle B) and "avoid unwise or unclear commitments" (integrity; Principle C).

Self-Care

The final sentence describing the principle of beneficence states that "Psychologists strive to be aware of the possible effect of their own physical and mental health on their ability to help those with whom they work." This was inserted in recognition of the close relationship between ethical misconduct and impairment. According to Koocher and Keith-Spiegel (1998) about one-half of the psychologists who were disciplined by the APA Ethics Committee appeared to have committed their misdeed in the context of some personal crisis or stress. Taken to its logical conclusion, it would appear that one-half of the serious ethical violations of psychologists could be eliminated if psychologists were receiving adequate self-care.

The enforceable ethical Standard 2.06 requires psychologists to be alert to early stages of impairment and take appropriate action if they discern themselves to be impaired. However, the aspirational principle goes beyond that and addresses what psychologists can do to avoid being impaired or what they can do to maximize their professional effectiveness. No enforceable standard could dictate rules of self-care such as ensuring that psychologists get enough sleep, watch their diet, exercise, seek out appropriate health care, and so forth. However, it is a goal to which psychologists can aspire. The Ethics Code does a valuable service to the public and the profession by including this one sentence.

FIDELITY AND RESPONSIBILITY

The principle of fidelity means that psychologists are faithful to their primary obligation to serve their clients/patients. According to Kitchener, it means "truthfulness, promise keeping, and loyalty" (1984, p. 51). Fidelity can also be manifested when psychologists protect client/patient confidentiality and direct the course of treatment to benefit their clients/patients and not third parties. Also, the ethical standards dealing with abandonment, boundary violations, and multiple relationships are based, in part, on the moral principle of fidelity.

The first sentence of Principle B states "Psychologists establish relationships of trust with those with whom they work." They clarify their professional roles and consult, refer, and cooperate with others as needed. Fidelity applies both to professional obligations to individuals and to society as a whole. The enforceable Standard 3.08 ("Psychologists do not exploit persons over whom they have supervisory, evaluative, or other authority") reflects the general principle of fidelity.

Collegial Concern

Finally, the description of Fidelity and Responsibility states that "they are concerned about the ethical compliance of their colleagues' scientific and professional conduct." The Ethics Code does not describe how psychologists are to express this concern. However, if the principles of beneficence and respect for people's rights and dignity are considered together, then it appears that the optimal manner to operationalize this obligation is through respectful and charitable engagement with colleagues.

Although no psychologist can be responsible for the behavior of another, each psychologist can contribute to a collegial and helpful environment within the profession. Psychologists can be sensitive about any ethical concerns that may arise, discuss ethical concerns with colleagues, and be proactive about addressing them. They can help to ensure a collegial atmosphere in which people feel free to seek advice on ethical issues.

INTEGRITY

Integrity means internal consistency in behavior, words, actions, and intent. Consequently, psychologists demonstrate integrity when they "promote accuracy, honesty, and truthfulness in the science, teaching, and practice of psychology" (Principle C). Similarly, "psychologists do not steal, cheat, or engage in fraud, subterfuge, or intentional misrepresentation of fact" (Principle C). The enforceable Standard 5.01a ("Psychologists do not knowingly make public statements that are false, deceptive, or fraudulent concerning their research, practice, or other work activities. . . .") reflects the general principle of integrity.

Deception

The integrity principle states that

> In situations in which deception may be ethically justifiable to maximize benefits and minimize harm, psychologists have a serious obligation to consider the need for, the possible consequences of, and their responsibility to correct any resulting mistrust or other harmful effects that arise from the use of such techniques.

This sentence could apply to deception in research, or it could apply to cases in which psychotherapists withhold information from clients/patients for clinical reasons.

The caution concerning deception research is based on several factors including the way that deception, by its very nature, contradicts the principles of honesty and informed consent, and often brings discomfort to subjects (Fisher, 2000). Certainly deception should never be used for trivial reasons, but sometimes it may be the only way to address a legitimate research question. Deception in research is considered in the enforceable Standards 8.07 and 8.08. For professional psychologists, deception may be clinically indicated for some vulnerable clients/patients.

JUSTICE

Justice can be viewed in different ways. Distributive justice refers to the fair and equitable distribution of resources of services. Formal or procedural justice refers to equal treatment (Beauchamp & Childress, 2001). This aspirational principle includes both concepts. That is, "fairness and justice entitle all persons to access to and benefit from the contributions of psychology" as well as "equal quality in the processes, procedures, and services being conducted by psychologists." It would not be possible to put distributive justice within the enforceable standards. However, enforceable Standard 3.01 ("In their work-related activities, psychologists do not engage in unfair discrimination. . . .") reflects the general principle of formal justice.

RESPECT FOR PEOPLE'S RIGHTS AND DIGNITY

This aspirational principle is by necessity broad and overlaps with the other principles. For example, actions that are beneficent or that are conducted with respect for formal justice would ordinarily involve respect of the rights and dignity of the recipients. However, this general principle contains several concepts that the other aspirational principles do not cover, including respect for the rights of individuals to confidentiality and privacy and an effort by psychologists to overcome the effect of biases in their work. Furthermore, the principle gives special attention to client/patient autonomy.

Respect for Autonomy

Autonomy means the freedom to think or choose as long as one's choice does not infringe upon the rights of others. "Personal autonomy is, at the minimum, self-rule that is free from both controlling interference by others and from limitations, such as inadequate understanding, that prevent meaningful choice" (Beauchamp & Childress, 2001, p. 58). Psychologists should treat clients/patients as autonomous and independent agents who can participate as full partners in determining treatment goals and methods.

The aspirational section states that psychologists should respect the rights of individuals to self-determination. It also encourages psychologists to protect the rights and welfare of individuals "whose vulnerabilities impair autonomous decision-making." Enforceable Standard 3.10a ("They obtain the informed consent of the individual or individuals using language that is reasonably understandable") reflects concern for client/patient autonomy.

The overriding of client/patient autonomy is called paternalism (literally, it means assuming the role of the pater or father). Respect for client/patient autonomy is so important, however, that paternalistic interventions should be rare and even then only to the narrowest possible extent to fulfill other moral obligations.

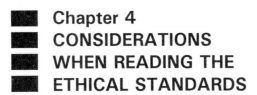

Chapter 4
CONSIDERATIONS
WHEN READING THE
ETHICAL STANDARDS

The next chapter reviews each of the standards of the Ethics Code in detail. Our commentaries give more attention to those areas in which psychologists are more vulnerable to some kind of disciplinary action, and we offer practical suggestions as to how psychologists may reduce their risks of being charged with an ethics complaint.

In addition, we emphasize the relationship between the aspirational ethical principles and specific ethical standards. Because ethics should be more than just avoiding disciplinary actions, we urge psychologists to consider how they can use their ethical principles to help them live up to their ethical potential.

DISCIPLINARY GROUNDS
AGAINST PSYCHOLOGISTS

No comprehensive registry exists that records all of the disciplinary actions taken against psychologists by the APA Ethics Committee, state licensing boards, state ethics committees, institutional disciplinary boards, and malpractice insurance carriers. The development of such a registry is not likely to ever occur because the various boards, committees, and courts summarize their findings in different ways or consider such information to be proprietary and do not share it. Nonetheless, we have information from several sources that can inform us of the high risk areas of practice for psychologists.

According to the Association of State and Provincial Psychology Boards data bank, 33% of the disciplinary actions were based on unethical multiple relationships (including sexual improprieties); 30% for unprofessional/unethical/negligent practice; 8% for fraudulent acts; 4% for breach of confidentiality; 4% for inadequate supervision; 4% for inadequate record keeping; and 4% for impairment (Reaves, 2001).

Over a 5-year period (1996 to 2000), the APA Ethics Office (Report of the Ethics Committee, 1997, 1998, 1999, 2000, 2001) reported that about 34% of their disciplinary actions were for loss of licensure or for a disciplinary action by another jurisdiction; 19% were for sexual misconduct; 7% for insurance or fee problems; 6% for nonsexual boundary violations; and 4% for breaches of confidentiality. In addition 7% arose out of child custody disputes and 2% involved psychologists practicing outside of their area of competence.

In summary, disciplinary actions occurred because of violations of sexual boundaries, nonsexual multiple relationships, incompetence, breaches of confidentiality, abandonment, inadequate supervision, and inadequate record keeping. In addition, many complaints arose in the context of child custody disputes.

STRATEGY FOR
IMPLEMENTING ETHICAL IDEALS

Although some psychologists who are disciplined for ethical misconduct have personality disorders or serious character flaws, it is inaccurate to attribute all (or even most) ethical violations to character defects. Any psychologist, given the right circumstances, might make an ethical mistake. The goal is to minimize the likelihood of making an ethical mistake and maximize the likelihood of living up to ethical ideals.

We have identified six "I"s that appear to be associated with charges of professional misconduct: incompetence, impairment, insensitivity and impulsiveness, ignorance, and incomplete documentation (Bricklin, Knapp, & VandeCreek, 2001). Incompetence is addressed in our coverage of Standards 2.01 and following dealing with competence, and impairment is reviewed in our commentary dealing with Standards 2.06 and 7.04. However, it is appropriate to comment here briefly on the other "I"s.

Insensitivity and Impulsivity

Sometimes complaints arise out of insensitive or impulsive actions by psychologists. Periodically reports of ethics complaints reference actions on the part of psychologists that caused or reflected the lack of a strong psychologist/client/patient relationship. For example, a psychologist who fails to consider the unique cultural features relevant to the client's/patient's presenting problem may be showing insensitivity. Or the psy-

chologists who fail to appreciate the extent of their negative countertransference risk making an impulsive and countertherapeutic comment to a
client/patient.

Self-Awareness Prevents a Lapse*

A psychologist was treating a frustrating client/patient who was
highly needy and lacking in basic social skills. Because of her poor
social skills and her inability to process social information adequately, the client/patient had few social support systems. The
psychologist was aware of her negative countertransference and
sometimes processed her feelings through her professional consultation group. Consequently, she was able to keep her interactions
focused on meeting the treatment needs of her client/patient.

Ignorance

We may assume that readers of this book are attempting to reduce
any errors that could be caused by ignorance of existing ethical standards
or laws. However, the effort to become fully aware requires an understanding of relevant state laws. For example, licensing laws usually specify
the scope of the practice of psychologists, exemptions to the licensing
law, standards for supervisors, and other issues directly relevant to the
practice of psychology. Other state laws specify the criteria for reporting
suspected child abuse, the standards and procedures for involuntary civil
commitments, age of consent for minors, standards for expert witnesses,
and more. Compendiums of such laws exist in several states (e.g., *Pennsylvania Law and Psychology*, Knapp, VandeCreek, & Tepper, 2000),
and APA, under the editorship of Bruce Sales and Michael Miller, has
initiated a project of compiling a book on law and mental health for each
state.

Incomplete Documentation

The APA ethical standards require adequate documentation in order
for psychologists to facilitate the provision of services by other professionals, allow research protocols to be replicated, meet institutional requirements, ensure accurate billing, and ensure compliance with the law
(Standard 6.01). Although the ethical standards do not mention this, prudent psychologists also keep records in order to provide self-protection in
the event of an ethics, licensing board, or malpractice complaint.

---

*The details in these vignettes have been substantially altered to protect the privacy of the persons involved.
Many vignettes represent composites of situations that have been encountered by two or more psychologists.

Nothing can compare with the value of good records in helping psychologists protect themselves in the event of a complaint. Courts give great weight to medical records. The general assumption is that the records accurately reflect the nature of the psychologist/client/patient interaction. If events are not documented, or are not documented in sufficient detail, the determination of fact then shifts to determining the credibility of the psychologist versus that of the complainant ("he said" versus "she said"). This fact substantiates the wisdom of the axiom among malpractice defense attorneys: "If it isn't written down, it did not occur."

ASPIRATIONAL ETHICS AND
SUPEREROGATORY OBLIGATIONS

The Ethics Code contains high ideals (aspirational principles) and the mandatory or minimal standards (ethical standards). However, it is impossible to completely separate aspirational from enforceable ethics. Psychologists attempting to provide the highest level of services are also ensuring that they are fulfilling their mandatory duties. For example, some psychologists may feel a sense of responsibility to assist disaster survivors, but they cannot fulfill that aspirational goal unless they also possess the skills necessary to deliver an effective intervention, as required by the standards of the Ethics Code.

As part of meeting their aspirational goals psychologists may impose supererogatory obligations upon themselves. These obligations are freely chosen, in contrast with mandatory obligations, which are incumbent upon all psychologists. Most psychologists, like most other professionals, are guided by a desire to do more than just enough to get by. They may express this beneficence through providing pro bono or low cost services, focusing their practices on persons who have traditionally been underserved, by striving to be highly competent with a particular client/patient population, or increasing the knowledge base of the profession.

The decisions concerning how to express supererogatory obligations need to consider the underlying philosophical systems or beliefs that guide individual behavior. Psychologists who reflect on the personal meaning of their work should become better at identifying and living up to their highest goals.

For example, a competent and successful psychologist became aware of the sufferings of victims of torture in Third World countries. She regularly treated these survivors in her practice for little or no money. Her actions reflect a deliberate decision to live out her deeply held values.

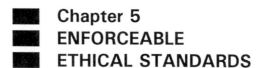

Chapter 5
ENFORCEABLE
ETHICAL STANDARDS

The enforceable ethical standards are divided into 10 sections. With each section, we review the content of each standard. We identify the moral foundation for the standard and review relevant risk management techniques for ensuring adherence to the standard.

The first section deals with Resolving Ethical Issues. Some of the major issues addressed within this section are the processes to follow when the Ethics Code conflicts with the laws or organizational demands. This section also considers informal and formal resolutions of ethical violations that come to the attention of psychologists, cooperation with ethics committees, and other issues related to the adjudication process.

1. RESOLVING ETHICAL ISSUES

This section provides information about the responsibilities of, and restrictions on, psychologists when using the Ethics Code to protect the public. Specifically, it covers how psychologists can proceed when learning of the misuse of their work (Standard 1.01), dealing with conflicts between the Ethics Code and the law or organizational demands (1.02, 1.03), and learning of misconduct by other psychologists (1.04, 1.05). It also covers the responsibilities of psychologists to the Ethics Committee (1.06, 1.07), and to those charged with ethics complaints (1.08).

The ethical standards in this section are based, to a large extent, on General Principle A, Beneficence and Nonmaleficence, in that psychologists "seek to safeguard the welfare and rights of those with whom they interact professionally." They are also based on General Principle B, Fidelity and Responsibility, in that psychologists "uphold professional standards of conduct. . . . [and] are concerned about the ethical compliance of their colleagues' scientific and professional conduct." Furthermore they are based on General Principle C, Integrity, in that psychologists "seek to promote accuracy, honesty, and truthfulness in the science, teaching, and practice of psychology." Finally, General Principle E, Respect for People's Rights and Dignity, is relevant in that psychologists "are aware that special safeguards may be necessary to protect the rights and welfare of persons."

Psychologists have a responsibility to protect the public when they learn of misrepresentations of their own work or of unethical conduct on the part of other psychologists. However, the responsibility to protect the public is not absolute and must be balanced against the responsibility to protect client/patient confidentiality and the rights of psychologists to be free of frivolous complaints and to be assumed to be innocent until an Ethics Committee determines otherwise.

This section reorganized the standards of the 1992 Ethics Code, but only makes a few minor changes to them. One significant change is that psychologists may not deny other psychologists employment, advancement, or admission to academic or other programs only because an ethics complaint has been filed. Of course psychologists may deny employment and so forth to other psychologists on the basis of other factors and if the case has been resolved against them. The 1992 Ethics Code only prohibited such discrimination on the basis of a sexual harassment allegation.

1.01   Misuse of Psychologists' Work

If psychologists learn of misuse or misrepresentation of their work, they take reasonable steps to correct or minimize the misuse or misrepresentation. [This standard is similar to Standard 1.16b of the 1992 Ethics Code.]*

The modifier "reasonable" means that psychologists must use their judgment on how to respond based on the context of the situation. For example, it may be useful to consider how a reasonably prudent psychologist would respond in a similar situation. According to this standard, a disciplinary action would not be based on the outcome in which a psychologist's work has been misused (which is often out of the control of the psychologist), but upon the quality of the effort of the psychologist to correct the problem.

---

*We will indicate whether the standard is identical, similar, overlaps with, or is related to a standard in the 1992 Ethics Code, or a new standard. At times similar standards will have only one or two words changed for grammatical purposes or to ensure consistency in wording with other standards. At other times, the changes may be substantive. We indicate that a standard is related to a standard in the 1992 Ethics Code (APA, 1992) if it deals with the same general topic, but involves a major change. Some degree of interpretation is involved in determining whether the change is major or minor.

This is one of the few standards in which the obligations of the psychologist arise only when they learn or become aware of the misrepresentation. Most standards are evoked when the psychologists are the actors and would necessarily be aware of their own actions.

Although psychologists should avoid getting involved with those who would misrepresent their work, sometimes these situations cannot be avoided. For example, the publisher of a book may make statements without the awareness of the psychologist and print them on the jacket of the books. If the psychologist learns of the misrepresentation, then he or she should take "reasonable steps" to correct that misrepresentation. The exact nature of the redress depends on the situation. It may not be possible for the psychologist to get the publisher to retract copies of a book. However, the psychologist could ensure that future printing and editions correct the misrepresentation.

Prudent psychologists can reduce the likelihood that they would be caught in such traps if they think ahead before making commitments, such as book contracts, and asking for some degree of review, control, or input into the promotional materials.

1.02 Conflicts Between Ethics and Law, Regulations, or Other Governing Legal Authority

If psychologists' ethical responsibilities conflict with law, regulations, or other governing legal authority, psychologists make known their commitment to the Ethics Code and take steps to resolve the conflict. If the conflict is unresolvable via such means, psychologists may adhere to the requirements of the law, regulations, or other governing legal authority. [This standard is similar to Standard 1.02 in the 1992 Ethics Code.]

This standard differs from Standard 1.02 of the 1992 Ethics Code in that the 1992 Ethics Code makes references to "law" whereas the 2002 Ethics Code makes references to "law, regulations, or other governing legal authority" (such as a court order). Although regulations and court orders are technically laws, the change should help clarify the obligations of psychologists.

The following is an example of a conflict between the Ethics Code and a legal authority.

A Court Order Appears to Violate Client/Patient Confidentiality

In a trial, a court orders a psychologist to testify against the wishes of her client and in apparent violation of her state's privileged communication statute. In this particular case, the psychologist informed her client's/patient's attorney of the order. The attorney for the client successfully argued against the admission of the testimony of the psychologist.

Here the only obligation of the psychologist is to make known her reservations and concerns and take steps to resolve them. However, there is no guarantee that all psychologists will be that fortunate. Even if the client's/patient's attorney had not been successful, however, the psychologist would not be disciplined by an ethics committee for complying with a court order.

The Ethics Code adopts a middle ground in these types of situations. On the one hand, psychologists should not passively follow the statute or court decision regardless of what it says, its impact on their clients/patients, or its apparent conflict with the Ethics Code. On the other hand, the Ethics Code does not necessarily require psychologists to disobey the law. Instead it requires psychologists to try to do something to reconcile the problem.

1.03   Conflicts Between Ethics and Organizational Demands

If the demands of an organization with which psychologists are affiliated or for whom they are working conflict with this Ethics Code, psychologists clarify the nature of the conflict, make known their commitment to the Ethics Code, and to the extent feasible, resolve the conflict in a way that permits adherence to the Ethics Code. [This standard is similar to Standard 8.03 in the 1992 Ethics Code.]

Many psychologists work in institutions such as schools, health maintenance organizations (HMOs), or prisons that may have policies contrary to the letter or spirit of the Ethics Code. The standard for psychologists when faced with conflicts between the Ethics Code and organizational demands is the same as for when psychologists are faced with conflicts between the Ethics Code and the law. That is, psychologists are required to take a middle ground and attempt to resolve the issues. They are not automatically subject to disciplinary sanctions because they followed the demands of their institutions, but they do have some responsibility to try to correct the problems.

For example, many Air Force psychologists have experienced conflicts with the Ethics Code and their institutional responsibilities. Some may be required to comment on the fitness for duty of persons whom they have not evaluated, or to reveal information that they believe should have been kept confidential (Orne & Doarman, 2001). Similarly, psychologists employed by correctional systems may have to obey rules that contravene their roles as helping professionals. For example, a correctional psychologist may be asked to participate as a member of a disciplinary board for an inmate who may eventually require mental health treatment (Weinberger & Sreenivasan, 1994). Psychologists working in hospitals may face financial and institutional pressure to admit or discharge clients/patients for reasons other than client/patient need (Pope, 1990). School psychologists are sometimes "asked" to violate the confidentiality of their adolescent clients, disseminate copyrighted test information into the public domain, falsify test results, or misclassify children. Here is an example of a conflict faced by a school psychologist.

A Carefully Worded Report

A school psychologist received a memo from her superior stating that she may not recommend neurological, ophthalmological, or other medical services in any psychological report that she writes for the school. The school psychologist believed that she is being required to withhold information that may alert the parents to the possibility of a coexisting or complicating medical condition.

School psychologists in this situation need to make known their commitment to the Ethics Code and to seek a modification of the district's policy. The issue prompting this memo was the fact that the schools may be required to provide or pay for "related services" which are tailored to the educational needs of the students and reasonably calculated to afford them "full educational opportunity." Sometimes parents and school districts disagree concerning the extent to which medical concerns are related to the school performance of children. On the one hand, a child who needs glasses could hardly be expected to perform adequately in school. On the other hand, a child may benefit from braces on her teeth, but this is probably not related to her school performance. However, it is often unclear the extent to which other medical or psychological problems impact on the child's school performance.

One school psychologist who effectively negotiated with the school district acknowledges the district's concerns about funding "unrelated" services. She was able to address both the concerns of the school and to fulfill her ethical obligations to her students and their parents. Her reports began with a statement that the report deals only with educational issues and is not a comprehensive psychological evaluation of the child. She reports verbally to the parents if she believes that the child needs a referral to a specialist.

The spread of managed care organizations (MCOs) has made institutional conflicts more common. Many psychologists in independent practice have to decide how to respond to an imposition by a managed care company that restricts their therapeutic options or otherwise appears to compromise the quality of client/patient care. The exact response depends on many contextual factors and no algorithm of rules can guide the psychologist on how to respond. However, the frequency of these issues highlights the importance of being educated on the content of the Ethics Code so that psychologists can better discern when a conflict arises and also in ethical decision making so that they will be better able to think through their responses.

1.04   Informal Resolution of Ethical Violations

When psychologists believe that there may have been an ethical violation by another psychologist, they attempt to resolve the issue by bringing it to the attention of that individual, if an informal resolution appears appropriate and the intervention does not violate any confidentiality rights that may be involved. (See also Standard 1.02, Conflict Between Ethics and Law, Regulations, or Other Governing Legal Authority, and 1.03, Conflicts Between Ethics and Organizational Demands.) [This standard is similar to Standard 8.04 in the 1992 Ethics Code.]

1.05   Reporting Ethical Violations

If an apparent ethical violation has substantially harmed or is likely to substantially harm a person or organization and is not appropriate for informal resolution under Standard 1.04, Informal Resolution of Ethical Violations, or is not resolved properly in that fashion, psychologists take further action appropriate to the situation. Such action might include referral to state or national committees on professional ethics, to state licensing boards, or to the appropriate institutional authorities. This standard does not apply when an intervention would violate confidentiality rights or when psychologists have been retained to review the work of another psychologist whose professional conduct is in question. (See also Standard 1.02, Conflict Between Ethics and Law, Regulations, or Other Governing Legal Authority.) [This standard is similar to Standard 8.05 in the 1992 Ethics Code.]

At times otherwise conscientious psychologists may commit an ethical breach out of ignorance. For example, one psychologist advertised a referral fee for those who referred clients/patients to his marital dysfunction clinic. This psychologist had misinterpreted the APA consent agreement with the FTC which prohibited referral fees. A brief phone call to the psychologist resulted in him expressing his thanks and discontinuing the advertisement.

Such easily corrected mistakes differ substantially from those that harm clients/patients.

A Serious Transgression

A psychologist accepted a new client/patient who revealed that she had just discontinued a sexual relationship with her former psychotherapist. The relationship appeared to exacerbate her preexisting depression.

About 50% of professional psychologists have treated a client/patient who was sexually exploited by a previous mental health professional (Pope, 1994). Very often these psychologists wonder about their ethical responsibilities when treating clients/patients who have been sexually exploited by a previous health care provider. Often the new psychologist feels angry or embarrassed after hearing a credible story of sexual exploitation and wants to report the offending psychotherapist to an ethics committee or licensing board.

However, the desire to punish should not take precedence over the right of clients/patients to make their own decisions and to control confidentiality. The clients/patients must decide for themselves how or whether to pursue a legal complaint. Psychologists are not permitted to report the sexual exploitation to anyone (licensing boards, ethics committees, etc.) without the consent of the client/patient.

This does not mean that the new psychologist should ignore the reality of the sexual abuse which should be considered in the treatment of the client/patient. When therapeutically appropriate the new psychologist should inform the client/patient that the sexual contact with the former psychologist was a breach of fiduciary responsibility and violated the minimal acceptable standards of the profession. In addition, the new psychologist should inform the client/patient of the various disciplinary avenues that are available, including the time limits and general nature of each formal disciplinary avenue.

In Standard 1.04 the phrase "when psychologists believe" makes the ethical action dependent on the subjective state of mind of the psychologist. Consequently, an important issue arises concerning the degree of certainty that psychologists must have before they are required to act. Hearing a rumor third hand about a psychologist who allegedly has a drinking problem is much different than personally observing a psychologist who is drunk at work. Unfortunately, the Ethics Code provides little guidance for psychologists concerning the degree of certainty required.

However, as a risk management rule we would suggest that psychologists adopt a lower standard of certainty when attempting an informal resolution (such as calling the psychologist in question and asking about the concern) and a higher standard when attempting a formal resolution (such as reporting a psychologist to a licensing board). Psychologists incur little harm when they receive a polite inquiry from another psychologist expressing concern. On the other hand, psychologists, even if innocent of any wrong doing, can incur great hardship when they are reported to a licensing board.

1.06   Cooperating With Ethics Committees

Psychologists cooperate in ethics investigations, proceedings, and resulting requirements of the APA or any affiliated state psychological association to which they belong. In doing so, they address any confidentiality issues. Failure to cooperate is itself an ethics violation. However, making a request for deferment of adjudication of an ethics complaint pending the outcome of litigation does not alone constitute noncooperation. [This standard is similar to Standard 8.06 in the 1992 Ethics Code.]

This standard makes it a violation, in and of itself, for a psychologist to fail to cooperate with the investigation of an ethics committee. Without this provision any psychologist could evade scrutiny simply by refusing to comply with requests for a response to a complaint.

Failure to cooperate with state or provincial psychological association ethics investigations and related proceedings has been added to this standard as a violation. In addition it is important to note that many state licensure boards adopt the APA Ethics Code or a variant of it, and, as such, it would be a violation of the licensure board's code if a psychologist failed to cooperate with a licensure board's inquiry as well, even if the psychologist was not a member of APA or a state or provincial psychological association.

1.07   Improper Complaints

Psychologists do not file or encourage the filing of ethics complaints that are made with reckless disregard for or willful ignorance of facts that would disprove the allegation. [This standard is similar to Standard 8.07 in the 1992 Ethics Code.]

Sometimes emotions get raised in the process of complaints and countercomplaints. In those situations it could be tempting to file complaints for the purposes of getting even. However, a complaint based only on revenge does not further any social good, ties up resources of ethics committees, and only leads to an atmosphere of further recrimination and ill-will. Standard 1.07 requires a minimal amount of prudence before filing a complaint.

The comparable standard from the 1992 Ethics Code prohibited such allegations if they were "intended to harm the respondent rather than to protect the public." That phrasing was dropped because the intentions or feelings of the psychologist filing the charges should be irrelevant. What is relevant is whether the allegations are likely to be true.

1.08 Unfair Discrimination Against Complainants and Respondents

Psychologists do not deny persons employment, advancement, admissions to academic or other programs, tenure, or promotion, based solely upon their having made or their being the subject of an ethics complaint. This does not preclude taking action based upon the outcome of such proceedings or considering other appropriate information. [This standard is related to Standard 1.11b of the 1992 Ethics Code.]

Standard 1.11b of the 1992 Ethics Code only prohibited discrimination against those charged with sexual harassment. The 2002 standard extends the ban against discrimination against any psychologist merely charged with an ethics complaint. Of course, actions may be taken against persons when such charges have been substantiated. This standard also protects "whistle blowers" or those who file reports.

2. COMPETENCE

This section of the Ethics Code requires psychologists to be competent in their services, teaching, and research (2.01a), to take efforts to maintain their expertise (2.03), and base their decisions on the foundation of scientific or professional knowledge of the discipline (2.04). Other provisions deal with competence when treating specific populations where age, gender, culture, and so forth impact the quality of treatment (2.01b); moving into new areas of work (2.01c); providing services to underserved populations (2.01d); implementing innovative treatments (2.01e); assuming forensic roles (2.01f); and dealing with emergencies (2.02). The fac-

Table 4: Standard for Competence

Area	*Responsibility*
2.01a - general competence	competence through education, training, supervised experience, consultation, study, or professional experience
2.01b - diverse populations	when it is "essential for effective implementation of their services or research," psychologists must either (a) get training, experience, consultation, or supervision to ensure competence; (b) refer; or (c) treat if there are extraordinary circumstances
2.01c - new populations, techniques, or technologies	undertake relevant education, training, supervised experience, consultation, or study
2.01d - services not available "compassionate exception"	may provide services to ensure that they are not denied, but must make reasonable effort to ensure competence using relevant research, training, consultation, or study
2.01e - emerging area	act to protect clients/patients
2.01f - assuming forensic roles	adopt standards appropriate to forensic roles
2.02 - emergencies	may provide service to ensure that it is not denied

tors to be considered in practicing with competence are shown in Table 4 (above). Other principles in this section deal with services that are supervised or delegated to others (2.05); or when emotional problems threaten the quality of services (2.06).

The standards of competence are based on General Principle A, Beneficence and Nonmaleficence. That is, psychologists should work to benefit those with whom they work and strive to avoid harming them. This requires an understanding of when interventions could be reasonably expected to benefit clients/patients or organizations.

These standards are highly similar to those in the 1992 Ethics Code except that a "compassionate exception" can be made in emergencies (2.02) or when psychologists are asked to provide treatment to individuals outside of their areas of competence (Standard 2.01d). Greater emphasis is placed on sensitivity to the impact of cultural, disability, or other diversity factors on competence of a psychologist (2.01b). Finally this Ethics Code requires psychologists to ensure the competency of individuals to whom they delegate work (2.05).

2.01   Boundaries of Competence

(a)   [General Rule of Competence.] *Psychologists provide services, teach, and conduct research with populations and in areas only within the boundaries of their competence, based on their education, training, supervised experience, consultation, study, or professional experience.* [This standard is similar to Standard 1.04a of the 1992 Ethics Code.]

As it applies to professional psychology, the question of competence may refer to the use of a technique (assessment, hypnosis, biofeedback, etc.), or skills working with particular problem areas (marital therapy, child management, etc.), a particular population (children, geriatrics, etc.), or some combination thereof (pediatric neuropsychology, etc.). Considerations in working with diverse populations are covered in Standard 2.01b. Considerations in working with techniques that are new to the practitioner are covered in Standard 2.01c.

In addition, competence may refer to emotional competence (Pope & Brown, 1996) or to the psychologists' ability to withstand the transference, countertransference, vicarious traumas, frustrations, or other emotional difficulties associated with professional practice. It also refers to the ability to express compassion and empathy, demonstrate positive regard, show congruence or genuineness, and manage countertransference reactions and other qualities which appear related to good patient outcomes (Steering Committee, 2001). Emotional competence is not discussed in the Ethics Code except as it relates to impairment which is covered in Standard 2.06 (Personal Problems and Conflicts) and 7.04 (Student Disclosure of Personal Information).

The general rule is that psychologists can ascertain if they have become proficient in a certain area of practice after submitting their work to external feedback. The most obvious example of external feedback is when students attend doctoral programs in psychology and submit their performance to the feedback of faculty and clinical supervisors. It becomes more difficult for practitioners to demonstrate competence in areas or with techniques after they have left their doctoral programs.

Generally speaking it is not sufficient to claim competence in a new domain of practice only after reading books or attending workshops. Taking these steps provides no guarantee that psychologists have actually acquired the knowledge and skills found in those books or workshops. Furthermore, the psychologist might not have read the specific books or attended the specific workshops designed to provide a comprehensive overview of the field. Finally, competent performance in a new domain may require actual skills as opposed to just factual knowledge. For example, individual work with children requires psychologists to have a personal style appropriate for children. It may require nuances of body language, tone of voice, and choice of vocabulary that are best acquired through direct contact with children, as opposed to just reading about them.

Unlike professional psychologists, teaching psychologists can earn no specialty credentials for competency. The primary oversight for teachers comes from the hiring institution. It is sometimes difficult to determine how much of a stretch psychologists can make between their formal academic training and their teaching responsibilities. Does one graduate course in social psychology qualify a psychologist to teach social psychology to undergraduates? To graduate students? What if the course was taken 5 years ago? 15 years ago? What if sudden illness on the faculty leaves a vacuum in the department and this psychologist is the most qualified person available to teach it? Sometimes faculty members will have to make a compassionate exception of their own because they will be pressed into teaching courses in which they did not have the optimal academic preparation. Nonetheless, those psychologists who then undertake appropriate study or consultation will be able to fulfill their responsibilities under the Ethics Code.

Good research requires a knowledge of the literature, research design skills, and research ethics. The Ethics Code does not intend to discipline psychologists for running a poorly designed study that could not get published in a peer review journal or for using an inappropriate statistical test. At worst it would be considered a waste of time, not an ethical violation. However, the burden for ensuring competence increases as the potential for harm to the subjects increases. If the research entailed the delivery of services, such as a treatment for a mental illness, then researchers would be held to the standards of minimal competence required of all practitioners who deliver such services.

In addition, the work of psychologists must be based on the knowledge foundation of the discipline or profession of psychology (2.03) and psychologists must make ongoing efforts to maintain their expertise in areas of their work (2.04). Past training, in the absence of ongoing readings, study, experience, or workshops, is not sufficient to maintain competence if the standard of practice in a particular area has shifted.

> *(b)* [Competence With Special Populations.] *Where scientific or professional knowledge in the discipline of psychology establishes that an understanding of factors associated with age, gender, gender identity, race, ethnicity, culture, national ori-*

gin, religion, sexual orientation, disability, language, or so-cioeconomic status is essential for effective implementation of their services or research, psychologists have or obtain the training, experience, consultation, or supervision necessary to ensure the competence of their services, or they make appropriate referrals, except as provided in Standard 2.02, Providing Services in Emergencies. [This standard is similar to Standard 1.08 of the 1992 Ethics Code.]

Effective treatments are geared to the unique needs of the individual. One extreme position is that demographic variables never have an impact on treatment. The other extreme position is that only persons of one particular ethnic group, gender identity, disability, and so on, can treat persons of that same ethnic group, gender identity, disability, and so forth. The Ethics Code adopts a middle position in which egregious misconduct is punishable, but frivolous complaints have no chance of survival.

It is true that data have not yet established empirical bases by which to match psychotherapists or treatments to clients/patients based on their age, gender, gender identity, race, ethnicity, culture, national origin, religion, sexual orientation, disability, language, or socioeconomic status. For example, most psychotherapy outcome research has been conducted with European-Americans, despite recent National Institutes of Health requirements that its funded research must include members of ethnic minority populations. Consequently, it is not known how much the outcome studies done with predominately European-American clients/patients will generalize to ethnic minority populations. Indeed, determining the external validity of these studies is difficult because of the diversity of ethnic minority populations (e.g., individuals who fit into the broad category of "Asian/Americans" may represent widely diverse national backgrounds), the variation with which individuals have been acculturated to American society, or the possibility that the individual has a bicultural or biracial identity. Also, a demographic match may not be meaningful from a cultural perspective. For example, a highly acculturated non-Chinese-speaking Chinese-American may have little understanding of the culture of a recent Chinese-speaking immigrant (Lam & Sue, 2001). Nonetheless these factors are relevant to treatment planning. Hall (2001) states that

Although competent therapists consider individual client characteristics on a case-by-case basis, the therapist unfamiliar with ethnic minority cultures may easily overlook or misunderstand constructs that may be more highly emphasized in ethnic minority than majority cultures. (p. 506)

Similar questions about the degree of external validity could be made about persons because of their age, socioeconomic status, religion, or sexual orientation. Consequently, this standard requires that psychologists be competent, refer, or obtain supervision when special knowledge is "essential for effective implementation of their services or research." Exceptions are permitted for emergencies (2.02).

Allison et al. (1996) reported that most recent graduates in Counseling Psychology had some course work or supervised experience with diverse populations (ethnic minorities, sexual minorities, physically impaired) and limited their services to their self-reported areas of competence. However, about 8% of those psychologists reported treating diverse individuals whom they were not competent to treat. It is hoped that these psychologists are performing these services under the exceptions provided in Standard 2.02.

Religiously sensitive psychotherapy requires a framework of sensitivity and openness to the faith orientation of the client. At times it may be necessary to distinguish between the religious practices of the client/patient and psychopathology.

Sincere Religion or Extreme Pathology?

A client/patient in a charismatic religious group displayed great evangelical zeal which carried over into his work, where the enthusiasm alienated some of his fellow workers and disrupted work production. The treating psychologist had to determine whether this behavior was initiated and maintained because it was culturally valued or if it was a manifestation of the early signs of hypomania.

(c) [Moving Into New Areas.] *Psychologists planning to provide services, teach, or conduct research involving populations, areas, techniques, or technologies new to them undertake relevant education, training, supervised experience, consultation, or study.* [This standard is similar to Standard 1.04b of the 1992 Ethics Code.]

Competent psychologists may want to develop expertise in areas of psychology that they did not study in graduate school. Psychologists can obtain proficiency credentials in some areas such as biofeedback certification. In other areas, no such credentials exist. Moreover, there may not be a uniformly agreed upon sequence of experiences, study (set of readings, workshops, or classes), or examination for psychologists so that they can become proficient in other areas. Although these psychologists may self-prescribe a course of readings and continuing education programs, we recommend that psychologists should not consider themselves competent in a new domain until they have had another psychologist who is proficient in that field monitor or supervise them.

Belar et al. (2001) present a series of self-assessment questions for psychologists before they move into clinical health psychology. However, the same self-assessment process can be useful for psychologists moving into other new domains as well. Some of the questions include whether the psychologist knows the scientific basis (biological, social, cognitive/affective, developmental) in the relevant domain, has the clinical skills, understands the treatment milieu, and knows the related ethical and legal issues. Perhaps the most important recommendation they make is for psychologists to "become an apprentice to an experienced psychologist. Pay for consultation or volunteer services in return for opportunities for shadowing the expert in relevant clinical settings" (p. 138).

> (d) [When Services Are Not Available.] *When psychologists are asked to provide services to individuals for whom appropriate mental health services are not available and for which psychologists have not obtained the competence necessary, psychologists with closely related prior training or experience may provide such services in order to ensure that services are not denied if they make a reasonable effort to obtain the competence required by using relevant research, training, consultation, or study.* [This standard is new.]

This standard, as does 2.02, deals primarily with psychologists who work in geographical areas in which a wide range of mental health services are not available. Although psychologists may provide services to anyone in an emergency, this standard deals with nonemergency services. For nonemergency services in underserved geographical areas, psychologists can provide services in closely related areas provided that they make a reasonable effort to obtain the necessary competence. A key issue concerns what is "closely related prior training or experience."

It is difficult to give fixed rules for determining how closely related the training should be. Certainly, a psychologist with expertise in dealing with young adults may be presumed to have skills that could be useful to late adolescents, at least some of the time. Beyond the "one step removed" decisions, it may be necessary to do a utilitarian calculus and determine if the expertise of the psychologist is likely to benefit the client/patient, depending on the specific condition of the client/patient, and the burden that would occur if he or she were to wait until a more qualified professional was identified.

Helping a Family in Need

A psychologist with experience with adult obsessive compulsive disorder (OCD) was asked to consult with a family where a child was suspected of having OCD. This family lived in a rural area, had limited financial resources, and would have had to travel more than an hour to locate a qualified professional (during winter months, they might not be able to make appointments at all). The psychologist agreed to accept the client/patient, but with the understanding that he would be consulting on a regular basis with a psychiatrist who was proficient in the psychological treatments for children with OCD.

> *(e)* [Emerging Areas.] *In those emerging areas in which generally recognized standards for preparatory training do not yet exist, psychologists nevertheless take reasonable steps to ensure the competence of their work and to protect clients/patients, students, supervisees, research participants, organizational clients, and others from harm.* [This standard is similar to Standard 1.04c of the 1992 Ethics Code.]

This standard attempts to balance two concerns. First, it attempts to ensure that psychologists do not haphazardly apply every passing technique on their clients/patients without considering the research base supporting its efficacy. The ethical principle of nonmaleficence (do not harm) requires nothing less.

On the other hand, it does not ask psychologists to withhold possibly efficacious treatments or techniques while researchers debate the nuances of existing outcome studies. The ethical principle of beneficence (working to promote the welfare of others) requires psychologists to use techniques that they believe would help their clients/patients.

Psychologists may ask where should they set the threshold for accepting a new therapeutic technique. In recent years psychologists have expressed an interest in new techniques, such as telephone therapy, internet therapy, massage, nutritional supplements, herbal or holistic treatments, facilitated communication, metronome therapy, auditory integration therapy, and so on. Some of these techniques may be on the cutting edge of health care, may acquire empirical support, and may be eventually taught as part of the professional training of psychologists. Or, they may acquire acceptance as providing some benefit, perhaps as an adjunctive treatment, for a few clients/patients under some circumstances. Other new techniques may be therapeutically inert or iatrogenic, have no empirical support, and should be considered quackery. Nonetheless, many health care professionals and clients/patients are expressing an interest in novel treatments. For example, Druss et al. (1998) found that many depressed clients/patients had sought out nontraditional or alternative medications and some were on both prescription antidepressants and alternative medications.

Before agreeing to use an experimental technique, psychologists need to evaluate it critically and to understand its limitations. They need to ask themselves if these techniques have a reliable theoretical base (i.e., is it based on a generally accepted theory, not just any theory). What is the state of the outcome literature? Does the methodology account for a possible placebo effect or other confounding factors? Which clients/patients would benefit from this technique? It should be remembered that a technique that benefits one client/patient may not necessarily benefit another client/patient.

In addition, psychologists should ask themselves if they are sufficiently trained in the technique. Does it fall within the purview of the practice of psychology? Could the treatment be iatrogenic? If appropriate, has the client's/patient's primary care physician been informed about the treatment? Has the psychologist consulted with peers about the use or application of this technique? Are clients/patients informed about the innovative nature of the treatment? Is the progress of the clients/patients measured and their welfare monitored throughout the course of treatment? Will the clients/patients be discouraged from trying more conventional approaches if the experimental one fails? This last point is especially important. Not only will the clients/patients have wasted their time if the treatment is inert, they may be so discouraged that they will not take advantage of more acceptable treatments with a better record of success. In other words, inert treatments may be harmful. Failure to attend to any one of these questions could create problems for both the psychologist and the client/patient.

For example, one psychologist placed an ad in a newspaper in which he claimed that he had "miraculous results" using magnets to treat depression. In addition to having a misleading advertisement, this psychologist was using a technique that has no empirical support. In fact, the only study in the literature found that a placebo group had better outcomes than the treatment group.

A Sensitive Clinical Decision

A psychologist was treating a client/patient who revealed that she was also taking a herbal antidepressant. Although the psychologist respected her client's/patient's right to make that decision, she carefully explained the outcome literature with this remedy (which was mixed), asked the client/patient to monitor the dosage of the herbal drug she was taking, informed the client/patient about prescription drug alternatives, asked her to talk it over with her family physician, regularly asked about her use of the herbal drug, and monitored her progress.

This psychologist was aware that her outright disapproval of the herbal remedy could impair her relationship with the client/patient. She was also aware that, for some clients/patients, this particular herbal remedy may have some benefit. However, herbal remedies sometimes are not sold in standardized doses so it is not always clear that the amount taken would have any therapeutic benefit (Cirigliano & Sun, 1998). In addition, cases have been reported where clients/patients have taken doses which were toxic or which interacted with prescription medications. Coordination with a treating psychopharmacologist is important.

Another emerging area is that of therapy through telephone, e-mail, or other telehealth interventions. The 2002 Ethics Code deliberately made few direct references to the electronic transmission of information. There will be many developments in e-health or telehealth over the life of the 2002 Ethics Code, and APA did not want to address the ethical conduct with today's technology only to find those provisions outdated in the near future. Consequently, references to innovative therapies are made on the basis of general principles that psychologists need to apply, using professional judgment, consultation, and reliance on informed sources.

Nonetheless, the existing technologies in telephone and e-mail therapy do create some ethical problems. Telephone therapy differs from crisis intervention or the occasional between-therapy phone contact. Proponents of telephone therapy claim it is a way to help persons who have difficulties traveling, such as those who are blind, have panic disorder with phobic avoidance, or mobility problems. However, telephone therapy alone may raise concerns whether the psychologist could perform an adequate assessment or conduct therapy without the benefit of visual cues. Furthermore, high quality outcome data on this mode of intervention is lacking. Finally, it is unclear which licensing board should have authority to regulate the practice. Should the authority to regulate rest with the state in which the client/patient resides or the state in which the psychologist lives? In the absence of outcome data, it may be prudent to rely on reasonable inferences about the potential limitations of telephone-only therapy (Haas, Benedict, & Kobos, 1998) such as the inability to read nonverbal cues or the temptation for the psychologist to become distracted during the conversation. Some of the same concerns could apply to therapy conducted by e-mail. However, e-mail is complicated by the limits to confidentiality inherent in some e-mail systems.

(f) [Assuming Forensic Roles.] *When assuming forensic roles, psychologists are or become reasonably familiar with the judicial or administrative rules governing their roles.* [This standard overlaps with Standard 7.06 of the 1992 Ethics Code.]

Forensic work requires specialized knowledge and expertise. Although any psychologist could treat a client/patient who later ends up in court, this standard only applies when psychologists voluntarily take forensic assignments. Such psychologists are expected to know the rules governing their forensic roles. Two important source documents that guide psychologists doing forensic work are the *Specialty Guidelines for Forensic Psychologists* from Division 41 Society for Law and Psychology (Committee on Ethical Guidelines for Forensic Psychologists, 1991) and the *Guidelines for Child Custody Evaluations in Divorce Proceedings* (APA, 1994). In addition, psychologists need to know the laws of their state or province, especially concerning the role of expert witnesses and the general protocol for court reports and appearances.

2.02 Providing Services in Emergencies

In emergencies, when psychologists provide services to individuals for whom other mental health services are not available and for which psychologists have not obtained the necessary training, psychologists may provide such services in order to ensure that services are not denied. The services are discontinued as soon as the emergency has ended or appropriate services are available. [This standard is new.]

Psychologists may, at times, accept clients/patients out of a sense of compassion, even though they might not have the training or expertise typically required to work with them. This is especially likely to occur in rural, inner city, or other traditionally underserved areas. Nonetheless, even in those situations, psychologists should take steps to increase the likelihood of favorable outcomes with their clients/patients.

A Needy Client/Patient

A rural Midwestern psychologist was asked to treat a seriously disturbed refugee from Nigeria whose entry into the United States had been sponsored by a local church. The psychologist lacked proficiency in French, the primary language of his prospective client/patient, and had no knowledge of the prospective client's/patient's culture, but there probably was no mental health professional in the whole state with those qualifications.

This particular psychologist, however, was able to locate a social worker from another city who worked through a refugee association and was able to provide useful consultation on relevant cultural factors. The intent of this standard is to permit psychologists to respond compassionately in emergency settings even if they do not otherwise meet the qualifications needed to provide the service.

In many rural and other underserved communities, services referred often means services denied. Because of the travel required to get to the next closest mental health professional, many clients/patients either must see this psychologist or no one. The problem can be especially acute when clients/patients, such as the one in the preceding example, are in great emotional turmoil or even exhibit life endangering behaviors.

Here is an example of a psychologist who was able to fulfill her responsibilities.

An Unwanted Assignment

Due to a sudden budget shortage, a psychologist working in an underserved public clinic was assigned the responsibility of running the groups for older adults. She had never worked with older clients/patients before. Although the clinic made a commitment to hire a geriatric psychologist, this psychologist still had responsibility for this group for 2 months. She consulted closely with the geriatric psychiatrist assigned to the clinic and engaged in extra readings and study to ensure adequate care for her clients/patients.

Within recent years, psychologists have been paying greater attention to the issue of cultural competence. Diversity needs to be considered when delivering psychological services. Once again, there is little substitute for submitting one's work to external feedback. Although few psychologists are outright bigots, no psychologist can be expected to have extensive experience with members of all of the other cultural groups in North America, and they may not understand their unique perspectives and needs.

2.03 Maintaining Competence

Psychologists undertake ongoing efforts to develop and maintain their competence. [This standard is similar to Standard 1.05 of the 1992 Ethics Code.]

Psychological knowledge becomes obsolete over time. Psychologists need both formal and informal continuing education to keep pace with the latest developments in the field. Most state boards of psychology require continuing education as a condition of licensure renewal. However, that requirement is just the educational floor. Psychologists who follow the aspirational principles do more than the minimum required.

2.04 Bases for Scientific and Professional Judgments

Psychologists' work is based upon established scientific and professional knowledge of the discipline. (See also Standards 2.01e, Boundaries of Competence, and 10.01b, Informed Consent to Therapy.) [This standard is similar to Standard 1.06 of the 1992 Ethics Code.]

In order to fulfill their responsibilities to provide competent services, psychologists need to base their work on the established scientific and professional knowledge of the discipline. The exact phrasing of this standard is important. It does not require psychologists to rely entirely upon scientific studies to inform their treatment decisions. As much as psychologists would like to have scientific bases for everything they do, the reality is that much of what is accepted as a professional standard is based on clinical intuition or tradition.

For example, scientific evidence shows that cognitive-behavioral interventions can produce substantial and clinically significant symptom reduction for a high percentage of clients/patients with uncomplicated panic attacks. There is less evidence concerning its efficacy with clients/patients with comorbid axis I or axis II disorders. However, the psychologists using cognitive-behavioral therapy with a panic disorder client/patient with a coexisting personality disorder may apply additional treatment techniques or interventions that were not included in the original cognitive-behavioral protocol for the treatment of panic disorder. In other words, professional judgment must supplement the scientific knowledge base.

2.05 Delegation of Work to Others

Psychologists who delegate work to employees, supervisees, or research or teaching assistants or who use the services of others, such as interpreters, take reasonable steps to (1) avoid delegating such work to persons who have a multiple relationship with those being served that would likely lead to exploitation or loss of objectivity; (2) authorize only those responsibilities that such persons can be expected to perform competently on the basis of their education, training, or experience, either independently or with the level of supervision being provided; and (3) see that such persons

perform these services competently. (See also Standards 2.02, Pro-
viding Services in Emergencies; 3.05, Multiple Relationships; 4.01,
Maintaining Confidentiality; 9.01, Bases for Assessments; 9.02, Use
of Assessments; 9.03, Informed Consent in Assessments; and 9.07,
Assessment by Unqualified Persons.) [This standard is similar to
Standard 1.22 of the 1992 Ethics Code.]

Psychologists are responsible for the quality of services provided by
the people whom they supervise. Psychologists should delegate only those
responsibilities that their supervisees can perform competently. Training
centers typically accept trainees from many different programs and the
skill level of the trainees will vary greatly. Indeed, Procidano et al. (1995)
found that 89% of the graduate departments of psychology that were surveyed reported having a student who had serious professional deficiencies, limited clinical skills, or personality/emotional problems in the last 5
years.

Supervising psychologists should determine the adequacy of preparation and level of skill of trainees even though previous supervisors and
sponsoring academic departments may claim that the students have superior skills. Adequate preparation means emotional competence, technical
skills, and understanding the unique cultural issues in the population receiving services (Vasquez, 1994).

The same obligations to ensure quality applies to all employees, even
those who are not undergoing the supervision required for licensure or
another credential. From a risk management perspective, it is prudent for
psychologists/employers/supervisors to have office policies, training programs (including refresher courses), regular staff meetings, and an objective system for monitoring the quality of the performance of their staff.
Any breach by one staff member will reflect badly on the psychologist
(Woody, 2000).

Whenever possible, psychologists should attempt to get professional
interpreters when the client/patient is not proficient in the psychologists'
language. In some large cities, it may be relatively easy to find an interpreter for a common foreign language. However, the ability to find such
an interpreter may also depend upon how common the language is. If no
trained interpreter can be found, then it may be acceptable to use another
person with fluency, such as an instructor of the foreign language (Fortuny
& Mullaney, 1998). Fortuny and Mullaney state that friends or relatives
of family members or facility staff should never be used as translators
because of their potential to contaminate information collection. This statement may be too extreme as there may be emergencies or other unusual
situations when such persons have to be used.

2.06   Personal Problems and Conflicts

(a)   [Refraining From Practice When Impaired.] *Psychologists refrain from initiating an activity when they know or should know that there is a substantial likelihood that their personal problems will prevent them from performing their work-related activities in a competent manner.* [This standard is similar to Standard 1.13a of the 1992 Ethics Code.]

(b)   [Seeking Assistance When Impaired.] *When psychologists become aware of personal problems that may interfere with their performing work-related duties adequately, they take appropriate measures, such as obtaining professional consultation or assistance, and determine whether they should limit, suspend, or terminate their work-related duties. (See also Standard 10.10, Terminating Therapy.)* [This standard is similar to Standard 1.13c of the 1992 Ethics Code.]

Impairment refers to the ongoing inability to perform the functions of a psychologist at a competent level due to a psychological or physical disability. Impairment needs to be distinguished from distress and incompetence. Distress refers to psychological or physical problems which, although subjectively disturbing, do not prevent the psychologists from performing adequate work. Incompetence refers to the inability to perform adequately as a psychologist because of the lack of knowledge or technical skills. Incompetence is addressed in Standards 2.01, 2.03, and elsewhere in the Ethics Code.

The estimates of impairment, of course, vary with the definition of impairment. However, even if we take a narrow definition of impairment, we could argue that at least 3% of psychologists will, at some time in their careers, have a psychological or physical disability that substantially limits their ability to perform the minimal functions of their profession adequately (other researchers have suggested higher rates, see for example, Thoreson, Miller, & Krauskopf, 1989).

In any event, the standard states that impairment is, in and of itself, grounds for disciplinary actions. Psychologists who know or should know that they are impaired have a responsibility to withdraw from their work or seek supervision to ensure the quality of their work and to get help for their problem.

Fortunately, many state and provincial psychological associations (SPPAs) have created colleague assistance programs designed to help psychologists who have such difficulties (Barnett & Hillard, 2001). In addition, there is growing literature on the stressors facing health care professionals and ways that individuals and institutions can help reduce distress, prevent impairment, or assist in making the job as pleasant and desirable as possible. Also, in recent years the professional literature has encouraged psychologists to focus on general self-care, which means anticipating and learning to handle these stressors and to focus on positive self-care. This focus on positive self-care is especially important in the professional practice of psychology where emotional competence is directly relevant to the quality of the work product.

This standard deals with impairment. However, many psychologists may acquire, because of stress or other personal or situational factors, a noticeable decline in effectiveness that does not cause them to become incompetent. Nonetheless, a reduced ability to empathize with patients, or to handle countertransference feelings may result in a decline in positive patient outcomes. "For therapists to be effective, it is essential that they care for themselves so that they are better able to care for clients" (Lambert & Barley, 2001, p. 359).

3. HUMAN RELATIONS

This section of the Ethics Code on human relations deals with several issues including the necessity to avoid harming others through unfair discrimination (3.01), sexual harassment (3.02) and other harassment (3.03), and a general prohibition against harming others (3.04). In addition, it addresses the need to avoid harmful or exploitative multiple relationships (3.05) and conflicts of interest (3.06), and to clarify roles when services are being provided at the request of a third party (3.07). Furthermore, it prohibits psychologists from exploiting those over whom they have supervisory or other evaluative authority (3.08), urges them to cooperate with other professionals when necessary to benefit their clients/patients (3.09), requires psychologists to give informed consent to consumers of their services (3.10), including organizations (3.11), and to make reasonable efforts to plan for the continuity of needed services in the event of an anticipated interruption in those services (3.12).

These standards are based primarily on General Principle A, Beneficence and Nonmaleficence. That is, psychologists have an obligation to avoid harming others such as through harassment or harmful multiple relationships. In addition, the General Principle E, Respect for People's Rights and Dignity (respect for client/patient autonomy) becomes relevant in implementing the principles of informed consent (Standard 3.10). It is the goal of that standard to give as much decision making as is reasonable to the consumers of psychological services.

Most of these standards were also found, in varying forms, in the 1992 version of the Ethics Code. However, the major changes are that the new version clarifies that not all multiple relationships are necessarily harmful and it specifically includes informed consent obligations to organizational clients as well as individual clients.

3.01 Unfair Discrimination

In their work-related activities, psychologists do not engage in unfair discrimination based on age, gender, gender identity, race, ethnicity, culture, national origin, religion, sexual orientation, disability, socioeconomic status, or any basis proscribed by law. [This standard is similar to Standard 1.10 of the 1992 Ethics Code.]

3.02 Sexual Harassment

Psychologists do not engage in sexual harassment. Sexual harassment is sexual solicitation, physical advances, or verbal or nonverbal conduct that is sexual in nature, that occurs in connection with the psychologist's activities or roles as a psychologist, and that either (1) is unwelcome, is offensive, or creates a hostile workplace or educational environment, and the psychologist knows or is told this or (2) is sufficiently severe or intense to be abusive to a reasonable person in the context. Sexual harassment can consist of a single intense or severe act or of multiple persistent or pervasive acts. (See also Standard 1.08, Unfair Discrimination Against Complainants and Respondents.) [This standard is similar to Standard 1.11a of the 1992 Ethics Code.]

3.03 Other Harassment

Psychologists do not knowingly engage in behavior that is harassing or demeaning to persons with whom they interact in their work based on factors such as those persons' age, gender, gender identity, race, ethnicity, culture, national origin, religion, sexual orientation, disability, language, or socioeconomic status. [This standard is similar to Standard 1.12 of the 1992 Ethics Code.]

These three standards (3.01-3.03) are fairly straightforward. The prohibition against unfair discrimination is designed to protect members of diverse or minority groups from harmful activities by psychologists. Standard 3.02 defines sexual harassment and prohibits it.

Some psychologists may wonder why APA did not adopt a more precise definition of sexual harassment in 3.02. APA recognizes that the legal definition of sexual harassment may change over time and that agencies that employ psychologists will have their own specific policy and definition of sexual harassment. Standard 3.02 provides general guidance for psychologists while recognizing that some psychologists will be guided by other more specific definitions.

Standard 3.03 prohibits psychologists from knowingly harming or demeaning others. This is one of the few standards in which the subjective state of mind of the psychologist becomes relevant. It is implicitly recognized that psychologists may inadvertently act in an insensitive manner toward an individual because of her or his age, gender, gender identity, and so on.

3.04 Avoiding Harm

> *Psychologists take reasonable steps to avoid harming their clients/ patients, students, supervisees, research participants, organizational clients, and others with whom they work, and to minimize harm where it is foreseeable and unavoidable.* [This standard is similar to Standard 1.14 of the 1992 Ethics Code.]

From a practical perspective in enforcing the Ethics Code, Standard 3.04 is seldom charged in isolation. More often it is cited in combination with other standards. Nonetheless, it may have some educational value.

Standard 3.04 deals with more generic harm than the specific Standards 3.01 to 3.03, which are limited to discrimination or harassment based on diversity, or general sexual harassment. The standard is not intended to punish psychologists any time a client/patient feels discomfort. It is possible that psychologists may need to confront clients/patients with some unpleasant news or unpleasant feedback concerning their behavior. Although there may be some short-term discomfort with that feedback, it would not be considered harmful, as long the psychologist used reasonable judgment in providing the feedback or attempted to minimize foreseeable and unavoidable harm.

Unwelcome But Needed Feedback

A client/patient was both enraged and in agony after his wife said she was thinking about filing for a divorce. In order for the goals of therapy to be met (which was to save the marriage), the psychologist needed to confront the client/patient with some of his behavior patterns (insensitivity, coarseness, etc.) that probably contributed to his wife's reaction.

Unpleasant News

For sound clinical reasons, a treatment team in a nursing home made the decision that the psychologist should tell the client/patient that his wife had just died. It is foreseeable that the client/patient would be very upset by this news, but every effort was made to soften the blow to him.

There is no intent on the part of the Ethics Code to "punish the messenger" or otherwise impair the ability of psychologists to perform their jobs, which may, on occasion, mean delivering unpleasant news or causing patients some discomfort.

3.05 Multiple Relationships

(a) [General Rule on Multiple Relationships.] *A multiple relationship occurs when a psychologist is in a professional role with a person and (1) at the same time is in another role with the same person, (2) at the same time is in a relationship with a person closely associated with or related to the person with whom the psychologist has the professional relationship, or (3) promises to enter into another relationship in the future with the person or a person closely associated with or related to the person.*

A psychologist refrains from entering into a multiple relationship if the multiple relationship could reasonably be expected to impair the psychologist's objectivity, competence, or effectiveness in performing his or her functions as a psychologist, or otherwise risks exploitation or harm to the person with whom the professional relationship exists.

Multiple relationships that would not reasonably be expected to cause impairment or risk exploitation or harm are not unethical. [This standard is related to Standard 1.17a of the 1992 Ethics Code.]

Multiple relationships are dealt with several times in the Ethics Code, including standards dealing with student disclosure of information (7.05), sexual intimacies with students and supervisees (7.07), clarifying roles in couples or family therapy (10.02), sexual intimacies with current clients/patients (10.05), sexual intimacies with relatives of current clients/patients (10.06), therapy with former sexual partners (10.07), and sexual intimacies with former therapy clients/patients (10.08). All of the other standards appear to expand upon, but do not contract, the essential provisions of 3.05. Each of those standards will be discussed separately in this book.

Multiple relationships (boundary conflicts or role conflicts) have represented about half of the ethical violations brought before the APA Ethics Committee. Most of the alleged violations were egregious actions such as sexual contact between psychologist and client/patient and would be covered by the new Standard 10.05 rather than this standard.

The prohibition against harmful multiple relationships is one example where conflicts of interests may harm clients/patients, students, research subjects, organizational clients, or other recipients of the services of psychologists. In other standards the Ethics Code considers conflicts of interest with clients/patients (bartering, 6.05), students (credit for research/publications, 8.12b), and research participants (students decline to participate in research, 8.04).

Definition of Multiple Relationships. This standard is one of the few in which the Ethics Code defines a term. A multiple relationship could be a relationship that is concurrent, consecutive, or consecutive and premised upon promises made during the therapeutic relationship. For example, a concurrent multiple relationship exists when psychologists have a social or business relationship with clients/patients at the same time they have a professional relationship. In a consecutive relationship, psychologists have a social or business relationship either before or after the professional relationship with their clients/patients.

The standard explicitly states that not every multiple relationship is necessarily harmful ("Multiple relationships that would not reasonably be expected to cause impairment or risk exploitation or harm are not unethical"). This is one of the few times that the Ethics Code states what is explicitly ethical. The interpretation of the word "reasonably" again takes on importance. The issue is whether a reasonable psychologist would be aware of countertransference, transference, or other clinical contraindications that would make harm or exploitation foreseeable.

Not every contact with a client/patient outside of the office is necessarily an ethical violation. For example, it could be clearly appropriate for psychotherapists to conduct some therapeutic techniques, such as in vivo desensitization, outside of the office. Also, incidental or unavoidable contacts with clients/patients that occur outside the office are not intrinsically unethical.

According to this standard, it could even be ethical for psychologists to enter into a treatment relationship with a person with whom they have a current or consecutive business or social relationship, as long as the relationship is not exploitative or clinically contraindicated.

Handling Multiple Relationships. Despite the clarification that loosened the restrictions against multiple relationships, psychologists still need to be careful about entering into concurrent multiple relationships and should be sensitive to the effects of subtle multiple relationships.

Concurrent or Consecutive Multiple Relationships. From a risk management perspective, psychologists should not minimize the possibility that their own self-interest could blind them to the dangers of entering into a multiple relationship. Also, even conscientious and scrupulous psychotherapists need to watch certain behaviors which, in and of themselves, are harmless, but which clients/patients could misinterpret. Even if the psychologist reaches the goal of having a completely objective attitude toward the client/patient, the client/patient might not be able to reach or maintain that attitude toward the psychologist.

Other multiple relationships are consecutive in that a social or business relationship developed before the professional relationship has started or after the professional relationship has ended. Anderson and Kitchener (1996) conducted a nonrandom survey of psychologists and identified numerous posttherapy contacts between psychologists and clients/patients. Some of the contacts were brief (attending the wedding of an ex-client/patient) and others were more intense (the development of a social or business relationship). At times they occurred because they were unavoidable (the psychologist and the former client/patient lived, worked, shopped, or worshiped in the same vicinity). At other times the contact was initiated by the client/patient and at other times by the psychologist.

Let's Do Lunch

At the last session of brief therapy, a female client/patient asked her psychologist if they could have lunch together. The psychologist said she would think it over, and eventually notified her ex-client/patient that such a meeting would not be ethical. The now former-client/patient fumed over the "betrayal" and filed a complaint alleging that the therapist had "groomed" her for a posttreatment social relationship by her excessive use of self-disclosure.

In hindsight the initial hesitation of the psychologist had allowed her ex-client/patient to invest herself in their expected posttherapy relationship. Only after treatment ended did the psychologist fully understand the unresolved transference issues. Although the psychologist was successful in defending herself against the complaint, she wished she had handled the situation differently (i.e., that she had not hesitated in declining the lunch invitation and had used the opportunity to address the transference issues).

According to Pipes (1997), it is important for psychologists to weigh several factors when considering posttherapy relationships, such as the possibility that the client/patient may need to return to therapy, that some clients/patients remain vulnerable to exploitation even after termination, that the client/patient or psychologist may have strong transference or countertransference feelings, or that the trustworthiness of psychologists in general may be threatened when such relationships become public.

Although the Ethics Code does not require it, psychologists may find it useful to apply the same criteria to nonsexual social or business contacts as the APA Ethics Code applies to sexual contacts with former clients/patients after 2 years. It may be useful for psychologists to consider developing social/business relationships with former clients/patients only if they can demonstrate that there is no exploitation based on an analysis of relevant factors including the amount of time that has passed since therapy terminated, the nature and duration of therapy, circumstances of the termination, the client's/patient's personal history and current mental status, or the likely impact on the client/patient.

Anderson and Kitchener (1998) also suggest that psychologists think in terms of their personal virtues when considering whether to enter into a posttermination social relationship. Psychologists who act out of the traits of prudence (practical wisdom), integrity, respectfulness, compassion, and trustworthiness will be better able to appreciate the ethical risks involved and act in a manner that considers the welfare of the former client/patient.

Overt or Subtle Multiple Relationships. Boundary violations include the overt, such as social relationships with a client/patient, and the subtle, in which the boundaries are weakened by just-noticeable gradients of behavior. The APA Ethics Code is intended to provide redress for the overt or exploitative boundary violations.

However, it is sometimes difficult to draw a clear line between the overt and subtle boundary crossings. Subtle boundary crossings include many actions on the part of the psychologist, but the more common ones are hugging, gift giving (or receiving), and excessive therapist self-disclosure. In reality, many psychologists are flexible in their maintenance of boundaries and may, depending on the needs of the client/patient and the context of therapy, disclose personal information, extend therapy beyond the scheduled time, express their personal feelings toward their clients/patients, or engage in social amenities such as the discussion of current events (Johnston & Farber, 1996).

Subtle boundary crossings also could occur when discussing religious issues with clients/patients. For example, it could be quite appropriate for psychologists to speak to clients/patients about religious issues and to use religious language to describe psychological concepts, but problems may arise if clients/patients perceive psychologists as imposing their religious beliefs on them or assuming the role of a denominational representative (Richards & Potts, 1995).

Although these actions are, in and of themselves, usually harmless or perhaps even helpful, it is prudent for psychologists to think carefully about these subtle boundary crossings. Some overly sensitive clients/patients have misconstrued therapeutically indicated or innocuous behaviors such as scheduling clients/patients for the last appointment of the day, extending sessions beyond the scheduled time (even if it appears therapeutically indicated), self-disclosing (even if minor and intended as therapeutic), calling clients/patients on the telephone between sessions, or using sexually explicit language, even if it is appropriate to the client's/patient's presenting problem.

Many of these boundary crossings can be analyzed in terms of the transference and countertransference issues that they represent. To a large extent therapists need to be free to use their discretion and judgment in making decisions about these boundaries. The desire to keep firm boundaries, or the extent to which psychotherapists feel flexible in modifying them, reflects more therapeutic discretion and risk management than it represents a minimal standard of care or a per se ethical violation. The Ethics Code has not been written to unnecessarily restrict the judgment of psychologists. Indeed, Barrett and Berman (2001) found that selective therapist self-disclosure (directed at client/patient welfare) led to reduced symptoms of client/patient distress and led clients/patients to like their therapists more. Similarly, Bridges (2001) noted that "when psychologically attuned and patient centered, intentional disclosure opens up space for deep therapeutic engagement between therapist and patient" (p. 21). A balance needs to be drawn between selective and patient-focused self-disclosure (Hill & Knox, 2001) and too much self-disclosure that may result in a weakened therapeutic alliance (Ackerman & Hilsenroth, 2001).

At times a boundary crossing may reflect a mishandling of transference or countertransference issues such as when the client/patient views the self-disclosure of the therapist as moving their relationship from a professional to a social one. This does not mean, however, that the boundary crossing could not be harmful or that a psychologist could not be disciplined for engaging in a pattern of subtle boundary crossings which, on the whole, would give a reasonable person the impression that the relationship was transformed from a professional to a personal one. However, the pattern needs to be obvious, and isolated decisions on the part of psychologists to cross a boundary in a nonexploitative manner for clinical reasons should not be grounds for disciplinary actions.

However, from a risk management perspective there is always a concern that these boundary crossings may be the first steps toward developing more serious sexual boundary violations. Typically the allegation of sexual contact involves no other evidence but the client's/patient's word against that of the psychologist. However, often the Ethics Committee will reach a judgment on the basis of other boundary violations. Sexual contact usually occurs in the context of multiple nonsexual violations (Simon, 1992). For example, in their retrospective study of clients/patients who had sexual relationships with their psychotherapists, Somer and Saadon (1999) found that many of those psychotherapists had hugged their clients/patients, or disclosed personal information that was unrelated to client/patient needs. Also, Lamb and Catanzaro (1998) found that psychologist sexual offenders (those who engaged in sexual boundary violations with clients/patients) were more likely than psychologist nonoffenders to have engaged in nonsexual boundary violations, such as developing a social or business relationship with a client/patient.

We recommend a reasonable balance between boundaries and therapeutic effectiveness. Just because exploitative psychologists tend to blur boundaries does not mean that all subtle boundary crossings are necessarily harmful or unethical. It may be therapeutically necessary for a psychologist to talk about sports to a treatment resistance adolescent male as a way of making him feel comfortable in therapy. It could be construed as abject rudeness for a psychologist to refuse a token gift of Christmas or Hanukkah cookies or to refuse to accept a trinket from a child client/ patient. The caution about subtle boundary crossings is not that psychologists should develop a rigid and defensive stance against them. The caution is that psychologists should use clinical judgment as to when such boundary crossings may be therapeutically indicated or harmful (Guthiel & Gabbard, 1993, 1998).

> *(b)* [Unavoidable Multiple Relationships.] *If a psychologist finds that, due to unforeseen factors, a potentially harmful multiple relationship has arisen, the psychologist takes reasonable steps to resolve it with due regard for the best interests of the affected person and maximal compliance with the Ethics Code.* [This standard is similar to Standard 1.17c of the 1992 Ethics Code.]

Standard 3.05b acknowledges that some multiple relationships with clients/patients or former clients/patients are unavoidable. Psychologists (especially in small towns or rural areas) may have chance encounters with clients/patients because of overlapping business or social relationships. In addition, the family of the psychologist may encounter clients/patients in any of the previous situations. For rural psychologists the question is not if these relationships will occur, but when (Schank & Skovholt, 1997). As the community becomes smaller or more remote, the likelihood of such encounters increases (Roberts, Battaglia, & Epstein, 1999). In frontier communities (less than 6.6 persons per square mile), psychologists may depend on their clients/patients to provide needed services. For example, their clients/patients may be the only ones in an area to sell gasoline or repair cars.

Psychologists who anticipate random meetings with their clients/patients can notify them of the "you first" rule by which the clients/patients retain control of whether they will recognize their psychologist in a nontherapeutic context. This rule allows clients/patients to introduce themselves first thereby ensuring that they can control the situation depending on their companions, the settings, or their personal degree of comfort.

These discussions can do much to reduce potential problems. For example, Barnett (1999) reported doing an intake interview of a child and his parents one day, only to see them on the sidelines of his child's soccer practice the next day. His discussions about chance encounters with the mother helped preserve a working therapeutic relationship. Although they were able to differentiate "soccer parent" from therapist roles, "we did revisit these issues several times during treatment to be sure there was no adverse impact on the client/patient or the treatment relationship" (p. 20).

Templeman (1992) found that psychologists in rural Oregon had more random encounters with their clients/patients than psychologists in urban Portland. About 91% of the psychologists in rural Oregon had experienced at least one passing contact with a client/patient in the past 30 days, and 51% of them were treating clients/patients who currently lived in their neighborhood. Sandifer (1989) wrote that

> psychologists working in most areas of Mississippi must . . . deal with such circumstances as taking their child to the first day of school to discover that an ex-client is the child's new fifth grade teacher. They must become adept and alert in their client scheduling practices so that neighbors do not run into each other in the waiting room. (p. 7)

Unavoidable multiple relationships can also occur in "small communities" in urban areas. For example, it is common for gay, lesbian, or bisexual professionals to have relatively small social circles, even in urban areas. Often gay, lesbian, or bisexual psychologists find themselves treating individuals with whom they have mutual acquaintances and they risk encountering each other through one of these social circles.

A Psychologist Uses Good Judgment

At the time when a psychologist was treating a woman for a mild depression, the psychologist's teenage son told her that he was taking a girl to the high school prom. The psychologist quickly realized that the girl was the daughter of her client/patient.

During the next psychotherapy session the psychologist told her client/patient that she would keep the dating relationship of their children separate from the therapy. The explanation was framed positively, "This is your time and I don't want anything to detract from your recovery." Later in the week the psychologist called her client/patient on the phone to coordinate transportation for the date. In this case, the relationship was remote enough and the client/patient was healthy enough so that no extraordinary complications occurred (and the children had a good time).

Here is another example:

An Embarrassing Discovery

Another psychologist had worked with a client/patient for three sessions when the psychologist realized that she was treating a woman who was once married to her second cousin many years ago (they subsequently divorced). The psychologist informed the client/patient of her belated realization of their relationship. The psychologist believed it was better for her to initiate the topic than to risk having the client/patient discover the relationship and wonder if the psychologist had known it all along.

Sometimes institutional policies lead to an unavoidable relationship. For example, a school psychologist was required to have lunch duty and needed to discipline a student whom she had evaluated earlier in the year. Psychologists working in the military, law enforcement, or correctional facilities have unique demands placed upon them. They may be called to consult in life/death situations, such as hostage negotiations, or coach police during the interrogations of prisoners whom they once treated or evaluated. Psychologists in those situations need to consider Standard 1.03 as well as their agency's standards.

(c) [Forensic Multiple Relationships.] *When psychologists are required by law, institutional policy, or extraordinary circumstances to serve in more than one role in judicial or administrative proceedings, at the outset they clarify role expectations and the extent of confidentiality and thereafter as changes occur. (See also Standards 3.04, Avoiding Harm, and 3.07, Third-Party Requests for Services.)* [This standard is similar to Standard 7.03 of the 1992 Ethics Code.]

The general rule is that psychologists should avoid mixing treatment and forensic relationships. However, that is not always possible. Sometimes psychologists will treat patients who have been court ordered for treatment and the court will require some accountability for their services. At other times, psychologists will be working in small towns where no one else is available to provide treatment for a person the psychologist has evaluated (or vice versa). Finally, psychologists may be treating patients who, in the course of therapy, become involved in litigation and the information of the treating psychologist is relevant to the outcome of the court proceeding.

Court Ordered Treatment. Sometimes courts request accountability for clients/patients they have referred for treatment. For example, clients/patients may be court ordered for treatment because they are parents under the supervision of children and youth services. The court may expect the psychologist to provide information relevant to the disposition of the children, and it also expects the psychologist to provide meaningful treatment. This places the psychologist in the position of having loyalties to both the clients/patients and the court.

It is possible that the demands of the court for all relevant information may conflict with the role of a treating professional who desires to maintain confidentiality. The courts may not appreciate the traditional policy of complete confidentiality. The court might not have assurance that the treatment fulfilled the conditions of the court unless it had some access to the information about the treatment (Kearney, 1998). The worry of the court is, of course, that the clients/patients may persist in the problematic behavior. However, the psychologist's ability to help the client/patient becomes limited if the psychologist does not have a trusting relationship with her or him in the first place.

The best solution in this conundrum is to establish a policy of confidentiality ahead of time that would fulfill the conditions of the referring party while honoring the principle of confidentiality as much as possible. The policy should be clear to both the client/patient and the referring agency.

Small Communities. In unusual situations, such as in a small community, multiple involvements may be unavoidable. The *Specialty Guidelines for Forensic Psychologists* states that "the forensic psychologist takes reasonable steps to minimize the potential negative effects of these circumstances on the rights of the party, confidentiality, and the process of treatment and evaluation" (Committee on Ethical Guidelines for Forensic Psychologists, 1991, IV, D 2). Also, at times, psychologists may need to provide emergency mental health services to clients/patients being evaluated. In such cases, forensic psychologists "attempt to avoid providing further professional forensic services to that defendant unless that relationship is reasonably unavoidable" (VI, D 2).

Any psychotherapist who moves from the role of therapist jeopardizes the treatment relationship. It will prove difficult to discuss the client candidly in public on one day and then pick up treatment where it was left off the next week.

Therapy Clients/Patients Who Need Forensic Services. Some clients/patients are involved in litigation when they enter therapy. They may have initiated a lawsuit involving an accident (automobile, tripping on the sidewalk, etc.), wrongful termination of employment, sexual harassment, child custody, domestic abuse, or some other issue. At times they may present for therapy with an apparently routine disorder (depression, problem with children, etc.), but soon after treatment begins, they may try to solicit the involvement of the therapist in their court case. Nothing is wrong, of course, with treating clients/patients who are involved in litigation. However, these clients/patients need to know that the confidentiality of the sessions may be compromised if they enter their mental health as an issue in litigation.

Furthermore, the very process of litigation for emotional damages has, in and of itself, subtle pressures to maintain a sick role. The process of questioning and continuing to focus on their problems may undercut the natural process of recovery and dissuade the clients/patients from putting the trauma in the past and getting on with their lives.

Psychologists should try to identify these clients/patients early. At the beginning of treatment, psychologists can ask all clients/patients if they are involved in current litigation, and all clients/patients who have recent physical injuries or who request help with their child's problems can be asked for more details about their life circumstances and the possibility of litigation. Second, if litigation does appear unexpectedly in the course of therapy, psychologists need to communicate clearly to the client/patient the nature of their involvement. For example, some conscientious psychologists cite the APA *Guidelines for Child Custody Evaluations in Divorce Proceedings* (APA, 1994) which generally forbid moving from a treatment to an evaluation relationship for children involved in custody disputes. It is preferable for the treating psychologist to maintain only that role and to insist that another psychologist be hired to conduct the forensic evaluation.

General Principles Relevant to Multiple Relationships. Several moral principles underlie the cautions against harmful or exploitative multiple relationships. Competent psychologists show respect for the autonomy of their clients/patients (refrain from creating dependency or being paternalistic), are beneficent (act to further the welfare of the client/patient) and nonmaleficent (avoids doing things which harm the client/patient), and are faithful to their promises of putting the client's/patient's welfare first, following through on the treatment relationship, and respecting the laws governing the psychologist-client/patient relationship.

In legal terms, psychologists have a fiduciary relationship with their clients/patients. Legally, "fiduciary" is "a broad term for someone who has a duty to act for the benefit of someone else. He [sic] must subordinate his personal interests to that duty in the event that there is a conflict" (Gilmer, 1973, p. 129). As can be seen, the moral values underlying the psychologist-client/patient relationship are similar to the fiduciary concept found in the law.

3.06   Conflict of Interest

> *Psychologists refrain from taking on a professional role when personal, scientific, professional, legal, financial, or other interests or relationships could reasonably be expected to (1) impair their objectivity, competence, or effectiveness in performing their functions as psychologists or (2) expose the person or organization with whom the professional relationship exists to harm or exploitation.* [This standard is similar to Standard 1.17b of the 1992 Ethics Code.]

The standard needs to be read in conjunction with Standard 3.05. Psychologists should avoid taking on responsibilities where either previous, current, or future relationships could be harmful or exploitative.

3.07   Third-Party Requests for Services

> *When psychologists agree to provide services to a person or entity at the request of a third party, psychologists attempt to clarify at the outset of the service the nature of the relationship with all indi-*

viduals or organizations involved. This clarification includes the role of the psychologist (e.g., therapist, consultant, diagnostician, or expert witness), an identification of who is the client, the probable uses of the services provided or the information obtained, and the fact that there may be limits to confidentiality. (See also Standards 3.05, Multiple Relationships, and 4.02, Discussing the Limits of Confidentiality.) [This standard is very similar to Standard 1.21a of the 1992 Ethics Code.]

Often third parties ask psychologists to perform services. These may occur, for example, when psychologists are conducting evaluations at the request of a prospective employer or when conducting a court ordered evaluation. In those situations psychologists need to clarify their roles ahead of time and explain the probable use of the information generated by the evaluation.

An Important Evaluation

A psychologist evaluated a prospective employee for the local police department. The applicant, who was rejected as being psychologically unfit, claimed he was uninformed of the purpose of the evaluation and insisted upon seeing a copy of the test report.

Here the psychologist had appropriately reviewed the limits of confidentiality with the client/patient and the probable use of the information. He reminded the prospective employee that he had signed a statement noting that the results would be sent only to the police department and that he would not be receiving a copy of them. The psychologist had adequate documentation to show that the allegation was unfounded.

3.08   Exploitative Relationships

Psychologists do not exploit persons over whom they have supervisory, evaluative, or other authority such as clients/patients, students, supervisees, research participants, and employees. (See also Standards 3.05, Multiple Relationships; 6.04, Fees and Financial Arrangements; 6.05, Barter With Clients/Patients; 7.07, Sexual Relationships With Students and Supervisees; 10.05, Sexual Intimacies With Current Therapy Clients/Patients; 10.06, Sexual Intimacies With Relatives or Significant Others of Current Therapy Clients/Patients; 10.07, Therapy With Former Sexual Partners; and 10.08, Sexual Intimacies With Former Therapy Clients/Patients.) [This standard is similar to Standard 1.19a of the 1992 Ethics Code.]

Some actions, such as sexual relationships with students or supervisees, are clearly exploitative and are forbidden by this and other standards. Other actions, such as paying employees less than minimum wage or breaking a contract, would engender no discussion that they are exploitative. However, it can sometimes be difficult to distinguish when a relationship has been exploitative. The term exploit means to use a person improperly, unjustly, or meanly for personal advantage. What is unjust may be, in part, in the eye of the beholder.

Is This Relationship Unfair?

A recent doctoral graduate complained that his psychologist/employer, who only paid him $15 an hour for conducting therapy, was exploiting him. The employer countered that the recent graduate had little ability to generate income on his own (since he was not licensed), and was getting valuable supervision, and that he should not have taken the job in the first place if he did not like the financial arrangements.

Certainly one can sympathize with the plight of the recent graduate. On the other hand, it does not seem fair to discipline the supervising psychologist just because her employee did not choose an employment setting wisely or lacked marketable skills or credentials.

3.09 Cooperation With Other Professionals

When indicated and professionally appropriate, psychologists cooperate with other professionals in order to serve their clients/patients effectively and appropriately. (See also Standard 4.05, Disclosures.) [This standard is very similar to Standard 1.20b of the 1992 Ethics Code.]

Psychologists may treat clients/patients who are being treated concurrently by other health care professionals. However, it may help the client/patient for the psychologist to have contact with those professionals. For example, when a client/patient is being treated simultaneously with psychotherapy and psychopharmacology, the psychologist should communicate with the treating psychopharmacologist. A recent study found that more than one-half of the psychotherapy clients/patients seen by psychologists were receiving psychotropic medications (Borkovec et al., 2001). In addition, psychologists should cooperate and provide information to future health care professionals. For example, if a client/patient needs a copy of her past records, it would be expected that the psychologist would provide it. Of course, the standard does not limit itself to cooperating with just health professionals. Other professionals, such as attorneys, may have legitimate reasons to receive information from psychologists.

The Ethics Code does not explicitly require psychologists to obtain the past records of their clients/patients. However, from the standpoint of risk management psychologists should try to get past treatment records.

Getting Past Records Might Have Helped

A psychiatrist was treating a client/patient who, in the course of therapy, seriously assaulted his paramour. In the ensuing litigation, the court ruled that the previous records would have revealed the client's/patient's past history of assaulting his girlfriends and that the failure to obtain those records led the psychiatrist to make a treatment plan which fell below acceptable professional standards.

However, some clients/patients will present seemingly good reasons for refusing to allow the release of past records, such as abuse on the part of the previous psychotherapist or a sense that their previous psychotherapist did not understand their problems, or like them personally. At times these reports by the client/patient may be accurate, but they may also distort past treatment and be designed to hide an accurate report of their past manipulative behaviors. Reports by patients of past misconduct by previous psychotherapists should not be an automatic barrier against retrieving the past records. Even if the client/patient reports of abuse are accurate, the records of previous psychotherapists may still contain some useful clinical information.

Recently some psychologists have balked at having to bear the expense of copying and mailing out records of former clients/patients. Nothing precludes a psychologist from charging a fee for this service, if such a fee arrangement had been explained to the client/patient at the beginning of therapy. It could be argued that sending past records or providing brief consultations with future health care professionals is an implied part of the treatment relationship. Consequently, the average client/patient would not expect to be charged for that service. Clients/patients need to be informed of the costs ahead of time.

3.10   Informed Consent

> (a)   [General Rule for Informed Consent.] *When psychologists conduct research or provide assessment, therapy, counseling, or consulting services in person or via electronic transmission*

or other forms of communication, they obtain the informed consent of the individual or individuals using language that is reasonably understandable to that person or persons except when conducting such activities without consent is mandated by law or governmental regulation or as otherwise provided in this Ethics Code. (See also Standards 8.02, Informed Consent to Research; 9.03, Informed Consent in Assessments; and 10.01, Informed Consent to Therapy.) [This standard is related to Standards 4.01d and 4.02a of the 1992 Ethics Code.]

Informed consent is one of the most important concepts found in the APA Ethics Code. It is based, among other things, upon the moral principles that require respect of the dignity and rights of people and respect for client/patient autonomy. Except for highly unusual situations, such as when clients/patients are in extreme distress, psychologists should trust the ability of clients/patients, students, organizational clients, and research participants to decide what would be helpful to them.

Informed consent means the full and active participation of clients/patients in treatment decisions. However, it is not meant to imply that the client/patient is passively consenting to something presented by the psychotherapist. Optimally, the client/patient and psychotherapist are collaborating to identify and reach mutually agreed-upon goals. The phrase "client/patient participation" probably better reflects the underlying goals and values behind this standard. Nevertheless, for purposes of this discussion, the authors will use the traditional term, informed consent.

In addition to representing an ethical obligation, informed consent also reflects good clinical practice. The informed consent process is an opportunity to engage the client/patient in the therapeutic process, improve expectations, and encourage adherence to treatment. According to Stromberg, Stone, and Claiborn (1993), "viewing informed consent as a means of sharing power with the client can have clinical significance, especially for those clients who have been previously victimized. For such clients, issues of power and control can be of central concern" (p. 159). Indeed, in an analogue study, T. Sullivan, W. Martin, and Handelsman (1993) found that "clients may be more favorably disposed to therapists who take the time and effort to provide [informed consent] information" (p. 162). The authors concluded that "doing ethical practice and doing good therapy are not mutually exclusive" (p. 163).

Standard 3.10 initiates the presentation on informed consent, although it is referenced throughout the entire Ethics Code. Standard 3.10a defines informed consent and 3.10b describes assent (agreement from persons who are legally unable to give consent). However, other standards expand upon the concept of informed consent as well, including 4.02 (discussing limits of confidentiality), 4.03 (obtaining consent for image recording), and 6.04 (information about fees). There are also specific informed consent standards dealing with therapy (10.01, 10.02, 10.03), assessment (9.03), teaching (5.03, 7.02, 7.03a, 7.04), research (8.02, 8.03, 8.05, 8.07b, 8.07c), and organizational consulting (3.11). A complete list of references to informed consent is found in Table 5 (pp. 82-83). Exceptions to informed consent are found in Table 6 (p. 84).

Standard 3.10 defines the essential prerequisites of informed consent. The person must have the capacity to give consent, have received information relevant to the decision, be aware of the voluntary nature of her or his participation, and have been given the opportunity to ask questions about participation.

The nature of the specific communication should vary according to the sophistication and needs of the client/patient, but a general rule is to ask, "What would the average person want to know about the procedure?" Here the case law regarding informed consent in medical malpractice can guide psychologists on the general standards that they should use when considering informed consent. In recent years courts dealing with informed consent have ruled that clients/patients should have the opportunity to learn the risks and benefits of treatment procedures. According to *Canterbury v. Spence* (1972),

> [The] physician has duty, as facet of due care, to warn of dangers lurking in proposed treatment and to impart information which patient has every right to expect; reasonable explanation required means generally informing patient in nontechnical terms as to what is at stake, i.e., the therapy alternatives open to him, goals expected or believed to be achieved, and risks which may ensue from particular treatment and no treatment. (p. 773)

However, in *Cobb v. Grant* (1972), another court clarified, "Patient's interest in medical information does not extend to lengthy polysyllabic discourse on all possible complications; [a] minicourse in medical science is not required" (p. 2). In summary, psychologists should provide information, in lay terms, concerning the alternatives, goals, and risks of the treatment.

The legal principles supplement what is specifically enumerated in Standard 3.10 concerning the essential ingredients of informed consent. In addition, when conducting psychotherapy, Standard 10.01a requires that psychologists inform prospective clients/patients of "the nature and anticipated course of therapy, fees, involvement of third parties, and limits of confidentiality." Although not specifically enumerated in the Ethics Code, psychologists may include additional information that, in their experience, their clients/patients often want to know. Most importantly, however, informed consent is a process; it is not a pro forma statement only given to clients/patients at the beginning of services.

Informed consent represents an ongoing dialogue between psychologist and client/patient and not merely the rote dissemination of a predetermined set of facts. Thus, the information provided at the beginning of treatment may be insufficient as treatment progresses, treatment plans change, or new clinical issues unfold. Ongoing discussions regarding treatment, therefore, may be warranted.

In deciding what information to give to clients/patients, it may be helpful to consider the moral principles of respecting client/patient autonomy and respecting the dignity of others that underlie the informed consent imperative. A continual awareness of these principles may help psychologists to develop the informed consent process that best meets the legitimate concerns of their clients/patients.

Service brochures or informed consent forms may be helpful if they supplement, not replace, the dialogue between psychologist and client/patient. Such forms can include basic information about billing policies, scheduling appointments, policy on cancellations, common exceptions to confidentiality, and so forth. With the implementation of the Health Insurance Portability and Accountability Act (HIPAA; Health and Human Services, 2002) in 2003, all professionals providing health care will need to distribute a privacy statement, as well.

A Psychologist Who Is Too Cautious

A psychologist developed a 12-page, single-spaced consent form that covered virtually every possible contingency including a statement that the client/patient understood that this was a professional relationship and "will not attempt to enter into a social or romantic relationship with Dr. M, misconstrue his remarks as sexual in nature, have romantic dreams or fantasize about Dr. M, or in any manner whatsoever allow sexual feelings to enter into the relationship."

In addition to its great length and cumbersome wording, which ensured that it would not be carefully read, the references to sexual thoughts or feelings were inappropriate. A client/patient would certainly wonder why the psychologist had such an intense interest in sex. Furthermore, the stern prohibition on sexual fantasies almost guarantees that some of them will occur. Gordon (1993) claims that overly inclusive disclosure agreements

---

Table 5: Standard for Informed Consent

General Rules Applicable to All Psychologists

3.10a   obtain consent using language that is understandable, unless mandated
          by law
3.10d   informed consent is documented
4.02a   limits of confidentiality and foreseeable use of information generated
4.02c   discuss limits of confidentiality when using electronic transmissions
4.03   permission obtained before recording voices or images
6.04a   informed of compensation and billing arrangements
6.04d   limits on funding can be anticipated

Therapy (All Therapy)

10.01a   the nature and anticipated course of therapy
          fees (see also 6.04a)
          involvement of any third parties
          limits of confidentiality (see also 4.02)
          opportunity to ask questions and receive answers

Therapy (Special Types of Therapy)

10.01b   experimental or developing treatment
          nature of treatment potential risks
          alternatives available
          voluntary nature of participation
10.01c   trainee is in supervision and must give name of supervisor
10.02   in couple or family therapy who are the clients/patients,
              nature of relationship psychologist will have with each client/patient,
              probable uses of services provided or information obtained
10.03   in group therapy, informed of limits of confidentiality and
              rules and responsibilities of all parties

Assessment

9.03a   nature and purpose of assessment
          fees
          involvement of third parties
          limits of confidentiality
          opportunity to ask questions and receive answers
9.03c   if using an interpreter, obtain consent of client/patient

---

Table 5: Standard for Informed Consent *(Continued)*

Forensic

3.10c   if court ordered, psychologists so inform clients/patients and inform them
           of limits of confidentiality
9.03b   use language understandable by client/patient if decisional capacity is
           questioned or if mandated by court

Teaching

7.02   accurate descriptions of training programs
7.03a   accurate descriptions of course syllabi (although may be modified if
           students can still meet the educational requirements)
7.04   inform students ahead of time if the course or program has
           experiential requirements
5.03   workshops and nondegree programs describe themselves accurately

Organizational Consulting

3.11   nature and objectives of services
           the intended recipients
           which individuals are clients
           relationship to each person
           uses of services provided and information obtained
           who has access to information
           limits to confidentiality

Research

8.02a   purpose of research, expected duration, and procedures
           right to decline to participate
           foreseeable consequences of not participating
           reasonable factors that would influence participation
           any possible research benefits
           limits of confidentiality
           incentives to participate
           to whom they should address questions about rights
           opportunity to ask questions and receive answers
8.02b   experimental nature of treatments (see also 10.01b)
           method of assignment to experimental or control groups
           services available to control groups
           treatment alternatives if an individual does not wish to participate
8.03   permission to record voices or imaging
8.07b   do not deceive about potential for distress

Table 6: Informed Consent Exceptions*

All Psychologists

3.10b   when dealing with persons legally incapable of giving consent,
        psychologists must take other precautions such as providing information,
        obtaining assent, considering best interests and preferences of clients/
        patients, and gaining permission from authorized individual if appropriate
4.02b   when to discuss confidentiality if not feasible or contraindicated at the
        onset
6.02b   if entering confidential information into a nonconfidential database,
        psychologists must use coding
6.04a   fees, as early as feasible

Research

8.03   (for recording voices or images) naturalistic observations in public places
        and unlikely to cause harm; research involves deception and permission
        obtained upon debriefing
8.05   normal educational practices, curricula, or classroom management in
        educational settings; naturalistic observations, anonymous questionnaires,
        archival research in which disclosure would not put participants at risk of
        criminal or civil liability; or organizational research related to job or
        organizational effectiveness and employability is not at risk and
        confidentiality is protected; or where permitted by law or institutional
        regulation
8.07   research using deception and deceptive quality is justified by scientific
        worth of project and nondeceptive alternatives are not available

Assessment

9.03a   mandated by law; routine educational, institutional, or organizational
        assessment; or the purpose is to assess decisional capacity
9.03b   use language understandable by client/patient if decisional capacity is
        questioned or if mandated by law

Therapy

10.01a if not feasible

Organizational Consulting

3.11b   inform individuals at the outset if they are unable to provide information
        because of law or their organizational roles

---

*These are exceptions to the rule that informed consent must always be obtained, or always must be obtained
before the start of research, therapy, assessment, or other services.

"communicate an effort to control inappropriate impulses that are not expected to occur in the professional relationship. . . . This implies that the therapist is not to be relied upon on the basis of her maturity or trustworthiness" (p. 105).

Informed consent forms may be especially important when certain techniques are used. For example, clients/patients may have misconceptions about hypnosis, and the psychologist may have to go to great lengths to correct these false beliefs. Some clients/patients mistakenly believe, for example, that hypnosis can retrieve lost memories with great accuracy. Of course, this is not true. Although subjects tend to have a high degree of confidence in hypnotically refreshed memories, these memories are more likely to be contaminated or inaccurate. Other techniques that involve discomfort, such as flooding, or which are experimental should be accompanied by detailed information to the client/patient. A handout on the limitations to and the therapeutic context of the techniques may supplement the information given verbally to the client/patient.

Psychologists can make several mistakes when implementing the informed consent requirement. One mistake is to place undue reliance upon a written form. Handelsman et al. (1995) found that a sample of consent forms used by mental health professionals in Colorado had a readability scale of 15.74, which was at the level of a college senior. Many clients/patients likely were unable to understand the forms that were submitted to them. Practitioners who rely solely on written forms may be neglecting the most important aspect of informed consent, namely talking with clients/patients about their expressed or anticipated concerns.

Another mistake is the failure to tailor the information to the needs of the client/patient. Extensive discussions about the law surrounding the limits to confidentiality may have a chilling effect on clients/patients and leave them confused and frustrated. A detailed description of the exceptions to confidentiality necessitated by a child protective services law, for example, would probably be unnecessary when working with a childless couple.

A third mistake is the failure to appreciate that informed consent is especially crucial in forensic assessments. In forensic relationships, it may be prudent to reiterate the essential nature of the relationship (limits to confidentiality, possible expert testimony) each time the psychologist has contact with the client/patient.

When implemented properly, informed consent fulfills both the clinical demands and the ethical obligations of the psychologist. It is not a concept to be feared or avoided. Disseminating information to clients/patients and obtaining the agreement to engage in the treatment process is a strong first step towards a positive therapeutic outcome.

In fact, there is some evidence that the ability to form a therapeutic alliance and to develop a set of shared goals (Horvath, 2001) is positively related to good client outcomes. Informed consent, or patient participation, may reflect good clinical practice.

> *(b)* [General Rule for Assent.] *For persons who are legally incapable of giving informed consent, psychologists nevertheless (1) provide an appropriate explanation, (2) seek the individual's assent, (3) consider such persons' preferences and best interests, and (4) obtain appropriate permission from a legally authorized person, if such substitute consent is permitted or required by law. When consent by a legally authorized person is not permitted or required by law, psychologists take reasonable steps to protect the individual's rights and welfare.* [This standard is similar to Standards 4.02b and 4.02c of the 1992 Ethics Code.]

The concept of informed consent is sometimes more honored in the breach than in the observance in relation to certain client/patient populations. For example, psychologists are often asked to evaluate clients/patients who are suspected of having a dementia or asked to treat adult clients/patients with moderate to profound mental retardation. These clients/patients may not have been legally adjudicated incompetent so that 3.10b does not technically apply. Nonetheless, it is important to look beyond the letter and into the spirit of these standards. The goal is to ensure the protection of those who do not have the capacity to make their own decisions. The informed consent process may require more discussion or explanation with a person who has mental retardation. Or the informed consent process may require the involvement of relatives or others who can help represent the wishes or best interests of the affected individual.

Under state laws clients/patients are considered competent to give consent unless they have been adjudicated incompetent. However, some such clients/patients are incapable of understanding the information regarding therapy, evaluation, or release of information conveyed by the treating psychologist. This is often true no matter how carefully the psychologist couches and explains the information. Nonetheless, many clients/patients will sign a valid consent form, and the psychologist will proceed with the evaluation or therapy and will release the confidential information in question.

The issue is further complicated by the fact that the psychologist might not be able to ascertain the ability of the clients/patients to understand the nature of the services being offered until the evaluation is well underway or even completed. A client/patient who initially presents as alert and intelligent may appear more and more demented as the evaluation continues. When psychologists feel uncertain about the ability of the client/patient to give informed consent, they should proceed with caution.

In addition to careful and honest documentation of any explanation offered to the client/patient with regard to the particular procedure or matter under consideration, psychologists are advised to consult with the client's/patient's family or any relatives. Even if the client/patient has not yet been adjudicated incompetent, informing relatives reduces misunderstandings and the likelihood that they will perceive the psychologist as having initiated an unnecessary health care procedure. Further, it would be wise to consult with colleagues as well as any other professionals treating the client/patient regarding the wisdom of proceeding with any procedure based on the cognitive capacities of the client/patient in question.

Finally, anytime the psychologist doubts the client's/patient's ability to give voluntary, informed consent, the psychologist should pay careful attention to communicating with the client/patient in a manner commensurate with her or his psychological capacity and should take care to protect her or his best interest. As in other cases where ethical dilemmas manifest themselves, honesty, as well as very careful documentation, is the best policy.

> *(c)* [Forensic Informed Consent.] *When psychological services are court ordered or otherwise mandated, psychologists inform the individual of the nature of the anticipated services, including whether the services are court ordered or mandated and any limits of confidentiality, before proceeding.* [This standard is new.]

Many of the principles of informed consent that apply to voluntary clients/patients also apply to court mandated services as well. In forensic evaluations, the court may order clients to submit to an evaluation against their will. In that sense the client/patient is not consenting to the evaluation. Nonetheless, the psychologist still has the responsibility to give the reluctant client/patient relevant information about the anticipated service and the future use of information. In addition to representing an ethical or legal obligation, informed consent also reflects good clinical practice. The informed consent process is an opportunity to engage the client/patient in the evaluative process, correct mistaken expectations, and encourage adherence to the evaluation. Certainly in a forensic environment, it would be necessary to explain how the role of the evaluator contrasts with the role of a psychotherapist.

As with other psychological services, informed consent represents an ongoing dialogue between the psychologist and client/patient and is not merely the rote dissemination of a predetermined set of facts. Thus, the information provided at the beginning of the evaluation may be insufficient as new clinical or legal issues unfold. The essential information on informed consent could be repeated at the start of each new assessment session. Brochures or informed consent forms may help if they supplement, not replace, the dialogue between psychologist and client/patient.

> *(d)* [Documentation of Informed Consent.] *Psychologists appropriately document written or oral consent, permission, and assent. (See also Standards 8.02, Informed Consent to Research; 9.03, Informed Consent in Assessments; and 10.01, Informed Consent to Therapy.)* [This standard overlaps with Standard 4.02a of the 1992 Ethics Code.]

This standard requires psychologists to note that appropriate informed consent procedures have been conducted with their clients/patients. It does not, however, require a specific signed consent form. Nonetheless, many psychologists believe it is prudent to have an informed consent form that patients can sign, indicating that they have read essential information about office practices, billing, confidentiality, and other details of service.

In addition to obtaining informed consent, the Health Insurance Portability and Accountability Act (HIPAA) imposes several additional responsibilities upon psychologists, including the development of a privacy statement, specific ingredients in the patient authorization forms (release of information forms), and a requirement that psychologists must train their employees concerning privacy and confidentiality issues. Furthermore, all practices must have a "privacy officer" and a mechanism by which clients/patients can express grievances. These HIPAA requirements will be discussed at appropriate places later in this book (see summary of HIPAA in Table 7, p. 89). In addition we present here general information on HIPAA and on the general consent requirement. As this manuscript goes to print, the American Psychological Association's Practice Organization (formerly the Practice Directorate), and the American Psychological Association Insurance Trust (APAIT) are in the process of developing and distributing sample privacy statements and other materials.

Although HIPAA only applies to those who transmit information electronically, we recommend that all psychologists consider themselves to be subject to HIPAA. HIPAA is based on an all-or-nothing principle; if psychologists even once for one patient transmit information electroni-

---

Table 7: Summary of Essential HIPAA Rules

---

1. *Applicability.* Most professional psychologists will be covered by HIPAA. The compliance date is April 14, 2003. Once psychologists are covered for one patient, they are covered for all patients.
2. *Privacy Statement.* Psychologists must give out a privacy statement to all patients.
3. *Staff Training.* Psychologists must train their staff members in confidentiality and privacy issues.
4. *Privacy Officer.* Every practice, even solo practices, must have a privacy officer. For a solo practice, the psychologist would be the privacy officer. The compliance activities are "scalable," meaning that the protective mechanisms required vary according to the size of the practice. What is required of a solo practitioner is far less than what is required of a large group practice.
5. *State Preemption.* State laws that are more protective of patient rights (from the standpoint of the patient) preempt HIPAA standards.

Final Note: Psychologists who belong to their state or national organizations have the benefit of resources that can help them to comply with HIPAA. Psychologists who do not belong to their state or national organizations are at a distinct disadvantage.

---

cally, then they are subject to HIPAA. Consequently, a solo practitioner who bills electronically or who employs a billing service which uses electronic billing is subject to HIPAA. Even an insurance or managed-care-free psychologist who submits information electronically to an insurance company for reimbursement on only one client/patient is subject to HIPAA.

One of the difficulties in understanding HIPAA is that the Department of Health and Human Services, the agency responsible for promulgating and interpreting HIPAA regulations, uses wording that is not consistent with that commonly used in the medical or psychological fields. For example, "authorizations," according to HIPAA, refers to what psychologists have traditionally considered to be "release of information forms."

3.11   Psychological Services Delivered To or Through Organizations

(a) [General Rule for Organizational Informed Consent.] *Psychologists delivering services to or through organizations provide information beforehand to clients and when appropriate those directly affected by the services about (1) the nature and objectives of the services, (2) the intended recipients, (3) which of the individuals are clients, (4) the relationship the*

*psychologist will have with each person and the organiza-
tion, (5) the probable uses of services provided and information obtained, (6) who will have access to the information,
and (7) limits of confidentiality. As soon as feasible, they provide information about the results and conclusions of such
services to appropriate persons.* [This standard is related to
Standard 1.07a of the 1992 Ethics Code.]

(b) [Law on Organizational Roles Preclude Informed Consent.] *If
psychologists will be precluded by law or by organizational
roles from providing such information to particular individuals or groups, they so inform those individuals or groups at
the outset of the service.* [This standard is identical to Standard 1.07b of the 1992 Ethics Code.]

This standard applies the informed consent principles to organizations. It is intended to supplement, not replace, Standard 3.10. The standards for informed consent in organizational consulting reflect the different demands on organizational consultants. Since the clients are legal en-
tities, as opposed to individuals, there is more of a need to specify the
intended recipient, which individuals are clients, and the relationship of
the consulting psychologists to each of those individuals. A comparison
of the informed consent requirements for therapy clients/patients and for
organizational clients is shown in Table 5 (pp. 82-83).

3.12 Interruption of Psychological Services

*Unless otherwise covered by contract, psychologists make reason-
able efforts to plan for facilitating services in the event that psychological services are interrupted by factors such as the
psychologist's illness, death, unavailability, relocation, or retirement or by the client's/patient's relocation or financial limitations.
(See also Standard 6.02c, Maintenance, Dissemination, and Disposal of Confidential Records of Professional and Scientific Work.)*
[This is related to Standard 4.08a of the 1992 Ethics Code.]

This standard clarifies that psychologists must anticipate ahead of time
the possibility that services will be interrupted. The 1992 Ethics Code had
such a requirement for psychologists who were providing therapy. The
2002 Ethics Code extends that requirement to all psychologists who are
providing services. More details on termination of therapy services can
be found in Standards 10.09 and 10.10.

4. PRIVACY AND CONFIDENTIALITY

This section contains a general statement on confidentiality (4.01), and tells psychologists what they need to discuss with clients/patients concerning confidentiality (4.02). Standard 4.03 requires psychologists to obtain consent for recording information about clients/patients. Psychologists must minimize intrusions on privacy in reports or consultations (4.04, 4.06). Standard 4.05 permits disclosures in limited situations without client/patient consent. Standard 4.07 permits psychologists to present confidential information in didactic presentations as long as the identity of the clients/patients is disguised.

These standards are based on the moral principles of General Principle A, Beneficence and Nonmaleficence, because the unwanted disclosure of information could harm clients/patients and General Principle B, Fidelity and Responsibility (faithfulness), because the trust in the psychologist client/patient relationship requires that psychologists honor the commitment to keep information confidential. In addition, General Principle E, Respect for People's Rights and Dignity, is relevant when it states that "psychologists respect . . . the rights of individuals to privacy, confidentiality, and self-determination."

Most of the standards in the 2002 Ethics Code are highly similar to those found in the 1992 Ethics Code. One difference, however, is that the 2002 Ethics Code created Standard 4.02c that requires psychologists to inform clients/patients of the risks to privacy and inherent limitations of confidentiality when transmitting information electronically.

4.01   Maintaining Confidentiality

Psychologists have a primary obligation and take reasonable precautions to protect confidential information obtained through or stored in any medium, recognizing that the extent and limits of confidentiality may be regulated by law or established by institutional rules or professional or scientific relationship. (See also Standard 2.05, Delegation of Work to Others.) [This standard is similar to Standard 5.02 of the 1992 Ethics Code.]

Confidentiality is a general term for the promises of psychologists to keep information about patients private. Confidentiality rules were originally found in the code of ethics of psychology and other mental health professions. However, they have now been embodied in legislation and case law. Psychologists who breach confidentiality could violate the licensing law in their state or be liable for damages in a malpractice suit.

Confidentiality is the cornerstone of effective psychotherapy. Clients/ patients may be reluctant to discuss their problems openly or may even decline to engage in therapy unless they receive some assurances of privacy. Of course confidentiality is not absolute and must be balanced by other ethical or legal requirements.

The obligations of professional psychologists can only be fully understood if the APA Ethics Code is read in conjunction with HIPAA, which establishes a minimal level of privacy that must be ensured by health care providers, institutions, and insurers. These levels of privacy may be overridden by state laws if those state laws provide greater protection for the public than the federal standards.

4.02   Discussing the Limits of Confidentiality

(a) [General Rule Regarding Discussions of Confidentiality.] *Psychologists discuss with persons (including, to the extent feasible, persons who are legally incapable of giving informed consent and their legal representatives) and organizations with whom they establish a scientific or professional relationship (1) the relevant limits of confidentiality and (2) the foreseeable uses of the information generated through their psychological activities. (See also Standard 3.10, Informed Consent.)* [This standard is similar to Standard 5.01a of the 1992 Ethics Code.]

(b) [When to Discuss Limits of Confidentiality.] *Unless it is not feasible or is contraindicated, the discussion of confidentiality occurs at the outset of the relationship and thereafter as new circumstances may warrant.* [This standard is identical to Standard 5.01b of the 1992 Ethics Code.]

It is important for psychologists to inform prospective clients/patients about any anticipated limits of confidentiality. As much as possible this should occur before or at the start of services. There are exceptions, such as when the client/patient is in an emergency when treatment starts. In those situations discussions of confidentiality, fees, and so forth may need to be deferred until the emergency passes.

HIPAA requires every health care provider to present clients/patients with a privacy statement that reviews, in language understandable to the average person, the relevant limitations on privacy. However, no one privacy statement is appropriate for all psychologists. The statements need to be modified according to the laws of each state and the unique needs of individual psychologists. The emphasis should be on promoting active discussion between the psychologists and their clients/patients and in emphasizing the importance of confidentiality to the psychologists. Privacy statements should supplement, not replace, discussions of confidentiality between psychologists and their clients/patients.

Special considerations with confidentiality may occur during the treatment of minor adolescents or in the use of information in forensic cases. Psychologists who treat adolescents have to be especially concerned about the rules of confidentiality. In most states adolescents who are under 18 or who have not yet graduated from high school do not have the right to seek treatment without the consent of their parents. In those states the parents control the release of information, including the right to know everything their minor child has stated. However, individual therapy with some adolescents is unlikely to succeed unless the clients/patients are given a "zone of privacy." Many psychologists make arrangements with the adolescents and parents ahead of time in which psychologists agree to treat the child only if the parents agree to waive their right to learn all of the information obtained in the counseling with the minor adolescent. Exceptions are made, however, for anything the minor adolescent reveals which, in the opinion of the psychologist, would indicate that the safety of the adolescent or others is in jeopardy. The consent of the parents to this arrangement should be truly informed. Parents may need to be reminded at the onset of the implications of their decision. It may mean that the psychologist may learn some important facts, such as about drug use or sexual behavior, which will not be revealed to the parents unless the safety of the adolescent or others becomes jeopardized.

It is also important to inform clients about confidentiality in forensic work. Clients who are referred for a forensic evaluation may not be aware of the consequences of the releases that they sign and the anticipated uses of the information gathered in the report. Special care should be taken to ensure that they understand the nature of what they are signing. Misunderstandings are more likely to occur if the forensic client has low intelligence, is confused about the nature of the judicial proceeding, or is under substantial stress.

> *(c)* [Confidentiality Risks With Electronic Transmissions.] *Psychologists who offer services, products, or information via electronic transmission inform clients/patients of the risks to privacy and limitations of confidentiality.* [This standard is new.]

Psychologists should be aware of the limited confidentiality inherent in e-mail or other electronic communications and inform clients/patients of those limits if they decide to use them.

A Wise Decision

The psychologists at a university counseling service were automatically given e-mail accounts by virtue of their status as professional employees of the university. Students easily learned of their e-mail addresses and began sending messages about scheduling appointments or concerns that arose between therapy sessions. As a consequence of these private (but nonconfidential) communications, the counseling center notified all students that e-mail messages were not confidential, would not necessarily be read by the psychologists between sessions, and that the psychologists were not permitted to respond by e-mail.

Unfortunately, electronically stored records of psychologists have sometimes been transmitted randomly as a result of viruses or other Trojan horse computer programs. In one case several dozen nonclients/patients received summaries of client/patient records or letters which had been stored in the hard drive of the psychologist's computer. Prudent psychologists will take special precautions to protect against such unwanted disclosures. Systematic problems are more likely to occur in hospitals or large group practices that use a computerized data recording system.

4.03 Recording

Before recording the voices or images of individuals to whom they provide services, psychologists obtain permission from all such persons or their legal representatives. (See also Standards 8.03, Informed Consent for Recording Voice and Images in Research; 8.05, Dispensing With Informed Consent for Research; and 8.07, Deception in Research.) [This standard is related to Standard 5.01c of the 1992 Ethics Code.]

This new standard recognizes the importance of protecting client/patient decision making when voice or image recordings are made. Such recordings are often done when psychologists are supervising others.

4.04 Minimizing Intrusions on Privacy

(a) [Limiting Information.] *Psychologists include in written and oral reports and consultations, only information germane to the purpose for which the communication is made.* [This standard is similar to Standard 5.03a of the 1992 Ethics Code.]

(b) [Discussion of Confidential Information.] *Psychologists discuss confidential information obtained in their work only for*

appropriate scientific or professional purposes and only with
persons clearly concerned with such matters. [This standard
is similar to Standard 5.03b of the 1992 Ethics Code.]

This standard deals with the issue of gratuitous information. Almost
by necessity, psychologists must include sensitive and private information in their reports and professional communications. This standard, however, deals only with information that is unnecessary or with communications to persons who have no appropriate interest in the information. Certainly psychologists should not hesitate to include germane information
in their reports and consultations. The standard only refers to unnecessary
or gratuitous information.

For example, a psychologist completed an evaluation of a client/pa-
tient and noted in the first sentence that the client/patient was "fat and
slovenly" and went on to describe his body odor and unattractive facial
features. The client/patient eventually saw the report, was angered at the
comments, and discontinued treatment. The comments about the appearance of the client/patient were irrelevant to the treatment goals.

4.05   Disclosures

(a)   [Consent for Disclosures.] *Psychologists may disclose confi-*
dential information with the appropriate consent of the orga-
nizational client, the individual client/patient, or another le-
gally authorized person on behalf of the client/patient unless
prohibited by law. [This standard is similar to Standard 5.05b
of the 1992 Ethics Code.]

(b)   [Disclosures Without Consent.] *Psychologists disclose confi-*
dential information without the consent of the individual only
as mandated by law, or where permitted by law for a valid
purpose such as to (1) provide needed professional services;
(2) obtain appropriate professional consultations; (3) protect
the client/patient, psychologist, or others from harm; or (4)
obtain payment for services from a client/patient, in which
instance disclosure is limited to the minimum that is neces-
sary to achieve the purpose. (See also Standard 6.04e, Fees
and Financial Arrangements.) [This standard is similar to
Standard 5.05a of the 1992 Ethics Code.]

Client/patient consent is generally required before information can be
disclosed to others (there are several exceptions, however). Although
Standard 4.05 does not require written consent, it is prudent to get the
consent in writing whenever possible. HIPAA has certain minimal crite-

ria that must be met before a release ("authorization" according to the terms of HIPAA) is valid. However, state laws may require features in these authorization forms that exceed the minimum established by HIPAA.

The standard also acknowledges that state or federal laws may create exceptions to confidentiality, such as when clients/patients may present imminent danger of harming themselves or others, or when psychologists suspect that the child coming before them in their professional capacity is an abused child (VandeCreek & Knapp, 2001). The standard does not identify all of the possible exceptions to confidentiality. Other exceptions include professional consultations (see Standard 4.06) or disclosing billing information to a bill collector or small claims court (see Standard 6.04e).

Over the years case law and statutory laws have established the responsibilities of psychotherapists to protect identifiable victims of harm from clients/patients. These may occur when clients/patients threaten physical harm against an identifiable third party (or class of individuals), when clients/patients are suicidal or a victim of suspected child abuse, or when they threaten to infect others with HIV.

The responsibilities of psychologists vary according to the specific statutes or court decisions of their states. Most states have adopted the "duty to protect" as first articulated in the *Tarasoff v. Regents of the University of California et al.* (1976) either through case law or through a "duty to warn" statute. Other states are silent on the obligations of psychologists and some do not permit psychologists to breach confidentiality to protect identifiable third parties (VandeCreek & Knapp, 2001).

Generally the obligations under a "duty to protect" can be divided into three steps: (a) assessing the degree of danger, (b) developing an appropriate treatment plan, and (c) implementing that treatment plan (Appelbaum, 1985). Fortunately, research and clinical evidence can guide psychologists work through each of these steps (Borum, 2000; Monahan & Steadman, 1996; Monahan et al., 2000; Otto, 2000). Even in states that permit or require psychologists to notify an intended victim or class of victims, it is desirable, as much as possible, to involve the client/patient in the decision to warn the identifiable victim. Although it is not always possible, the warning should be made with the client/patient present or at least with the consent of the client/patient. Binder and McNiel (1996) found that clients/patients who participated in the decision to warn were less likely to discontinue psychotherapy. When clients/patients were informed of the need or intention to protect an identifiable third party, they were more likely to continue in treatment, although a few did express anger at the warning being made.

Unlike a "duty to protect" situation, when a client/patient makes a serious threat of suicide, psychotherapists do not always have a duty to warn. Instead, psychologists need to balance the need to keep the client/patient involved in therapy versus the long-term need to protect the privacy of the client/patient. Psychologists must balance the benefits of informing family members or friends who can monitor the client/patient against the risks of harm to the therapeutic relationship.

Every state has a child protective service law that requires professionals to report suspected child abuse. Psychologists should be aware of at least three important features of the child protective services law in their state: (a) how their state defines child abuse, (b) the conditions that activate the duty to report, and (c) the definition of a perpetrator of child abuse. There is no substitute for knowing the exact law in one's state (VandeCreek & Knapp, 2001).

A final area of concern for psychologists concerns their responsibilities to breach confidentiality when treating HIV positive clients/patients who engage in high risk behaviors. State laws regarding reporting HIV status differ considerably from those regarding clients/patients who threaten to assault others. Psychotherapists in some states are prohibited from warning identifiable victims of persons who are HIV positive. In those states that do not have a confidentiality statute for HIV positive clients/patients, the case law on a "duty to warn" with HIV positive clients/patients is just emerging. Although we have been unable to find any case law finding psychologists liable for failing to warn an identifiable third party of the danger from the transmission of AIDS, such a case is conceivable in some jurisdictions based on longstanding precedents requiring physicians to notify identifiable third parties of contagious diseases (see review by Bateman, 1992).

Even in jurisdictions that permit or require a "duty to warn" with HIV positive clients/patients, psychologists need to ask themselves several questions before engaging in a "knee jerk" reaction to warn (California Psychological Association AIDS Committee, 1994). Does the psychologist know of an identifiable individual who is at an immediate risk? Do the victims know that they are at risk? Has the psychologist given adequate time to allow psychotherapy to work? Does the psychologist understand the reluctance on the part of the client/patient to disclose? Clients/patients may lack information about HIV or fear abandonment or social rejection (Kozlowski, Rupert, & Crawford, 1998). Effective psychotherapy can very often get the clients/patients to change behavior and/or to notify partners voluntarily. Attention should be given to the feelings and fears (such as the realistic fear of being the victim of domestic violence) which make disclosure difficult. In other words, many clini-

cal issues need to be considered before even considering breaking confidentiality. If the decision is made to break confidentiality, then psychologists are encouraged to involve the client/patient in the decision as much
as possible.

4.06   Consultations

> *When consulting with colleagues, (1) psychologists do not disclose
> confidential information that reasonably could lead to the identifi-
> cation of a client/patient, research participant, or other person or
> organization with whom they have a confidential relationship un-
> less they have obtained the prior consent of the person or organi-
> zation or the disclosure cannot be avoided, and (2) they disclose
> information only to the extent necessary to achieve the purposes of
> the consultation. (See also Standard 4.01, Maintaining Confidenti-
> ality.)* [This standard is similar to Standard 5.06 of the 1992 Ethics
> Code.]

Although it is desirable for psychologists to consult with others, the
privacy of the client/patient should be respected as much as possible. At
times the unique information about the client/patient that has to be disclosed to make the consultation worthwhile may cause the consultant to
surmise the name or identity of the client/patient. Nonetheless, psychologists will not give the name or identifying information about a client/
patient without the client's/patient's consent unless the disclosure was
unavoidable.

An Unexpected Identification

> A psychologist sought consultation on a difficult case. Although
> the psychologist revealed no identifying information about the cli-
> ent/patient, the consultant happened to be a distant relative of the
> client/patient and, halfway through the consultation, said, "I think I
> know this patient."

There was no culpability of the psychologist who sought the consultation
because it could not be anticipated that the consultant would be able to
identify the client/patient through relevant clinical details.

4.07   Use of Confidential Information for
Didactic or Other Purposes

> *Psychologists do not disclose in their writings, lectures, or other
> public media, confidential, personally identifiable information con-
> cerning their clients/patients, students, research participants, or-*

ganizational clients, or other recipients of their services that they obtained during the course of their work, unless (1) they take reasonable steps to disguise the person or organization, (2) the person or organization has consented in writing, or (3) there is legal authorization for doing so. [This standard is similar to Standard 5.08a of the 1992 Ethics Code.]

Psychologists often disseminate information through writings and professional presentations or when they teach college classes. The educational experience can often be greatly enhanced if reference is made to real-life situations and clients/patients. At times the discussion of the details is essential to convey the psychological principles involved. However, the privacy rights of clients/patients take precedence over the benefits of disseminating this information. Information that could lead to the personal identification of clients/patients should be eliminated in these public presentations unless the clients/patients have given their consent for its release. Changing the names of the persons involved might not be sufficient, especially if the gender, race, religion, physical disability, or unusual circumstances of the problem are not altered (Nagy, 2000).

Inadequate Precautions

A psychology instructor had a part-time practice in the community where the university was located. She often used case examples in her abnormal psychology class. Although the names of the clients/patients were never given, several students believed they knew the identity of one of her case examples.

It may be relatively easy to disguise very short vignettes, but it becomes harder to disguise detailed case studies. Obtaining truly informed and voluntary client/patient consent can be problematic, however, as the differential power status between the psychologists and clients/patients may lead the clients/patients to feel pressured to agree (Gavey & Braun, 1997). For that reason, some writers have created composite vignettes based on the experiences of many individuals (Herman, 1992). It would be a wise precaution never to give out actual test profiles of clients/patients in class, unless it was a case consultation as part of a practicum or internship.

5. ADVERTISING AND OTHER PUBLIC STATEMENTS

Psychologists do not knowingly make false statements about their work activities (5.01a) and do not make false statements about their credentials (5.01b). Psychologists promote their products through accurate statements (5.02a), describe their workshops accurately (5.03), and base public statements or public advice on accurate information (5.04). Finally, psychologists do not solicit testimonials from current clients or those who are vulnerable to exploitation (5.05) and do not engage in an in-person solicitation unless it is in the context of a disaster relief effort or as part of a collateral contact for existing clients/patients (5.06).

One moral value underlying the advertising rules is that of General Principle C, Integrity. It is expected that psychologists will be accurate and honest in their public representations. This honesty helps to ensure public confidence in the individual psychologist and the profession as a whole. Another moral value underlying the advertising rules is General Principle E, Respect for People's Rights and Dignity, which includes respect for client/patient autonomy ("psychologists respect the . . . rights of individuals to privacy, confidentiality, and self-determination"). It is assumed that clients/patients will be better able to choose the psychologist best for them if they are properly informed of relevant facts.

These standards are very similar to those found in the 1992 Ethics Code.

5.01   Avoidance of False or Deceptive Statements

(a)   [Public Statements About Work Activities.] *Public statements include but are not limited to paid or unpaid advertising, product endorsements, grant applications, licensing applications, other credentialing applications, brochures, printed matter, directory listings, personal resumes or curricula vitae, or comments for use in media such as print or electronic transmission, statements in legal proceedings, lectures and public oral presentations, and published materials. Psychologists do not knowingly make public statements that are false, deceptive, or fraudulent concerning their research, practice, or other work activities or those of persons or organizations with which they are affiliated.* [This standard overlaps with Standard 3.03a of the 1992 Ethics Code.]

(b)   [Public Statements About Credentials.] *Psychologists do not make false, deceptive, or fraudulent statements concerning (1) their training, experience, or competence; (2) their academic degrees; (3) their credentials; (4) their institutional or association affiliations; (5) their services; (6) the scientific or clinical basis for, or results or degree of success of, their services; (7) their fees; or (8) their publications or research findings.* [This standard overlaps with Standard 3.03a of the 1992 Ethics Code.]

By the very nature of their advertisements, brochures, public interviews, directory listing, or other public presentations, psychologists may make an impression on clients/patients even before meeting them. These impressions may either help and inform, or deceive and mislead. Consequently, the public presentations of psychologists are regulated by the APA Ethics Code and by state licensing boards.

However, under 5.01a, psychologists do not "knowingly" make false, deceptive, or fradulent public statements about their research, practice, or work activities. "Public statements" include advertising, product endorsement, grant applications, brochures, printed matter, directory listings, or other printed or oral presentations. Psychologists are not liable for statements that they did not know were false, deceptive, or fradulent.

However, the subjective standard of "knowing" does not apply to statements that psychologists make concerning their training, experience, competence, academic degrees, credentials, affiliations, and so on. It is assumed that all psychologists should be entirely accurate about these facts.

Psychologists should not make deceptive statements about academic degrees, credentials, or institutional affiliations or false or misleading statements about the scientific or clinical bases for, or results or degree of success of, their services. Although it is theoretically possible to make factually supported public statements about unusual skills or about the comparative desirability of offered services, this standard is difficult to meet. For example, a psychologist could advertise that she is the only psychologist with a specialty in children's issues in the county. That may be true at the time the Yellow Pages advertisement is sent in, but it may not be true in the near future when the composition or skills of the psychologists in the area changes.

Some forms of misleading advertisements are probably due to ignorance or not having thought out the implications of certain business names. For example, the name "Knapp and Associates" would be misleading if Samuel Knapp was the only professional affiliated with the group. The term "associates" suggests that more than one mental health professional works in the office and that clients/patients will have access to the resources of more than one mental health professional. However, some psychologists may see the term "associates," adopt it for their own practice with the full intention of eventually hiring an additional psychotherapist, but fail to consider what it conveys to the public.

A similar naivete may account for the overuse of the term "specialist." Dr. Knapp may refer to himself as a specialist in anxiety disorders if, indeed, he is a specialist in that field. However, the definition of a specialist is not uniformly agreed upon although generally specialists have a higher level of expertise than general practitioners and devote a substantial portion of their practice to the specialty area. It becomes especially suspicious if a psychologist claims to be a specialist in many areas. Psychologists may become "proficient" in many different areas, meaning that they have basic skills in those areas. However, being proficient in an area is a lower level of skill than being a specialist in that area.

The name, "VandeCreek International Psychological Services" would be deceptive if Leon VandeCreek did not really have an international practice. The adjective "international" conveys a large multinational organization with extensive resources and branches overseas. Having conducted one workshop at the APA Convention in Toronto in 1996 is not sufficient for psychologists to advertise their services as "international."

Psychologists can advertise through radio, television, billboards, leaflets, websites, business cards, brochures, newsletters, or other media. While most psychologists would not like to see their name, picture, or phone number on a billboard, it is not inherently unethical. The APA Ethics Code prohibits only public representations that are known to be false, misleading, fraudulent, or deceptive. Psychologists have wide discretion in what or how to advertise.

An Attention-Getting Advertisement

A complaint was received concerning a psychologist's advertisement in the Yellow Pages. It showed an attractive young woman, presumably the psychologist, with a beaming smile on her face throwing flowers into the air with her arms spread wide. The caption read "Bring Joy Back Into Your Life." Although some considered this advertisement gaudy, it was not unethical.

Although the woman pictured in the advertisement was attractive, the picture could not be characterized as risque or appealing to prurient interests. Nevertheless, the psychologist eventually discontinued the advertisement because she believed it attracted some male clients who were interested in challenging her professional boundaries.

(c) [Representing Degrees.] *Psychologists claim degrees as credentials for their health services only if those degrees (1) were earned from a regionally accredited educational institution or (2) were the basis for psychology licensure by the state in which they practice.* [This standard is similar to Standard 3.03b of the 1992 Ethics Code.]

Psychologists who provide mental health services may only use academic degrees from regionally accredited universities or that were the basis of their licenses. Some universities, especially nontraditional ones, have accreditation from their state education department or from an alternative accrediting body, but not from a regional accrediting association. Psychologists who graduated from one of those programs may refer to their degree if it was the basis upon which they received their license. The issue of degrees from unaccredited universities is, to our knowledge, only an issue in California where graduates from unaccredited universities have been able, at least until recently, to sit for the licensing examination.

This standard only applies to psychologists who are providing mental health services. Psychologists who are teaching, conducting research, or providing other services may represent degrees from unaccredited colleges and universities although some employers may forbid such activities.

It would be a mistake for psychologists-in-training or psychology interns to refer to themselves as "ABD" ("all-but-dissertation"). This acronym is used informally to apply to students who have completed all of their coursework except for the dissertation but have not yet earned their doctoral degree. It is an informal description, not a degree, and may not be used in advertising one's services.

Another misrepresentation could occur when psychologists supervise psychologists-in-training or other professionals. In a supervisory relationship, when the psychologist assumes responsibility for the work product of another person, the psychologist must ensure that the supervisees represent their credentials accurately.

A Naive Mistake

A young psychologist-in-training had arranged to do her postdoctoral training in a private practice. Before she actually started working, she made up business cards which included her name, degree, work address, telephone number, and areas of competence. The supervisor made her destroy those cards and print new ones which also included her professional status (psychologist-in-training) and the name of her supervisor.

In this situation the supervisor appropriately recognized that the failure to indicate the trainee status and the name of the supervisor could cause some clients/patients to conclude that the supervisee was a licensed and autonomous health care provider.

5.02 Statements by Others

(a) [Responsibility for Public Statements.] *Psychologists who engage others to create or place public statements that promote their professional practice, products, or activities retain professional responsibility for such statements.* [This is identical to Standard 3.02a of the 1992 Ethics Code.]

(b) [Compensation to Media Employees.] *Psychologists do not compensate employees of press, radio, television, or other communication media in return for publicity in a news item. (See also Standard 1.01, Misuse of Psychologists' Work).* [This is similar to Standard 3.02d of the 1992 Ethics Code.]

(c) [Identifying Advertising.] *A paid advertisement relating to psychologists' activities must be identified or clearly recognizable as such.* [This standard is similar to Standard 3.02e of the 1992 Ethics Code.]

Standard 5.02 deals with advertisements and the use of the media. Although psychologists may hire others to place public statements promoting their work activities, they retain the final responsibility for such statements. Psychologists do not compensate employees of the communication media for publicity on a news item. This does not preclude token gestures, such as paying for the lunch for a reporter (Canter et al., 1994). Paid advertisements must be recognized as such. This standard does not prohibit paying for advertising; it only precludes advertising which is not labeled as such.

5.03 Descriptions of Workshops and Non-Degree-Granting Educational Programs

To the degree to which they exercise control, psychologists responsible for announcements, catalogs, brochures, or advertisements describing workshops, seminars, or other non-degree-granting educational programs ensure that they accurately describe the audience for which the program is intended, the educational objectives, the presenters, and the fees involved. [This is similar to Standard 6.02c of the 1992 Ethics Code.]

Deception or misrepresentations should not be used when describing educational programs. However, the standard implicitly recognizes that psychologists should not be punished for decisions that are out of their control. Sometimes a nonpsychologist may override the judgment of a psychologist in determining what should be included in those publications. Under those situations, the psychologists should refer to Standard 1.03, dealing with conflicts between ethics and organizational demands.

5.04 Media Presentations

When psychologists provide public advice or comment via print, internet, or other electronic transmissions, they take precautions to ensure that statements (1) are based on their professional knowledge, training, or experience in accord with appropriate psychological literature and practice; (2) are otherwise consistent with this Ethics Code; and (3) do not indicate that a professional relationship has been established with the recipient. (See also Standard 2.04, Bases for Scientific and Professional Judgments.) [This standard is similar to Standard 3.04 of the 1992 Ethics Code.]

Media psychologists need to take care when they answer questions on radio or television talk shows, in newspaper columns, through informational websites, chat rooms, or other media. This standard requires that the same level of competence be used in providing advice as is used in providing direct treatment. Sensationalism should be avoided.

The presentations should adhere to the general standards of the Ethics Code. For example, they should not be false or misleading; they should be reasonably consistent with scientific or professional standards; and unqualified opinions should not be given without a direct examination of the individual in question (see Standard 9.01b).

In addition, the standard requires that psychologists do not indicate that a professional relationship exists between the advice seeker and themselves. It is assumed that when a professional relationship has been established, the information given would be tailored to the needs of the specific individual. However, this would not be possible with callers who present information in short formats (perhaps 5 minutes on the radio or a 300 word letter). Instead psychologists need to restrict their comments to generic information such as the common symptoms, anticipated course of a disorder, and general nature of treatments (Canter et al., 1994). They may say, "The description of your symptoms is consistent with that of a panic disorder. The essential characteristics of a panic disorder are. . . ." They may also say, "You may want to talk this over with a therapist" or give other statements that indicate that therapy is not being provided.

5.05 Testimonials

Psychologists do not solicit testimonials from current therapy clients/patients or other persons who because of their particular cir-

cumstances are vulnerable to undue influence. [This standard is similar to Standard 3.05 of the 1992 Ethics Code.]

Psychologists may use testimonials except from current psychotherapy clients or others who, because of their particular circumstances, are vulnerable to undue influence. It is sometimes difficult to determine when a former client/patient is vulnerable to undue influence. Certainly an argument could be made that clients/patients who appear at risk to need mental health services in the future would be subject to undue influence. However, no clear guidelines exist as to when or how to make this determination. Consequently, psychologists should proceed with caution before using testimonials.

The standard does not cover testimonials for psychological activities other than conducting therapy. For example, psychologists may include testimonials from other psychologists concerning the quality of their continuing education program or from clients concerning the quality of their organizational/industrial work.

5.06 In-Person Solicitation

Psychologists do not engage, directly or through agents, in uninvited in-person solicitation of business from actual or potential therapy clients/patients or other persons who because of their particular circumstances are vulnerable to undue influence. However, this prohibition does not preclude (1) attempting to implement appropriate collateral contacts for the purpose of benefiting an already engaged therapy client/patient or (2) providing disaster or community outreach services. [This standard is similar to Standard 3.06 of the 1992 APA Ethics Code.]

This is the psychological equivalent of ambulance chasing. However, this does not preclude making appropriate collateral contacts with significant others to benefit someone already in therapy. In addition, this standard allows psychologists to participate in community outreach programs (such as those designed to identify and assist homeless persons with serious or persistent mental illnesses) or in disaster relief services.

6. RECORD KEEPING AND FEES

This section deals with record keeping and fees. The standards on record keeping require psychologists to maintain confidentiality in creating, storing, and disposing of records (6.02a), protecting confidential information in databases (6.02b), and facilitating the transfer of records in the event of their death, disability, or retirement (6.02c). They may not withhold records needed for emergency services for nonpayment (6.03).

The standards require psychologists to make financial arrangements clear at the beginning of the relationship or as soon as possible thereafter as is feasible (6.04a), and not to misrepresent their fees (6.04c). Bartering is permitted unless it is clinically contraindicated or exploitative (6.05). Psychologists must take reasonable steps to ensure the accuracy of their reports to third-party payors (6.06) and may not take fees for referrals (6.07).

This section is based primarily on two moral principles. It is based on General Principle A, Beneficence and Nonmaleficence, in that records are to be kept, maintained, stored, and transferred, among other reasons, for the benefit of service recipients. Also, bartering may not be used if it is clinically contraindicated or exploitative, and referral fees are not permitted. In addition, these standards are based on General Principle C, Integrity, in that psychologists need to accurately represent their fees to their clients/patients and third-party payors.

Several changes to the 1992 Ethics Code should reduce the potential vulnerability of psychologists to ethics complaints. First, psychologists may withhold records solely on the basis that payment has not been received, except if the records are needed in an emergency (the 1992 standard required psychologists to send the records if they were imminently needed for treatment). However, HIPAA overrides this provision of the APA Ethics Code for psychologists who provide health care services.

In addition, the standard on bartering has deleted the phrase that psychologists do not ordinarily engage in bartering. It was believed that that statement unnecessarily tainted bartering. Furthermore, Standard 6.06 states that psychologists must take "reasonable steps" to ensure the accuracy of their statements to payors. In contrast, the 1992 Ethics Code required psychologists to state their fees accurately. The revision makes allowances for psychologists who make an honest error in their billing.

Finally, the 2002 revision eliminated old Standard 1.23b which required psychologists who had "reason to believe" that their records would be used in a legal proceeding to keep records in the "kind of detail and quality that would be consistent with reasonable scrutiny in an adjudicative forum." It was believed that a distinction needed to be made between those psychologists who willingly assumed forensic roles and other psychologists who, through circumstances beyond their control, got involved in a forensic proceeding. Psychologists who assume forensic roles would be expected to know their judicial role (see Standard 2.01f). However,

other psychologists may have therapeutic reasons for keeping the professional relationship (and the records) focused on therapy and not on the
forensic issues.

6.01 Documentation of Professional and Scientific Work and Maintenance of Records

*Psychologists create, and to the extent that the records are under
their control, maintain, disseminate, store, retain, and dispose of
records and data relating to their professional and scientific work
in order to (1) facilitate provision of services later by them or by
other professionals, (2) allow for replication of research design
and analyses, (3) meet institutional requirements, (4) ensure accuracy of billing and payments, and (5) ensure compliance with law.
(See also Standard 4.01, Maintaining Confidentiality.)* [This standard combines Standards 1.23a and 1.24 of the 1992 Ethics Code.]

This standard is unique in that it does not prohibit any specific behavior; instead it provides a rationale as to why records are needed. In addition to the five purposes mentioned, records also protect the psychologist
in the event of a charge of misconduct.

Receiving past records is considered a necessary part of the process
of developing an effective treatment plan. Although it is not specifically
required by the APA Ethics Code, psychologists should routinely ask cli-
ents/patients to sign release forms and obtain past treatment records. However, some clients/patients will present seemingly good reasons for refusing to allow the release of past records, such as past abuse on the part of
the previous psychotherapist. At times psychotherapists may write these
reports in ways that are designed to conceal their misconduct, but reports
of clients/patients of past misconduct by previous psychotherapists should
not be a barrier for attempting to retrieve the records. Even if the client's/
patient's reports of abuse are accurate, the records of previous psychotherapists may still contain some useful clinical information.

State boards of psychology and other state laws determine the length
of time that psychologists must keep records. After that time has expired,
psychologists may legally destroy their records. However, psychologists
may want to keep some records longer than the length required. Although
the statute of limitations on a malpractice suit varies from state to state, it
is typically 2 years or 2 years after the client/patient turns 18. Furthermore, some clients/patients may have legitimate needs for old records.
For example, a client/patient with a serious developmental disability may
need old records to demonstrate the lifelong history of that disability. Finally, it is prudent to keep records on some highly litigious clients/pa-

tients who may file a complaint before a licensing board that may have no statute of limitations.

The APA Ethics Code does not address the issue of client/patient access to records which is controlled by state law.

Record keeping is very important for forensic psychologists. The *Specialty Guidelines for Forensic Psychologists* states that the record keeping standard "is higher than the normative standard for general clinical practice" and that it should be the "best documentation possible under the circumstances" (Committee on Ethical Guidelines for Forensic Psychologists, 1991, VI, B). The records should contain information sufficient to justify the decisions made by the psychologist. Information contrary to the opinions of the psychologists should be included as well, including reasons that information did not change or influence the final opinions found in the report.

Psychologists who engage in forensic work should assume that another professional will review the records. Consequently, forensic psychologists should be prepared to send all of their notes and test data, including raw test data, to an appropriately qualified health care professional who will critically check the data for errors or alternative interpretations.

6.02   Maintenance, Dissemination, and Disposal of Confidential Records of Professional and Scientific Work

> *(a)* [Confidentiality of Records.] *Psychologists maintain confidentiality in creating, storing, accessing, transferring, and disposing of records under their control, whether these are written, automated, or in any other medium. (See also Standards 4.01, Maintaining Confidentiality, and 6.01, Documentation of Professional and Scientific Work and Maintenance of Records.)* [This standard is similar to Standard 5.04 of the 1992 Ethics Code.]

This standard requires psychologists to take reasonable precautions to protect the confidentiality of client/patient records. Standard 6.02a does not establish separate standards for records that are stored electronically. The Ethics Code does not attempt to anticipate the developments in electronic storage or transmission of information. Stories of leaks of confidential information stored on computers have been reported. One psychologist had her computer stolen (it had confidential information stored on it). Another psychologist had a virus that transmitted confidential client/patient information to people in her e-mail address book. Still another psychologist discarded her computer, but failed to purge the system of confidential client files. She mistakenly believed that erasing the file would be sufficient for destroying the record.

> (b)   [Confidentiality and Databases.] *If confidential information concerning recipients of psychological services is entered into databases or systems of records available to persons whose access has not been consented to by the recipient, psychologists use coding or other techniques to avoid the inclusion of personal identifiers.* [This standard is similar to Standard 5.07a of the 1992 Ethics Code.]
>
> (c)   [Transfer of Confidential Records.] *Psychologists make plans in advance to facilitate the appropriate transfer and to protect the confidentiality of records and data in the event of psychologists' withdrawal from positions or practice. (See also Standards 3.12, Interruption of Psychological Services, and 10.09, Interruption of Therapy.)* [This standard is similar to Standard 5.09 of the 1992 Ethics Code.]

Psychologists should take reasonable measures to protect their records in anticipation of retirement, disability, or death. The Ethics Code does not give specific instructions on how this is to be done. Nonetheless, some psychologists have written special wills in which they specify the handling of their records in the event of an untimely death or disability (Ragusea, 2002). It is preferable that the records be entrusted to another psychologist or other mental health professional who understands the procedures for handling confidential records.

In ordinary retirements, psychologists will have more time to dispose of records in an orderly fashion. They may destroy records as permitted by state law. They may write a letter to the last known address of their prior clients/patients informing them of their intention to retire and noting that they can have their records sent to a current health professional or allow them to be destroyed after the time specified in state law.

6.03   Withholding Records for Nonpayment

> *Psychologists may not withhold records under their control that are requested and needed for a client's/patient's emergency treatment solely because payment has not been received.* [This standard is similar to Standard 5.11 of the 1992 Ethics Code.]

The previous Code prohibited withholding records for nonpayment of fees if they are immediately needed by the client/patient. The term "immediately needed" was vague and appeared to place psychologists in a vulnerable position when they were asked to send records on clients/ patients who owed them money. Anecdotal evidence suggests that this occurs most commonly when assessments have been conducted, as opposed to ongoing therapy where the psychologist typically has more opportunity to address the nonpayment issue with the client/patient. The new standard gives psychologists greater flexibility in withholding records for nonpayment. However, some states specifically prohibit health care professionals from withholding records because of nonpayment.

However, professional psychologists can only understand the rules governing their behavior if they read this standard in conjunction with HIPAA. HIPAA distinguishes between psychotherapy notes and other more general records that include diagnosis, treatment dates, summary, and so on. HIPAA does not require psychotherapists to give copies of the psychotherapy notes to their clients/patients, but it does require them to give copies of the more general records to their clients/patients on request. HIPAA contains no provision that would allow health care professionals to withhold records for nonpayment. Consequently, psychologists would be required to send general records (but not psychotherapy notes) to clients/patients upon their request.

6.04   Fees and Financial Arrangements

(a) [Agreement on Fees.] *As early as is feasible in a professional or scientific relationship, psychologists and recipients of psychological services reach an agreement specifying compensation and billing arrangements.* [This standard is similar to Standard 1.25a of the 1992 Ethics Code.]

(b) [Fees and Law.] *Psychologists' fee practices are consistent with law.* [This standard is identical to Standard 1.25c of the 1992 Ethics Code.]

(c) [Accurate Representation of Fees.] *Psychologists do not misrepresent their fees.* [This standard is identical to Standard 1.25d of the 1992 Ethics Code.]

(d) [Limitations on Financing.] *If limitations to services can be anticipated because of limitations in financing, this is discussed with the recipient of services as early as is feasible. (See also Standards 10.09, Interruption of Therapy, and 10.10, Terminating Therapy.)* [This standard is similar to Standard 1.25e of the 1992 Ethics Code.]

(e) [Collecting Delinquent Debts.] *If the recipient of services does not pay for services as agreed, and if psychologists intend to use collection agencies or legal measures to collect the fees, psychologists first inform the person that such measures will be taken and provide that person an opportunity to make prompt payment. (See also Standards 4.05, Disclosures; 6.03, Withholding Records for Nonpayment; and 10.01, Informed Consent to Therapy.)* [This standard is similar to Standard 1.25f of the 1992 Ethics Code.]

Although psychologists may legally turn the bills of clients/patients over to bill collection agencies, it is desirable to avoid having to take that step. Attempts to collect unpaid bills are frequent precipitants of malpractice suits or ethics complaints, even if they are frivolous. Psychologists may decide that occasionally writing off unpaid bills is better than facing malpractice suits or ethics charges – even if such charges are frivolous. Psychologists can minimize this problem by being very proactive about requiring payment at the time the service is delivered.

Psychologists using collection services should limit their disclosures of information regarding the care of clients/patients to the minimum necessary to prove and collect debts. Typically, it is necessary to reveal only the name, address, and phone number of the client/patient, the name of the psychologist, and the amount of money owed. Similarly, information disclosed in small claims court can be restricted to the minimal essential information such as the client's/patient's name and address, the date of service, and the amount owed.

6.05   Barter With Clients/Patients

Barter is the acceptance of goods, services, or other nonmonetary remuneration from clients/patients in return for psychological services. Psychologists may barter only if (1) it is not clinically contraindicated, and (2) the resulting arrangement is not exploitative. (See also Standards 3.05, Multiple Relationships, and 6.04, Fees and Financial Arrangements.) [This standard is similar to Standard 1.18 of the 1992 Ethics Code.]

This standard was substantially revised from the 1992 Ethics Code, which stated that psychologists ordinarily refrain from bartering. However, it was believed that the 1992 caveat unnecessarily tainted bartering relationships which are common among some cultural groups. Of course bartering is prohibited if it is contraindicated or exploitative.

From a practical perspective, bartering goods presents fewer risks than bartering services. Goods may be inspected ahead of time and assigned a predetermined economic value, which will reduce the sense of exploitation. Furthermore, goods can be returned if they are defective; time cannot be returned. Woody (1998) cautions that an allegation of bartering sometimes occurs when the client/patient has given the psychologist a gift. Although the psychologist may interpret the gift as a symbolic gesture, the client/patient may interpret it as a way of fulfilling his or her financial debt.

Psychologists who barter may want to include, as a risk management procedure, a written agreement that specifies the worth of the object being bartered.

6.06   Accuracy in Reports to Payors and Funding Sources

In their reports to payors for services or sources of research funding, psychologists take reasonable steps to ensure the accurate reporting of the nature of the service provided or research conducted, the fees, charges, or payments, and where applicable, the identity of the provider, the findings, and the diagnosis. (See also Standards 4.01, Maintaining Confidentiality; 4.04, Minimizing Intrusions on Privacy; and 4.05, Disclosures.) [This standard is similar to Standard 1.26 of the 1992 Ethics Code.]

It is unethical for psychologists to willfully misrepresent their fees to third-party payors or to be negligent in their billing activities. It is not an ethical violation, in and of itself, only because a billing error was made. Psychologists need to use reasonable diligence in monitoring their billing services. This standard does not intend to hold psychologists responsible if a clerk willfully committed fraud behind the back of the psychologist. However, psychologists would be liable if they created a climate conducive to insurance fraud, such as telling billing personnel something to the effect that "I want my revenues increased. I don't care how you do it; just don't let me know about it."

6.07   Referrals and Fees

When psychologists pay, receive payment from, or divide fees with another professional, other than in an employer-employee relationship, the payment to each is based on the services provided (clinical, consultative, administrative, or other) and is not based on the referral itself. (See also Standard 3.09, Cooperation With Other Professionals.) [This standard is similar to Standard 1.27 of the 1992 Ethics Code.]

Referral fees are fees that are accepted for referring a client/patient to another practitioner for professional services. Although Ethics Codes before 1989 considered referral fees as unethical, APA rescinded its absolute position against referral fees under pressure from the Federal Trade

Commission. Now, the Ethics Code permits fees for referrals if these fees are made on the basis of services provided. Fees given only for referrals, however, are not ethical.

The prohibition against referral fees does not preclude the division of fees between employer and employee; nor does it preclude the division of fees in compensation for services rendered such as rent, secretarial services, or professional consultation. It could be appropriate, for example, for a psychologist to refer patients to other professionals who rent office space from them. However, the payment for the office space must be based on the value of the rent and not on the basis of a referral.

A Misleading Fee Arrangement

A psychologist with a part-time practice rented office space from another psychologist on an "as-used" basis. This meant that he paid the landlord/psychologist a flat fee for every hour that he used the office. However the landlord/psychologist charged him $40 an hour for every client/patient that he referred, but only $20 an hour for other clients/patients.

The higher rent for the clients/patients referred by the landlord/psychologist constituted a referral fee and is unethical.

7. EDUCATION AND TRAINING

Psychologists responsible for educational programs must take reasonable steps to ensure that they will provide the experiences necessary for students to obtain the credentials advertised by the program (7.01). They must also ensure that the descriptions of the program (7.02) and individual classes are accurate (7.03a). Teachers should present psychological information accurately (7.03b).

Psychologists may not require students to disclose personal information unless the requirement for such disclosures are clearly identified ahead of time or if it is necessary to evaluate a student who appears to be impaired (7.04). Faculty may not provide mandatory group or individual therapy to the students whom they may be evaluating (7.05b). Psychologists give students and supervisees timely and specific feedback (7.06a). They evaluate students and supervisees on the basis of objective performance measures that have been presented to the students ahead of time (7.06b). Psychologists may not have sexual relationships with students or supervisees in their department or those over whom they have supervisory responsibilities (7.07).

These standards are based on General Principle C, Integrity, in that psychologists need to present program descriptions, course requirements, and psychological information accurately. Also, they are based on General Principles A (Beneficence and Nonmaleficence) and B (Fidelity and Responsibility) in that psychologists attempt to avoid or manage conflicts of interest.

One of the major differences from the 1992 Ethics Code in this section is the addition of Standards 7.04 and 7.05, which limit the circumstances under which psychology programs may require their students to disclose sensitive personal information. The prohibition against sexual contact with students and supervisees is expanded to include sexual contact with any psychologist in the department or agency (7.07).

7.01   Design of Education and Training Programs

Psychologists responsible for education and training programs take reasonable steps to ensure that the programs are designed to provide the appropriate knowledge and proper experiences, and to meet the requirements for licensure, certification, or other goals for which claims are made by the program. (See also Standard 5.03, Descriptions of Workshops and Non-Degree-Granting Educational Programs.) [This standard is similar to Standard 6.01 of the 1992 Ethics Code.]

Psychologists who are responsible for training programs need to describe their programs accurately. This standard seeks to protect students from being exploited by training programs that could fail to take adequate steps to meet the requirements for licensure, certification, or other goals that the programs claim. Psychologists, for example, could not advertise that their programs would allow the students to become licensed, but then take no reasonable effort to ensure that those program goals are met.

7.02   Descriptions of Education and Training Programs

Psychologists responsible for education and training programs take reasonable steps to ensure that there is a current and accurate description of the program content (including participation in required course- or program-related counseling, psychotherapy, experiential groups, consulting projects, or community service), training goals and objectives, stipends and benefits, and requirements that must be met for satisfactory completion of the program. This information must be made readily available to all interested parties. [This standard is similar to Standard 6.02a of the 1992 Ethics Code.]

Training programs must represent their requirements accurately. Some of the program requirements that have caused problems for students in the past include participation in experiential groups or participation in counseling classes that require substantial self-disclosure. There is no problem with having such requirements. Indeed, many psychologists believe that such requirements are essential in order to provide meaningful training as a psychotherapist. However, the program materials should describe these requirements ahead of time so that prospective students are made aware of them.

7.03   Accuracy in Teaching

(a)   [Accuracy in Syllabi.] *Psychologists take reasonable steps to ensure that course syllabi are accurate regarding the subject matter to be covered, bases for evaluating progress, and the nature of course experiences. This standard does not preclude an instructor from modifying course content or requirements when the instructor considers it pedagogically necessary or desirable, so long as students are made aware of these modifications in a manner that enables them to fulfill course requirements. (See also Standard 5.01, Avoidance of False or Deceptive Statements.)* [This standard is similar to Standard 6.02b of the 1992 Ethics Code.]

(b)   [Presenting Psychological Information Accurately.] *When engaged in teaching or training, psychologists present psychological information accurately. (See also Standard 2.03, Maintaining Competence.)* [This standard is similar to Standard 6.03a of the 1992 Ethics Code.]

Psychologists who teach courses need to ensure that the course requirements are specified ahead of time and, if it is necessary to make changes in the course requirements, that students will be given an opportunity to fulfill the course requirements. Psychologists must also present class material accurately. There is obviously some discretion in what constitutes accuracy. A psychologist who, for example, has had extensive training and commitment to a psychodynamic model may appear to give more weight or credence to psychodynamic principles and less to other theoretical systems. Such biases are not likely to be viewed as ethical violations unless the course syllabus clearly specified that several theoretical models would be presented with equal enthusiasm or the instructor's bias clearly interfered with the instructor's ability to meet the course objectives and students' training was sacrificed. Again, the Ethics Code concerns itself with egregious behavior, not nuances of behavior where reasonable persons may disagree.

7.04   Student Disclosure of Personal Information

Psychologists do not require students or supervisees to disclose personal information in course- or program-related activities, either orally or in writing, regarding sexual history, history of abuse and neglect, psychological treatment, and relationships with parents, peers, and spouses or significant others except if (1) the program or training facility has clearly identified this requirement in its admissions and program materials or (2) the information is necessary to evaluate or obtain assistance for students whose personal problems could reasonably be judged to be preventing them from performing their training- or professionally related activities in a competent manner or posing a threat to the students or others. [This standard is new.]

Training programs that require disclosure on the part of students must make self-disclosure requirements known to students before they enroll in the program. However, this standard allows schools to make inquiries or require an evaluation or psychotherapy for students who appear to be impaired. Indeed, one of the primary obligations of training programs is to ensure that their students have the social and emotional competence to be adequate psychologists. Despite screening of candidates, most graduate programs will, at some time, admit a student who lacks the social skills or emotional strengths necessary to be a competent psychologist. Procidano et al. (1995) found that 34% of the graduate departments of psychology, in the last 5 years, had students whose personality/emotional problems were serious enough to impair their effectiveness as psychologists. It is the responsibility of doctoral programs to identify these students, help them address their problems, or direct them out of the profession.

An Especially Troublesome Problem

A doctoral student in a clinical psychology program had informed several of his friends that he intended to commit suicide, and he alleged that he had made an unsuccessful attempt last year. Although his course work was marginally acceptable, he began to make unusual or bizarre comments during his classes. A faculty member suspected that he may have or be developing a major depression or another serious mental disorder.

A faculty member had an understandable concern for the safety of this student and questioned his ability to perform adequately during the internship year. The faculty compassionately but directly confronted the student with his behavior, including his relationships with significant others (as that was a frequent topic of his ramblings) and his history of psychological treatment. They appropriately required the student to seek mental health evaluation and services before continuing in the program.

7.05 Mandatory Individual or Group Therapy

(a) [Conditions on Mandating Individual or Group Therapy.] *When individual or group therapy is a program or course requirement, psychologists responsible for that program allow students in undergraduate or graduate programs the option of selecting such therapy from practitioners unaffiliated with the program. (See also Standard 7.02, Descriptions of Education and Training Programs.)* [This standard is new.]

(b) [Avoiding Multiple Relationships Among Faculty Who Provide Individual or Group Therapy.] *Faculty who are or are likely to be responsible for evaluating students' academic performance do not themselves provide that therapy. (See also Standard 3.05, Multiple Relationships.)* [This standard is new.]

In the past, many programs required students to participate in courses which were, in part, a therapy group. In those settings many students felt compelled to disclose personal data that later could be used against them. The instructors who expected the disclosure could be the same instructors who graded the students in that or other courses.

Standard 7.05 gives students some protection against overly intrusive program requirements. However, the goal is to strike a balance between the rights of students and the need of the doctoral program to ensure the emotional competence of the students. Schools and training programs can still require individual or group psychotherapy, although students must be informed of this requirement ahead of time and the therapy cannot be given by persons who have evaluative authority over the students.

The standard applies to undergraduate and graduate programs. Faculty at postdoctoral programs, such as psychoanalytic training institutes, may conduct such group or individual therapy with their students.

7.06 Assessing Student and Supervisee Performance

(a) [Timely and Specific Feedback.] *In academic and supervisory relationships, psychologists establish a timely and specific process for providing feedback to students and supervisees. Information regarding the process is provided to the student at the beginning of supervision.* [This standard is similar to Standard 6.05a of the 1992 Ethics Code.]

(b) [Evaluation Based on Performance.] *Psychologists evaluate students and supervisees on the basis of their actual performance on relevant and established program requirements.* [This standard is identical to Standard 6.05b of the 1992 Ethics Code.]

This standard gives supervisors leeway in the nature of supervision and the means of evaluating student performance. However, it requires supervisors to inform the student or supervisee about the evaluation process at the beginning of supervision and to establish a timely and specific feedback process. The scenario to be avoided is one in which supervisees suddenly get informed that their performance is not adequate and they are being dismissed from the program or that they will receive an evaluation so poor that they will not be eligible to apply for an internship or for the licensing examination. Giving students feedback as they go through the program allows them to correct shortcomings, or at least gives them time to reconsider their careers and make other arrangements.

Programs need to balance the need to protect the public from incompetent psychologists with the need to protect students from capricious punishments from faculty members. The balance can best be struck if students receive specific and timely feedback about their performance.

Concerned Faculty

The faculty at Mid-Atlantic University evaluated all of the doctoral students each year on a number of dimensions including collegiality, social skills, and skill development. If a student received an unsatisfactory recommendation, then the faculty provided that student with a plan to remediate those deficiencies. The process informed students of their progress and alerted students early in the program if they were having problems.

7.07 Sexual Relationships With Students and Supervisees

Psychologists do not engage in sexual relationships with students or supervisees who are in their department, agency, or training center or over whom psychologists have or are likely to have evaluative authority. (See also Standard 3.05, Multiple Relationships.) [This standard is similar to Standard 1.19b of the 1992 Ethics Code.]

Students, especially graduate students, depend upon their teachers and supervisors for grades, letters of recommendations, and, to a large extent, the quality of their work life. Faculty and supervisors will have a difficult time remaining objective if they engage in dual relationships, especially sexual relationships, with students or supervisees (L. Sullivan & Ogloff, 1998). Nonsexual multiple relationships are handled through Standard 3.05a, which states that multiple relationships must be avoided if they impair objectivity or are exploitative. However, sexual relationships between supervisors or faculty and students are always forbidden.

In addition to the attention that has been given to the sexual relationships between psychologists and clients/patients, attention to the harmful impact of sexual relationships between supervisors and supervisees is growing. Pope, Levenson, and Schover (1979) reported that 9.4% of psychologists (16.5% women and 3% men) had sexual relationships with psychology educators and 5% (8% women and 2% men) had had sexual relationships with their supervisors. Robinson and Reid's (1985) survey of women psychologists found rates slightly lower than those found by Pope et al. (1979).

The educator or supervisor does not typically have the same influence over the student or supervisee as the psychologist has over the client/patient. Nevertheless, the educator or supervisor has influence in the form of grades, work conditions, or letters of recommendation. Furthermore, some supervisors have a style that requires substantial disclosure of emotions, background, and personal experience that approximates the disclosure found in psychotherapy.

8. RESEARCH AND PUBLICATION

Psychologists inform their host institutions about their research if necessary (8.01) and acquire informed consent from participants (8.02) except when it is conducted as part of a routine educational or organizational activity (8.05). Psychologists must obtain informed consent when recording voices or images in research, except in some unusual circumstances (8.03).

Subordinates and students must be free from coercion into participating in research (8.04) and the inducements to participate should not be such that are likely to be considered coercive (8.06). Deception in research is acceptable, but should be avoided if possible (8.07). Participants should be debriefed (8.08). Animal subjects in research should be treated humanely (8.09). Research results should not be falsified (8.10). Psychologists should not publish as original, data that has been published elsewhere (8.11). Psychologists should share their research data with others under some circumstances (8.14). Psychologists may not plagiarize (8.11), and reviewers should protect the confidentiality of the manuscripts they review (8.15). Standard 8.12 describes the criteria for determining authorship. Psychologists do not publish previously published data as original (8.13).

The moral principles underlying the standards in this section are primarily General Principle E (Respect for People's Rights and Dignity), but General Principle C (Integrity) and General Principle A (Beneficence and Nonmaleficence) also apply here. Scientific research benefits society. Information obtained from psychological research can be used to improve physical and mental health care, educational practices, and organizational functioning, and can inform public policy. However, a conflict may occur between the public benefit of the research and the career advancement of the researcher. Also, the manner in which research is conducted may raise ethical issues. The participants do not lose their rights only because of the possibility that the findings may benefit society as a whole. Instead, participants need to be treated with consideration and should be free to make informed decisions about their participation in the research.

Generally speaking, researchers should conduct themselves in accord with General Principle C, Integrity, in that they describe the experiments accurately to the participants and give them the opportunity for a debriefing session. Researchers should describe protocols involving treatments to participants/clients/patients, including any expectations of benefits to them. Exceptions to the Principle of Integrity are made when the research needs to use deception and alternate nondeceptive means are not available.

Finally, if the research involves treatment, then General Principle A, Beneficence and Nonmaleficence, should apply. That is, clients/patients should be treated with an effort to improve their well-being and to minimize harm.

This section contains several changes from the 1992 Ethics Code. It makes it explicit that researchers can dispense with informed consent under some limited circumstances (8.05). It also requires psychologists to try to minimize harm when they learn that participants have been harmed by the research (8.08c).

8.01   Institutional Approval

> *When institutional approval is required, psychologists provide accurate information about their research proposals and obtain approval prior to conducting research. They conduct the research in accordance with the approved research protocol.* [This standard is similar to Standard 6.09 of the 1992 Ethics Code.]

This standard requires psychologists to be candid about their research activities and not to conduct them surreptitiously. In addition, they are to conduct research in accord with generally accepted standards.

8.02   Informed Consent to Research

(a) [General Rule on Informed Consent to Research.] *When obtaining informed consent as required in Standard 3.10, Informed Consent, psychologists inform participants about (1) the purpose of the research, expected duration, and procedures; (2) their right to decline to participate and to withdraw from the research once participation has begun; (3) the foreseeable consequences of declining or withdrawing; (4) reasonably foreseeable factors that may be expected to influence their willingness to participate such as potential risks, discomfort, or adverse effects; (5) any prospective research benefits; (6) limits of confidentiality; (7) incentives for participation; and (8) whom to contact for questions about the research and research participants' rights. They provide opportunity for the prospective participants to ask questions and receive answers. (See also Standards 8.03, Informed Consent for Recording Voices and Images in Research; 8.05, Dispensing With Informed Consent for Research; and 8.07, Deception in Research.)* [This standard is similar to Standard 6.11b of the 1992 Ethics Code.]

(b) [Informed Consent With Intervention Research.] *Psychologists conducting intervention research involving the use of experimental treatments clarify to participants at the outset of the research (1) the experimental nature of the treatment; (2) the services that will or will not be available to the control group(s) if appropriate; (3) the means by which assignment to treatment and control groups will be made; (4) available treatment alternatives if an individual does not wish to participate in the research or wishes to withdraw once a study has begun; and (5) compensation for or monetary costs of participating including, if appropriate, whether reimbursement from the participant or a third-party payor will be sought. (See also Standard 8.02a, Informed Consent to Research.)* [This standard is new.]

Standard 8.02 expands on the informed consent requirements found in Standard 3.10. (See Table 5 on pp. 82-83.) The general requirements under 3.10 are that psychologists would use reasonably understandable language with persons who have the capacity to understand and to give voluntary consent, and have the opportunity to ask questions. Standard

8.02a adds other components of consent that should be given in research situations.

The general rules for getting consent are straightforward and are fairly routine when dealing with a university subject pool. However, the logistics of obtaining consent can be complicated, especially when treatments involve such vulnerable populations as those with serious mental illnesses, developmental disabilities, or dementias. The goal is to set consent standards that adequately protect the participants but do not stifle legitimate research with cumbersome extraneous requirements.

The specifics of how to obtain informed consent may vary with the population being studied. For example, persons with mental retardation may or may not be able to understand the salient features of what is being asked of them. At times it may be consistent with the spirit of informed consent to get substitute consent from family members or caregivers even if the person has not been legally declared incompetent. Nonetheless, even persons with mental retardation are often able to give consent that is truly informed if the concepts are explained to them adequately and they have the opportunity to have their questions answered. Many researchers have found the MacArthur Competence Assessment Tool for Treatment (MacCAT-T) useful in assessing the competence of individuals to consent to experimental treatments (Grisso & Appelbaum, 1998).

The goal of Standard 8.02b is to ensure the protection of the research participants in control groups when an experimental treatment is being evaluated. Researchers should explain the process of selection into the experimental and control groups, and options in the event that the participants do not wish to participate in the control group or wish to withdraw.

8.03   Informed Consent for Recording
Voices and Images in Research

Psychologists obtain informed consent from research participants prior to recording their voices or images for data collection unless (1) the research consists solely of naturalistic observations in public places, and it is not anticipated that the recording will be used in a manner that could cause personal identification or harm, or (2) the research design includes deception, and consent for the use of the recording is obtained during debriefing. (See also Standard 8.07, Deception in Research.) [This standard is similar to Standard 6.13 of the 1992 Ethics Code.]

Both clients/patients and research participants have choice and control over any recording of their voice or image (see also Standard 4.03). This rule does not apply to naturalistic observations of behavior in public places or when research involves deception and the psychologist obtains consent during the debriefing.

8.04   Client/Patient, Student, and Subordinate Research Participants

(a)   [Protection of Subordinate Research Participants.] *When psychologists conduct research with clients/patients, students, or subordinates as participants, psychologists take steps to protect the prospective participants from adverse consequences of declining or withdrawing from participation.* [This standard is similar to Standard 6.11c of the 1992 Ethics Code.]

(b)   [Research Participation as Course Requirement.] *When research participation is a course requirement or opportunity for extra credit, the prospective participant is given the choice of equitable alternative activities.* [This is identical to Standard 6.11d of the 1992 Ethics Code.]

Much research is conducted using subjects recruited from introduction to psychology courses. Although there may be some educational benefit in participating in these experiments, the major purpose is to provide subjects for the research of other students or faculty. Students should be given the opportunity to turn down or leave any experiment and accept equitable educational activities.

8.05   Dispensing With Informed Consent for Research

Psychologists may dispense with informed consent only (1) where research would not reasonably be assumed to create distress or harm and involves (a) the study of normal educational practices, curricula, or classroom management methods conducted in educational settings; (b) only anonymous questionnaires, naturalistic observations, or archival research for which disclosure of responses would not place participants at risk of criminal or civil liability or damage their financial standing, employability, or reputation, and confidentiality is protected; or (c) the study of factors related to job or organization effectiveness conducted in organizational settings for which there is no risk to participants' employability and confidentiality is protected or (2) where otherwise permitted by law or federal or institutional regulations. [This standard is related to Standard 6.12 of the 1992 Ethics Code.].

The general rule is to obtain consent for research although there are several types of situations in which this is not necessary. For example, a college or university may gather research on the SAT scores of its incoming freshmen class without having to obtain the consent of all of the students to do so. Or an organization may gather data on the relative productivity of one or more of its departments. In addition, psychologists may gather data from unobtrusive naturalistic observations, archival research, or anonymous questionnaires.

Routine Educational Data

A psychologist studied the relationship between attendance and grades in his introduction to psychology courses. There was no need to get consent for analyzing data (student grades) which were created as part of normal educational activity.

8.06 Offering Inducements for Research Participation

(a) [Excessive Inducements.] *Psychologists make reasonable efforts to avoid offering excessive or inappropriate financial or other inducements for research participation when such inducements are likely to coerce participation.* [This standard is similar to Standard 6.14b of the 1992 Ethics Code.]

(b) [Clarifying Nature of Services as an Inducement.] *When offering professional services as an inducement for research participation, psychologists clarify the nature of the services, as well as the risks, obligations, and limitations. (See also Standard 6.05, Barter With Clients/Patients.)* [This standard is similar to Standard 6.14a of the 1992 Ethics Code.]

Psychologists can reduce the likelihood of coerced participation by emphasizing the freedom of the person to decline participation, noting the availability of services elsewhere if participation is declined, and by having a readable consent form.

An example of an excessive or inappropriate inducement to research might be to give money to persons who abuse alcohol or other drugs with the foreknowledge that they would be likely to use the money to buy more alcohol or other drugs. Some monetary inducements that may seem small to middle-class Americans may appear substantial to those with limited incomes. An acceptable arrangement may be to give the persons who abuse alcohol or other drugs a voucher or gift certificate that can be redeemed at a restaurant or grocery store.

8.07 Deception in Research

(a) [General Rule on Deception in Research.] *Psychologists do not conduct a study involving deception unless they have de-*

> *termined that the use of deceptive techniques is justified by the study's significant prospective scientific, educational, or applied value and that effective nondeceptive alternative procedures are not feasible.* [This standard is similar to Standard 6.15a of the 1992 Ethics Code.]
>
> *(b)* [Deception About Pain or Distress.] *Psychologists do not deceive prospective participants about research that is reasonably expected to cause physical pain or severe emotional distress.* [This standard is similar to 6.15b of the 1992 Ethics Code.]
>
> *(c)* [Explanation of Deception to Participants.] *Psychologists explain any deception that is an integral feature of the design and conduct of an experiment to participants as early as is feasible, preferably at the conclusion of their participation, but no later than at the conclusion of the data collection, and permit participants to withdraw their data. (See also Standard 8.08, Debriefing.)* [This standard is similar to Standard 6.15c of the 1992 Ethics Code.]

Although deception research is not prohibited, these standards require psychologists to consider other nondeceptive research designs. When deception is used, the researcher must justify why deception was needed, debrief research participants as soon as possible, and give them an opportunity to withdraw their data if they so choose. The burden is on the psychologist to demonstrate the necessity of deception research.

Deception has been criticized on moral grounds (it is intrinsically undesirable to deceive people), methodological grounds (deception influences the way that subjects act), and policy considerations (deception undermines the trust that the public has in the discipline and profession of psychology) in that there may be a "reputation spill-over" as the public becomes aware that psychologists commonly deceive people in their research (Kimmel, 1998). Consequently, deception should be used only when other designs are inadequate to address the research question.

Psychologists may never deceive participants about physical discomfort or severe emotional distress. The term "severe" was added to eliminate the possibility of frivolous complaints. It is hard to imagine any experiment in which a participant could not claim some form of "distress" even if it was only mild boredom or annoyance. On the other hand, participants need to be protected from egregious behaviors that would be likely to inflict emotional pain on anyone.

8.08   Debriefing

(a)   [General Rule on Debriefing.] *Psychologists provide a prompt opportunity for participants to obtain appropriate information about the nature, results, and conclusions of the research, and they take reasonable steps to correct any misconceptions that participants may have of which the psychologists are aware.* [This standard is similar to Standard 6.18a of the 1992 Ethics Code.]

(b)   [Denying or Withholding Debriefing.] *If scientific or humane values justify delaying or withholding this information, psychologists take reasonable measures to reduce the risk of harm.* [This standard is identical to Standard 6.18b of the 1992 Ethics Code.]

(c)   [Minimizing Harm.] *When psychologists become aware that research procedures have harmed a participant, they take reasonable steps to minimize the harm.* [This standard is new.]

Psychologists should inform participants of the purpose of the study through a debriefing session or other debriefing methods. If deception is used or a reasonable possibility exists that the participants might misunderstand the nature or conclusions of the study, then psychologists need to attempt to correct these misconceptions. Of course, this does not need to be done if there are humane or scientific reasons for doing so. In addition, psychologists have a responsibility to minimize any harm caused by the research.

8.09   Humane Care and Use of Animals in Research

(a)   [Compliance With Laws and Standards.] *Psychologists acquire, care for, use, and dispose of animals in compliance with current federal, state, and local laws and regulations, and with professional standards.*

(b)   [Ultimate Responsibility of Psychologists.] *Psychologists trained in research methods and experienced in the care of laboratory animals supervise all procedures involving animals and are responsible for ensuring appropriate consideration of their comfort, health, and humane treatment.*

(c)   [Competence of Supervisees.] *Psychologists ensure that all individuals under their supervision who are using animals have received instruction in research methods and in the care, maintenance, and handling of the species being used, to the extent appropriate to their role. (See also Standard 2.05, Delegation of Work to Others.)*

(d) [Minimize Discomfort.] *Psychologists make reasonable efforts to minimize the discomfort, infection, illness, and pain of animal subjects.*

(e) [Subjecting Animals to Pain.] *Psychologists use a procedure subjecting animals to pain, stress, or privation only when an alternative procedure is unavailable and the goal is justified by its prospective scientific, educational, or applied value.*

(f) [Surgical Procedures.] *Psychologists perform surgical procedures under appropriate anesthesia and follow techniques to avoid infection and minimize pain during and after surgery.*

(g) [Terminating an Animal's Life.] *When it is appropriate that an animal's life be terminated, psychologists proceed rapidly, with an effort to minimize pain and in accordance with accepted procedures.* [These standards are similar to Standards 6.20a to 6.20i of the 1992 Ethics Code.]

Except for the deletion of one section, which was covered elsewhere in the Ethics Code, no changes were made in the ethical standards concerning the treatment of animals. Researchers must ensure the welfare of the animal subjects and may only inflict pain, stress, or privation upon them when no alternative research procedure is available and the goal can be justified by its prospective social value. When it is necessary to kill animals, it should be done rapidly with an effort to minimize pain. State and federal laws regarding the care of animals must be followed. More details on the specifics of protecting animal welfare can be found in *Guidelines for the Ethical Conduct in the Care and Use of Animals* (APA, 1993).

8.10   Reporting Research Results

(a) [Fabrication of Data.] *Psychologists do not fabricate data. (See also Standard 5.01a, Avoidance of False or Deceptive Statements.)* [This standard is similar to Standard 6.21a of the 1992 Ethics Code.]

(b) [Correction of Errors.] *If psychologists discover significant errors in their published data, they take reasonable steps to correct such errors in a correction, retraction, erratum, or other appropriate publication means.* [This standard is identical to Standard 6.21b of the 1992 Ethics Code.]

The scientific enterprise assumes the accuracy of the data reported. Needless to say, the scientific discipline of psychology would not advance if researchers were to falsify data. However, despite efforts by conscientious researchers, mistakes in reporting data may creep into a publication. When that occurs, the authors should take steps to correct the errors.

8.11 Plagiarism

Psychologists do not present portions of another's work or data as their own, even if the other work or data source is cited occasionally. [This standard is similar to Standard 6.22 of the 1992 Ethics Code.]

The scientific enterprise requires that authors receive credit for the work and ideas that they have developed. The standard applies to innovative ideas as well as to direct quotes.

8.12 Publication Credit

(a) [General Rule on Authorship.] *Psychologists take responsibility and credit, including authorship credit, only for work they have actually performed or to which they have substantially contributed. (See also Standard 8.12b, Publication Credit.)* [This standard is similar to Standard 6.23a of the 1992 Ethics Code.]

(b) [Awarding Credit for Authorship.] *Principal authorship and other publication credits accurately reflect the relative scientific or professional contributions of the individuals involved, regardless of their relative status. Mere possession of an institutional position, such as department chair, does not justify authorship credit. Minor contributions to the research or to the writing for publications are acknowledged appropriately, such as in footnotes or in an introductory statement.* [This standard is identical to Standard 6.23b of the 1992 Ethics Code.]

(c) [Authorship for Students.] *Except under exceptional circumstances, a student is listed as principal author on any multiple-authored article that is substantially based on the student's dissertation. Faculty advisors discuss publication credit with students as early as feasible and throughout the research and publication process as appropriate. (See also Standard 8.12b, Publication Credit.)* [This standard is similar to Standard 6.23c of the 1992 Ethics Code.]

One of the major goals of this standard is to eliminate honorary authors (those who receive authorship only because of their status although they did not do enough work to merit authorship) and ghost authors (those who receive no credit for their work although they made substantial contributions). Because authorship is usually a major criterion upon which faculty are hired or given promotions or tenure, it is important to ensure proper credit for awarding authorship.

This standard gives general guidelines for authors; the criteria for authorship are described in more detail in the *Publication Manual of the American Psychological Association* (5th ed.; APA, 2001). Some activities, such as developing the design, conducting the literature review, writing the first draft, or making substantial contributions to the final draft, all could warrant authorship. Such technical activities as collecting data or running subjects typically do not warrant authorship in and of themselves. Unfortunately, no clear algorithm can determine authorship in all situations, and participants may vary in their interpretation of the relative value of the different contributions.

Often the problems with publications involve research conducted between a student and a professor. On the one hand there is a desire to protect students who are in a power disadvantage and who risk having faculty usurp authorship for their work (L. Sullivan & Ogloff, 1998). The students may have done all of the legwork, written the proposal (with minimal input from the faculty member), run the subjects, analyzed the data, and written the report and article. The contribution of the faculty members were such that they should be second author, if an author at all.

On the other hand, some students inherit a lot of knowledge and experience from their faculty supervisors. The faculty may know the literature in the field of study very well to the point of directing the student to the appropriate sources (or even giving them copies of key articles or chapters), identifying the key research areas, helping to solicit subjects, directing or at least approving the research design, and assisting in the preparation of the dissertation or article. The contributions of the faculty member are such that she or he, not the student, deserves to be the primary author.

It is especially common in master's theses for professors to contribute more and, consequently, become more deserving of primary authorship. With master's theses, the professors typically know more of the relevant literature, methodology, and statistics and have the writing skills necessary to turn a thesis into a publication (Shadish, 1994).

In any event, it is desirable for those who conduct research to discuss their rules for determining authorship or credit for research well ahead of time. It is not desirable to wait after a student has spent 40 hours collecting and analyzing data to tell her that her contributions are not sufficient to merit authorship. Such information might have influenced her willingness to contribute so much time to the project. Such early discussions may be especially important when working with persons from other disciplines who may have different standards or traditions regarding authorship.

8.13 Duplicate Publication of Data

Psychologists do not publish, as original data, data that have been previously published. This does not preclude republishing data when they are accompanied by proper acknowledgment. [This standard is identical to Standard 6.24 of the 1992 Ethics Code.]

The presumption is that journal articles are based on original data unless otherwise specified. This standard attempts to avoid situations in which an author submits and/or publishes essentially the same article to two different journals. Publishing duplicate data wastes scarce journal space and may risk copyright violations. However, this does not preclude using portions of the data in subsequent publications. Canter et al. (1994) explain that the data could be published in abstracted form through a limited circulation publication (such as a university newsletter) without violating the intent of this standard.

Useful and Distinct Publications

A psychologist did important research on the dual process theory of memory. One of his seminal articles was published in the prestigious *North American Journal of Clinical Psychology*. He later published a more theoretical article which referenced his *North American Journal of Clinical Psychology* article including some paragraphs which were summaries or paraphrases of portions of the discussion section from that article.

This publishing sequence is done in accordance with the Ethics Code. The contents were sufficiently different to justify two articles. The prohibition is meant only to apply when data are published as original in two or more outlets.

8.14 Sharing Research Data for Verification

(a) [General Rule on Sharing Data.] *After research results are published, psychologists do not withhold the data on which their conclusions are based from other competent professionals who seek to verify the substantive claims through reanalysis and who intend to use such data only for that purpose,*

provided that the confidentiality of the participants can be protected and unless legal rights concerning proprietary data preclude their release. This does not preclude psychologists from requiring that such individuals or groups be responsible for costs associated with the provision of such information. [This standard is similar to Standard 6.25 of the 1992 Ethics Code.]

(b) [Sharing Data for Purposes Other Than Reanalysis.] *Psychologists who request data from other psychologists to verify the substantive claims through reanalysis may use shared data only for the declared purpose. Requesting psychologists obtain prior written agreement for all other uses of the data.* [This standard is new.]

Although the standard does not set a specific time frame, the APA's *Publication Manual* states that reviewers should keep data available for 5 years after publication of the research (APA, 2001). Also treatment manuals and other information related to the research should be kept for the same period of time. Generally, the person requesting the information should bear its costs. This standard does not supersede the confidentiality rights of the participants nor does it override any proprietary rights of the funder of the research.

Standard 8.14b is new. Although it is not required by this standard, it would be prudent to receive written approval to use the data for purposes other than reanalysis. Members of the ECTF were concerned that a sole reliance on oral communications alone could sometimes lead to misunderstandings.

8.15 Reviewers

Psychologists who review material submitted for presentation, publication, grant, or research proposal review respect the confidentiality of and the proprietary rights in such information of those who submitted it. [This standard is similar to Standard 6.26 of the 1992 Ethics Code.]

Editors and authors may not reference the work submitted for publication without the consent of the author until it is actually published. It is common for manuscripts to go through considerable changes from the first time they are submitted until the time they are published. It is not fair to the author to reference a less than final version of the work.

9. ASSESSMENT

The section on assessment requires psychologists to use reasonable skill in reaching their conclusions (9.01) and in using tests, especially when it involves the assessment of diverse populations (9.02). The informed consent requirement with assessments has exceptions delineated (9.03). Release of test data to qualified individuals is covered (9.04). Psychologists must use appropriate procedures when constructing (9.05) and interpreting tests (9.06). They do not promote the use of tests by unqualified persons, except trainees (9.07). Psychologists do not base their recommendations on outdated test results (9.08a) or use obsolete tests (9.08b). They use automated testing services appropriately (9.09). Psychologists take steps to ensure that explanations of the results are given to the individual tested (or a designated representative), except in certain situations (9.10). Psychologists must protect the security of test materials (9.11).

These standards are based on General Principle A, Beneficence and Nonmaleficence, in that psychologists should be competent to develop, administer, and interpret tests. General Principle E, Respect for People's Rights and Dignity, is also important in that it ensures that tests do not unfairly discriminate against others on the basis of cultural or demographic factors. Finally, General Principle B, Fidelity and Responsibility, is relevant here in that psychologists have responsibilities to society at large to protect test security.

The 2002 Ethics Code contains several important changes from the 1992 Ethics Code. First, psychologists may give opinions about persons they have not personally evaluated under some circumstances (9.01b). The special section on informed consent in assessments (9.03) supplements the general informed consent standard (3.10). New standards concern the release of raw test data to attorneys (9.04) and competence in developing tests (9.05). Several standards have been strengthened to ensure fair treatment in the assessment of members of diverse groups (9.02, 9.06).

9.01 Bases for Assessments

(a) [General Rule on Bases of Opinions.] *Psychologists base the opinions contained in their recommendations, reports, and diagnostic or evaluative statements, including forensic testimony, on information and techniques sufficient to substantiate their findings. (See also Standard 2.04, Bases for Scientific and Professional Judgments.)* [This standard is similar to Standard 2.01b of the 1992 Ethics Code.]

(b) [Opinions Without a Direct Examination.] *Except as noted in 9.01c, psychologists provide opinions of the psychological characteristics of individuals only after they have conducted an examination of the individuals adequate to support their statements or conclusions. When, despite reasonable efforts, such an examination is not practical, psychologists document the efforts they made and the result of those efforts, clarify the probable impact of their limited information on the reliability and validity of their opinions, and appropriately limit the nature and extent of their conclusions or recommendations. (See also Standards 2.01, Boundaries of Competence, and 9.06, Interpreting Assessment Results.)* [This standard is related to Standards 7.02b and 7.02c of the 1992 Ethics Code.]

(c) [Opinions Based on Record Review.] *When psychologists conduct a record review or provide consultation or supervision and an individual examination is not warranted or necessary for the opinion, psychologists explain this and the sources of information on which they based their conclusions and recommendations.* [This standard is new.]

Standard 9.01a is a competence standard that requires psychologists to base their conclusions (whether expressed in a report or any other communication) on sufficient information. However, the standard includes an important modification from the 1992 Ethics Code. The previous Ethics Code required that psychologists develop opinions only after face-to-face evaluations of individuals. That standard has been changed. Psychologists may now develop opinions based on second hand information if the attempt at a direct communication has failed and they appropriately note the limitations of their reports or if they have engaged in a records review and the source of the information is noted in their reports. This exception could occur when a psychologist conducts a psychological autopsy, responds to a hypothetical question on a forensic examination, or conducts a record review for a legitimate purpose.

9.02   Uses of Assessments

(a) [General Rule on Use of Assessments.] *Psychologists administer, adapt, score, interpret, or use assessment techniques, interviews, tests, or instruments in a manner and for purposes that are appropriate in light of the research on or evidence of the usefulness and proper application of the techniques.* [This standard is similar to Standard 2.02a of the 1992 Ethics Code.]

(b) [Relationship Between Assessment Instrument and Population Tested.] *Psychologists use assessment instruments whose validity and reliability have been established for use with members of the population tested. When such validity or reliability has not been established, psychologists describe the strengths and limitations of test results and interpretation.* [This standard is new.]

(c) [Language Preference and Competence.] *Psychologists use assessment methods that are appropriate to an individual's language preference and competence, unless the use of an alternative language is relevant to the assessment issues.* [This standard is new.]

Psychologists are obligated to use testing instruments as they were originally designed but may adapt them on the basis of research or evidence indicating the usefulness of the adaptation. Psychologists need to recognize limits to the certainty with which diagnoses, judgments, or predictions can be made about individuals and indicate significant reservations or limitations about the tests.

The use of assessment instruments with diverse populations requires special considerations. Cultural or racial factors appear to be related to the interpretation of many standardized psychological tests, and harm would occur if a test is used for a group for which no normative data have been obtained. Psychologists account for these limitations in their test interpretations.

Generally, psychologists give the assessment in the language that the client/patient prefers or is competent in, unless the purpose of the assessment is to determine the client's/patient's abilities in the use of English. Santiago-Rivera and Altarriba (2002) present a list of experiences and competencies that psychologists can assess to determine the linguistic abilities of an individual. The list includes information about (a) the length of time the person has lived in the United States, (b) countries in which the person has lived other than the native country and the United States, (c) the number of languages the person understands, speaks, reads, and/or writes, (d) the most fluent to least fluent languages the person knows, (e) the languages spoken at home, (f) the language spoken as a child and the age range when that language was spoken, and (g) the age when the person learned to speak and read each language. In addition, the psychologist may ask the person to rate (on a 10-point scale) her or his (a) comprehension of spoken language, (b) comprehension of written language, and (c) conversational skills.

9.03   Informed Consent in Assessments

(a)   [General Rule on Informed Consent in Assessments.] *Psychologists obtain informed consent for assessments, evaluations, or diagnostic services, as described in Standard 3.10, Informed Consent, except when (1) testing is mandated by law or governmental regulations; (2) informed consent is implied because testing is conducted as a routine educational, institutional, or organizational activity (e.g., when participants voluntarily agree to assessment when applying for a job); or (3) one purpose of the testing is to evaluate decisional capacity. Informed consent includes an explanation of the nature and purpose of the assessment, fees, involvement of third parties, and limits of confidentiality and sufficient opportunity for the client/patient to ask questions and receive answers.* [This standard is new.]

This standard delineates three exceptions to the informed consent requirement. Informed consent for assessments may be waived when testing is mandated by law (such as a court order) or government regulation; consent is implied because testing is conducted as a routine educational, institutional, or organizational activity; or the purpose of testing is to determine whether an individual is competent to make decisions.

Often employers or third parties requesting testing have not considered the strengths, limitations, or implications of psychological testing. The psychologist can help them clarify their goals and expectations.

An Inappropriate Request

A psychologist was invited to be a visiting professor at a theological seminary for 1 year. During that year she was asked to administer psychological tests to each seminarian. Upon discussion of this issue, she learned that different teachers had different goals for the testing. Some wanted it to help students identify appropriate careers for themselves, while others wanted to screen out students with serious pathology. Some wanted the testing started immediately; others wanted it to be started with the incoming class so that applicants would know about the testing requirement ahead of time.

The psychologist refused to do the testing. She noted that the testing would have placed her in a dual role (teacher and psychologist) with the students. She did, however, help the seminary clarify what it wanted from the psychological testing, develop an information sheet about testing to be given to future applicants, and assist them in finding an appropriate psychologist who could do that testing the next year.

(b) [Informed Consent in Forensic Assessments.] *Psychologists inform persons with questionable capacity to consent or for whom testing is mandated by law or governmental regulations about the nature and purpose of the proposed assessment services, using language that is reasonably understandable to the person being assessed.* [This standard is new.]

Although it may not be required to get the informed consent when conducting forensic assessments for persons for whom testing is mandated, psychologists should still explain the nature and purpose of the evaluation in terms that are reasonably understandable to the person being assessed. Forensic work differs considerably from traditional practice. One of the most important issues is that clients/patients should be informed of the nature and purpose of forensic work, including limits on confidentiality and probable use of the data. Just the fact of being a psychologist may lead some persons to assume that the psychologist is there to help them. If the psychologist provides any kind of feedback or demonstrates any empathy, then the clients/patients may take this as substantiating their perception that this is really a treatment relationship.

(c) [Use of Interpreters in Assessments.] *Psychologists using the services of an interpreter obtain informed consent from the client/patient to use that interpreter, ensure that confidentiality of test results and test security are maintained, and include in their recommendations, reports, and diagnostic or evaluative statements, including forensic testimony, discussion of any limitations on the data obtained. (See also Standards 2.05, Delegation of Work to Others; 4.01, Maintaining Confidentiality; 9.01, Bases for Assessments; 9.06, Interpreting Assessment Results; and 9.07, Assessment by Unqualified Persons.)* [This standard is new.]

Interpreters are agents of the psychologist and, as such, should be held to the same standards of confidentiality as other employees. Despite the best efforts of conscientious psychologists and interpreters, some imprecision may be inherent in the testing experience due to the very fact that the information had to be translated.

The job of an interpreter requires special skills. Errors could be made by interpreters who do not know the specific dialect of the client/patient being evaluated (e.g., there are numerous differences in the Spanish spoken by Americans of Cuban, Mexican, or Puerto Rican descent). Consequently, efforts should be made to ensure high quality interpreters. When, despite reasonable efforts, a psychologist cannot acquire a truly fluent interpreter (such as an interpreter who is fluent in Castilian Spanish but not in the dialects of the client/patient, or when a test has not been standardized in its translated version), limitations on the data should be noted.

9.04   Release of Test Data

(a) [Release of Test Data Pursuant to a Client/Patient Release.] *The term* test data *refers to raw and scaled scores, client/patient responses to test questions or stimuli, and psychologists' notes and recordings concerning client/patient statements and behavior during an examination. Those portions of test materials that include client/patient responses are included in the definition of* test data*. Pursuant to a client/patient release, psychologists provide test data to the client/patient or other persons identified in the release. Psychologists may refrain from releasing test data to protect a client/patient or others from substantial harm or misuse or misrepresentation of the data or the test, recognizing that in many instances release of confidential information under these circumstances is regulated by law. (See also Standard 9.11, Maintaining Test Security.)* [This standard is related to Standard 2.02b of the 1992 Ethics Code.]

(b) [Release of Test Data Required by Law.] *In the absence of a client/patient release, psychologists provide test data only as required by law or court order.* [This standard is new.]

Perhaps, the most commentary on any of the proposed revisions to the Ethics Code was received on Standard 9.04, dealing with the release of test data (test reports, summaries, client responses or products from the test, and psychologists' notes and observations during the test) and Standard 9.11, dealing with the release of test materials (the test manuals, instruments, protocols, test questions, or test stimuli). This contrasts to the 1992 Ethics Code when the most controversial standard dealt with sexual relationships with former clients/patients.

Standard 2.02b of the 1992 APA Ethics Code required psychologists to "refrain from releasing raw test results or raw data to persons, other than to patients or clients as appropriate, who are not qualified to use such information." Two concerns were used to justify the 1992 restriction against the release of test information to persons who were unqualified to use them, such as attorneys. The first concern was that they may misinterpret or misuse the information in conducting court cases. The second concern was that they may not respect copyright restrictions and might use the test stimuli or manuals to coach future clients in other cases (see review of these and other issues by Lees-Haley & Courtney, 2000). The first concern should not be given undue weight. Wise attorneys should know not to try to interpret the data themselves and would retain the expertise of a knowledgeable expert. Furthermore, the opposing party should have experts available to correct any misinterpretation the opposing attorney may present.

The second concern, however, appears more legitimate. This would be especially true if attorneys could obtain copies of the test questions or manuals. Anecdotal reports have arisen about attorneys who coach their clients on how to give favorable responses to the tests. A website for fathers involved in child custody litigation, for example, gives them suggestions on how to respond to certain psychological tests.

The 2002 Ethics Code dealt with this issue by distinguishing between test materials and test data. Standard 9.04 of the 2002 Ethics Code eliminates the requirement that psychologists keep test data (defined as "raw and scaled scores, client/patient responses to test questions or stimuli, and psychologists' notes and recordings concerning client/patient statements and behavior during an examination") out of the hands of persons unqualified to interpret them. However, it also allows psychologists to withhold test data if they believe doing so could harm a client/patient or violate test security. Consequently, the standard moves from a "must" standard to resist sending out the test data, or even the test report, to a "may" standard in which the clinical features and welfare of the client/patient and the security of the test can be considered.

Again, this is a standard that must be read in conjunction with HIPAA. HIPAA does not provide test reports or summaries the same protection that it does psychotherapy notes. Consequently, HIPAA would require psychologists to release client/patient testing reports, even if such a release would be clinically contraindicated. However, when this book was written, it was not clear what standards would apply concerning the release of other test data (actual responses or psychologists' notes and observations).

However, Standard 9.11 continues the requirement that psychologists protect the security of test materials (the test manuals, instruments, protocols, test questions, or test stimuli).

9.05 Test Construction

Psychologists who develop tests and other assessment techniques use appropriate psychometric procedures and current scientific or professional knowledge for test design, standardization, validation, reduction or elimination of bias, and recommendations for use. [This standard is similar to Standard 2.03 of the 1992 Ethics Code.]

The development and advertising of a test implies that basic issues of test construction have been followed.

An Unacceptable Test

A psychologist developed the "ABCDiary" Learning Inventory, which was a combination of various items that, on their face, appeared to be related to different ways of processing information. He placed it on a website where browsers could take it. Almost everyone who took the test ended up being recommended for one of his remedial programs in learning. The test was never validated nor was there any empirical evidence to suggest that the remedial programs would improve the participant's ability to learn.

The psychologist in this case was misleading consumers into thinking that his instrument had some proven utility. That was not the case. It was misleading and exploitative.

9.06 Interpreting Assessment Results

When interpreting assessment results, including automated interpretations, psychologists take into account the purpose of the assessment as well as the various test factors, test-taking abilities, and other characteristics of the person being assessed, such as situational, personal, linguistic, and cultural differences, that might affect psychologists' judgments or reduce the accuracy of their interpretations. They indicate any significant limitations of their interpretations. (See also Standards 2.01b and c, Boundaries of Competence, and 3.01, Unfair Discrimination.) [This standard is similar to Standard 2.05 of the 1992 Ethics Code.]

Automated tests do not replace the clinical judgment of the psychologist. Instead the psychologist must develop personalized interpretations based on the entire clinical picture of the client/patient. Psychologists should note the limitations of their interpretations.

9.07 Assessment by Unqualified Persons

Psychologists do not promote the use of psychological assessment techniques by unqualified persons, except when such use is conducted for training purposes with appropriate supervision. (See also Standard 2.05, Delegation of Work to Others.) [This standard is similar to Standard 2.06 of the 1992 Ethics Code.]

The appropriate use of psychological tests requires substantial skill derived from training and supervised experience. To outsiders the use of a psychological test may appear deceptively simple. It appears that all that is required is to add a few scores and look up the results in a textbook or to identify appropriate excerpts from a computerized printout. In reality, however, the appropriate use of psychological tests is far more complicated. Much harm can be done by the inappropriate use of these tests. Consequently, psychologists have a responsibility to restrict the use of these tests to those who know how to select, administer, and interpret them appropriately.

Determining who has such qualifications is not always easy. Some tests, especially screening instruments or vocational tests, have been specifically developed for the use by mental health counselors or social workers. The instruction manual of the test often identifies the appropriate credentials of the users. Turner et al. (2001) give more information on test user qualifications.

9.08 Obsolete Tests and Outdated Test Results

(a) [Outdated Test Results.] *Psychologists do not base their assessment or intervention decisions or recommendations on data or test results that are outdated for the current purpose.* [This standard is identical to Standard 2.07a of the 1992 Ethics Code.]

(b) [Obsolete Tests.] *Psychologists do not base such decisions or recommendations on tests and measures that are obsolete and not useful for the current purpose.* [This standard is similar to Standard 2.07b of the 1992 Ethics Code.]

Standard 9.08a deals with the issue of using test data for a client/patient that has become obsolete for that client/patient due to the passage of time. For example, a profile of an MMPI which was administered 10 years ago would be of questionable value for making treatment decisions for a client/patient today.

Standard 9.08b deals with the issue of using tests which are obsolete for the current purposes. Although the general preference is to use the most current test available, psychologists may have professional justifications for using an earlier version of a test. Much depends on the purpose for which the testing is being done. For example, an earlier version of a test may have more research justifying its usefulness with certain populations than the newer version. Or, using an older version of a test in a longitudinal study may result in a less extraneous variation than using a more current version. There may be other situations where the use of the earlier version of a test is professionally justified (Canter et al., 1994).

The issue of outdated test instruments was widely discussed when the MMPI was replaced with the MMPI-2. Even a few years after the MMPI-2 was released, 1995 data from National Computer Systems showed that 80% of test users were using the MMPI-2 (National Computer Systems, 1995). Although this is a large portion of the users, it would be hard to accuse the other 20% of engaging in ethical violations. Indeed, there were legitimate disagreements concerning the appropriate use of the MMPI versus the MMPI-2 (Butcher, 1996; Gordon, 1995). Of course, with any test the psychologist has a responsibility to report any limitations or reservations about the accuracy of the test results because of the nature of the testing conditions, the norms being used, or other relevant factors.

9.09 Test Scoring and Interpretation Services

(a) [Accurate Description of Testing Service.] *Psychologists who offer assessment or scoring services to other professionals accurately describe the purpose, norms, validity, reliability, and applications of the procedures and any special qualifications applicable to their use.* [This standard is similar to Standard 2.08a of the 1992 Ethics Code.]

(b) [Considerations in Selecting Testing Services.] *Psychologists select scoring and interpretation services (including automated services) on the basis of evidence of the validity of the program and procedures as well as on other appropriate considerations. (See also Standard 2.01b and c, Boundaries of Competence.)* [This standard is similar to Standard 2.08b of the 1992 Ethics Code.]

(c) [Retention of Ultimate Responsibility.] *Psychologists retain responsibility for the appropriate application, interpretation, and use of assessment instruments, whether they score and interpret such tests themselves or use automated or other services.* [This standard is similar to Standard 2.08c of the 1992 Ethics Code.]

Psychologists retain responsibility for the selection of the particular test, testing service, and the wording of the final report. Computerized assessments are readily available and are often user friendly. They can reduce the likelihood of computational or scoring errors and are much faster than an assessment done by hand. It is acceptable (and sometimes preferable) to rely on computerized assessments in assessing clients/patients. However, the psychologist still assumes full responsibility for the wording of the final report. Psychologists could not make a responsible report on a client/patient based on a computerized assessment alone. The interpretations derived from computerized services are based on group norms and do not necessarily apply to any one individual, are limited in the domain of questions they ask, and are not adjusted in light of the life circumstances of the client/patient.

9.10   Explaining Assessment Results

Regardless of whether the scoring and interpretation are done by psychologists, by employees or assistants, or by automated or other outside services, psychologists take reasonable steps to ensure that explanations of results are given to the individual or designated representative unless the nature of the relationship precludes provision of an explanation of results (such as in some organizational consulting, pre-employment or security screenings, and forensic evaluations), and this fact has been clearly explained to the person being assessed in advance. [This standard is similar to Standard 2.09 of the 1992 Ethics Code.]

Psychologists are required to give clients/patients feedback on the testing results, using language that is understood by laypersons. However, exceptions to these general rules exist. For example, a psychologist may be conducting a pre-employment examination to determine personality traits relevant to the suitability of an applicant for a particular position. The psychologist may not have to give feedback to that applicant if it is explained to the individual ahead of time. Similar arrangements may occur in forensic settings where the psychologist is employed by the court or one of the attorneys. Also, at times it may be more appropriate for a neuropsychologist to give the test results to a family member or a referring physician, as opposed to a client/patient who may not be able to understand what the results mean.

Sometimes psychologists may be asked to evaluate the tests of other psychologists, such as when there is a child custody evaluation. In reviewing these tests, the psychologists cannot definitively comment about the client/patient without having examined the client/patient ahead of time. They can, however, comment on the relationships of the raw data to the test interpretation. They could point out, for example, if the other psychologist made a computational or an interpretative error.

144 A Guide to the 2002 Revision of the APA's Ethics Code

9.11 Maintaining Test Security

> *The term* test materials *refers to manuals, instruments, protocols, and test questions or stimuli and does not include* test data *as defined in Standard 9.04, Release of Test Data. Psychologists make reasonable efforts to maintain the integrity and security of test materials and other assessment techniques consistent with law and contractual obligations, and in a manner that permits adherence to this Ethics Code.* [This standard is similar to Standard 2.10 of the 1992 Ethics Code.]

Test security can be compromised by inadequate office security, or by releasing data to unqualified persons (including take home tests). The APA Ethics Committee considered the issue of "take home" tests and concluded that it was not, in and of itself, an ethical violation to have clients/patients use a take home test. The decision depended on many circumstances. However, in some situations it could threaten the security of the test, the standardization of the testing process, and the usefulness of the test itself.

Although there is no blanket prohibition against having clients/patients take psychological tests home, several factors should be considered. First, giving the clients/patients tests to take home may result in their being used in a nonstandardized manner. Clients/patients may take too long to complete the test, work on the test over several days instead of at one sitting, ask their friends for input into some of the questions, or otherwise do things that would invalidate the results. Also, some clients/patients may share the test questions with others and cause the test items to leak into the public domain. On the other hand, in some situations it would be appropriate to give clients tests to take home.

Vocational Tests Help Returning Missionaries

A large denomination with an extensive missionary program with young adults offered them free vocational counseling upon their return to the United States or Canada. The counseling service with whom they contracted agreed to send a brief vocational battery to them in the field so they could complete it and have the results ready when they returned for debriefing at the denomination headquarters.

Here a home bound test did not seem contraindicated. There were no secondary gains that would encourage respondents to falsify results, and the logistics of getting to the young adults for face-to-face consultations were considerable. Nonetheless, psychologists should respect the privacy of psychological tests. It could do great harm to the integrity of the tests if items became available to the public.

10. THERAPY

The section on therapy includes specific informed-consent provisions that apply to therapeutic interventions (10.01), and special multiple relationship issues that could occur when working with families or couples (10.02) or group therapy (10.03). It also cautions appropriate concern when dealing with persons who are currently receiving services from others (10.04). There are prohibitions against sexual intimacies with current therapy clients/patients (10.05), with significant others or close relatives of current clients/patients (10.06), and with former clients/patients except under highly unusual circumstances (10.08). In addition, psychologists should not conduct therapy with former sexual partners (10.07). The responsibilities of psychologists are delineated in those circumstances where treatment may be interrupted (10.09) or terminated (10.10).

These standards are based on General Principle A, Beneficence and Nonmaleficence, in that clients/patients may be harmed if they have sexual contact with their therapists or are terminated from therapy abruptly. General Principle E, Respect for People's Rights and Dignity, is also important as reflected in the informed consent provision. That is, the assumption is that psychologists will respect the decisions of patients whether to enter therapy and the nature or degree of participation in therapy. Finally, General Principle B, Fidelity and Responsibility, supports the prohibitions against sexual conduct, the cautions against multiple relationships in family or couple therapy, and the precautions to use when terminating clients/patients.

Several changes in this section deal with clarifying issues that were implied, but not made explicit, in the 1992 Ethics Code. Standard 10.01b requires psychologists to inform clients/patients of the experimental nature of any treatment they may be offering. This requirement might have been inferred from some of the standards of the 1992 Ethics Code, but it was never stated explicitly. Another important change in this section concerns the cautions about potential conflicts of interest when conducting couple, family, or group therapy (10.02b and 10.03). Although these specific provisions had not previously been written in the past code, past codes were interpreted to prohibit psychologists from engaging in exploitative or harmful conflicts of interest. In addition, sexual relationships with significant others or close relatives of clients/patients (10.06) would have been handled as a multiple relationship in the previous code, although it was not specifically identified as an ethical violation.

The standard on termination of therapy allows more discretion for the treating psychologist (10.10), and permits psychologists to terminate clients/patients if their safety is endangered even if the client/patient is in need of more treatment. Generally speaking, psychologists conducting therapy make an obligation to provide pretermination counseling or to suggest alternative providers. However, these obligations do not apply when precluded by an action by a third-party payor or the client/patient.

Finally, the use of terms in this section needs to be explained. The 2002 Ethics Code deliberately uses of the word "therapy" instead of psychotherapy or counseling. The ECTF believed that the general term therapy would apply to all dimensions of health intervention such as psychotherapy, counseling, behavioral analysis, crisis intervention, career counseling, and other short-term targeted interventions.

The standards in this section are based largely on General Principle A, Beneficence and Nonmaleficence, in that psychologists should actively work to benefit their clients/patients and avoid harming them. They are also based on General Principle E, in that psychologists respect the decision-making capacity of their clients/patients.

10.01 Informed Consent to Therapy

(a) [General Rule on Informed Consent to Therapy.] *When obtaining informed consent to therapy as required in Standard 3.10, Informed Consent, psychologists inform clients/patients as early as is feasible in the therapeutic relationship about the nature and anticipated course of therapy, fees, involvement of third parties, and limits of confidentiality and provide sufficient opportunity for the client/patient to ask questions and receive answers. (See also Standards 4.02, Discussing the Limits of Confidentiality, and 6.04, Fees and Financial Arrangements.)* [This standard is similar to Standard 4.01a of the 1992 Ethics Code.]

(b) [Informed Consent With Emerging Areas.] *When obtaining informed consent for treatment for which generally recognized techniques and procedures have not been established, psychologists inform their clients/patients of the developing nature of the treatment, the potential risks involved, alternative treatments that may be available, and the voluntary nature of their participation. (See also Standards 2.01e, Boundaries of Competence, and 3.10, Informed Consent.)* [This standard is new.]

Standards 10.01a and 10.01b reiterate important information about informed consent. As noted in 10.01a, psychologists who are providing therapy need to inform clients/patients of the anticipated nature and direction of therapy, fees, and confidentiality. More general information on informed consent is given in the commentary on 3.10 (general informed consent).

The obligations for informed consent increase when psychologists are providing new, experimental, or innovative therapies. Under these circumstances, psychologists also need to inform prospective clients/patients of the experimental nature of the treatment, the potential risks involved, other more standardized alternative treatments that may be available, and the voluntary nature of their participation.

> *(c)* [Informed Consent With Supervisees.] *When the therapist is a trainee and the legal responsibility for the treatment provided resides with the supervisor, the client/patient, as part of the informed consent procedure, is informed that the therapist is in training and is being supervised and is given the name of the supervisor.* [This standard is similar to Standard 4.01b of the 1992 Ethics Code.]

Clinical supervision is a professional activity whereby the supervisors assume professional control and responsibility for the work product of others. Depending on the circumstances, it may or may not involve a commitment to teach professional skills to the supervisee. In a supervisory relationship, supervisees become extensions (hands and feet, so to speak) of the supervisor.

Clinical supervision differs from administrative supervision, which is primarily concerned with the nonclinical aspects of employment (hours worked, days off, salaries, general work assignments, etc.). Supervision also differs from consultation. Although many persons interchange the terms "supervision" and "consultation," they are distinct activities. Unlike supervisees, professionals receiving consultation are independent providers who may accept or reject the opinions of the consultants as they wish.

Finally, clinical supervision differs from what is commonly called "peer supervision," in which a group of professionals gets together for the purpose of discussing cases, critiquing the work of others, and exchanging information on assessment and treatment approaches. Although these groups are highly desirable and profitable, they are not really supervisory groups and could more accurately be called "peer consultation groups" because the participants retain the option of accepting or rejecting the advice of the other group members.

Clients/patients have a right to know if they are receiving services from a supervisee. The client's/patient's consent is especially important when the trainee is in the early stages of training because the client/patient may elect not to receive the service under these conditions. Knowledge of the supervised status of the trainee may also protect the supervisor. It is preferable that the client/patient call the supervisor with a concern early in treatment rather than having the supervisor learn about the discontent of the client/patient through a formal complaint. Furthermore, the trainee or supervisee status may be relevant to insurance reimbursement issues.

It is easy for clients/patients to misunderstand or misconstrue their therapists as acting in independent practice. Being introduced as "doctor," even though a person is a resident or a psychological trainee who is completing a year of postdoctoral supervision, may mislead the client/patient into believing that the practitioner is licensed to provide independent service. Consequently, no aspects of the practice, such as billing statements, business cards, signs on the office door, and so on, should mislead the client/patient into thinking the therapist is an independently practicing professional.

10.02 Therapy Involving Couples or Families

(a) [Clarifying Roles.] *When psychologists agree to provide services to several persons who have a relationship (such as spouses, significant others, or parents and children), they take reasonable steps to clarify at the outset (1) which of the individuals are clients/patients and (2) the relationship the psychologist will have with each person. This clarification includes the psychologist's role and the probable uses of the services provided or the information obtained. (See also Standard 4.02, Discussing the Limits of Confidentiality.)* [This standard is similar to Standard 4.03a of the 1992 Ethics Code.]

Psychologists need to clarify their roles and their relationships with all parties when conducting family or couples therapy. Two issues that commonly arise concerning the use of information concern the role of secrets in family or couples therapy and the rules for confidentiality with minors.

Sometimes family members reveal information in "secret" because they want to develop a special alliance between themselves and the psychologist. At other times they are afraid of the reactions of other family members, but they believe that this information is crucial for the success of therapy. Family therapists disagree concerning the optimal manner to handle family secrets. Some allow secrets; others do not. Nevertheless, the Ethics Code only requires therapists to attempt to clarify the policy regarding family secrets at the outset of therapy.

Confidentiality rules for minors depend largely on state law. Generally the ability to seek treatment independently implies the ability to have some control over the information generated from such treatment. Consequently, if parental consent is needed to institute treatment, then the parents also have a right to obtain information generated from such treatment. The Ethics Code requires psychologists to explain the rules of confidentiality at the outset of therapy.

Psychologists often develop agreements with parents to withhold parents' requests for information to allow the adolescent a greater sense of privacy and thus encourage a stronger therapeutic alliance. When discussing this issue with parents, psychologists need to be candid and note that the information generated (and withheld from the parents) may include such highly sensitive information as the use of drugs or sexual activity. One exception, which should be clearly spelled out to both the parents and adolescents, is that the psychologist may break confidentiality if it is necessary to protect the life and safety of the adolescent or others. This may require some discretion on the part of the psychologist as to when the high risk behavior of the adolescent reaches the threshold where parents need to be informed.

Upholding an Agreement I

A psychologist is treating an adolescent boy and has received the promise of the parents that they would respect confidentiality of the child unless there were situations that threatened the safety of the boy or others. The boy tells the psychologist that he intends to kill another student. The threat appears credible.

This situation highlights the need to be clear with parents and the adolescent about the limits of confidentiality and the nature of material that may be acquired during private sessions. The situation in the vignette above was clear. At other times psychologists may need to use considerable judgment in determining when the actions of the child are sufficiently dangerous to warrant notifying the parents.

Upholding an Agreement II

A psychologist is treating an adolescent girl and has received the promise of the parents that they would respect confidentiality of the child unless there were situations that threatened the safety of the girl or others. The girl tells the psychologist that she regularly has unprotected sex with a 25-year-old man. She does this without the knowledge of her parents.

In this situation there is danger to the girl, but more information is needed before it can be determined if it is imminent. The psychologist will have to consider whether the sexual behavior is truly voluntary, the degree of danger to the girl of contracting an STD (or even AIDS), the intent of the girl to continue the unwise relationship, and the likelihood that psychotherapy will help the girl to discontinue the behavior on her own. The final decision will depend on the answers to these and other clinical questions. If the decision is made to inform the parents, then the psychologist should, as much as possible, involve the girl in the decision as to how to inform her parents.

> (b)   [Clarifying Potentially Conflicting Roles.] *If it becomes apparent that psychologists may be called on to perform potentially conflicting roles (such as family therapist and then witness for one party in divorce proceedings), psychologists take reasonable steps to clarify and modify, or withdraw from, roles appropriately. (See also Standard 3.05c, Multiple Relationships.)* [This standard is similar to Standard 4.03b of the 1992 Ethics Code.]

At times psychologists who engage in couples or family therapy may find themselves in an apparent conflict of interest. For example, a psychologist may accept a couple in therapy and, for therapeutic reasons, also treat them individually. During the course of therapy, one of the participants may decide that her or his goal in therapy is to end the relationship, while the other participant may decide that her or his goal in therapy is to preserve the relationship. Psychologists would be in a conflict of interest if they continued the treatment without resolving the inherent conflict in the goals of the parties involved. Psychologists can handle these situations by obtaining a commitment from both parties ahead of time concerning their goals, and their intent to be open if their goals for therapy change.

10.03 Group Therapy

> *When psychologists provide services to several persons in a group setting, they describe at the outset the roles and responsibilities of all parties and the limits of confidentiality.* [This standard is new.]

Psychologists need to consider the unique aspects of group therapy and its impact on clients/patients. They need to ensure that clients/patients in the group will understand their roles and respect the privacy of other group members. When the clients/patients gather for the first meeting of the group, it is desirable to discuss the terms of participation, the purposes of the group therapy, and the kinds of sharing that will occur. Other information that should be discussed include whether the group is time-limited or ongoing. If ongoing, then the procedures for leaving the group should be discussed although all clients/patients have the right to leave at any time and for any reason. Although it is not a requirement of the Ethics Code, it may be a useful risk management strategy for psychologists to reinforce these concepts by having all group members sign an agreement promising to hold in confidence all matters discussed in the group and agree to a policy regarding extragroup interactions.

Psychologists should also inform the clients/patients of how they will handle confidentiality if clients/patients are being seen in both individual and group therapy. Conversely, psychologists need to avoid disclosing private or secret information about one client/patient to another client/patient in the group sessions. Disclosures should be limited to what the client/patient has chosen to reveal within the group sessions.

Finally, psychologists need to inform clients/patients that privilege in group therapy (and in marriage and family therapy) may be problematic. In some states the privileged communication statutes are worded in such a way to allow some courts to conclude that because the client shared information in the presence of third parties (beyond just the therapist) that the information was not truly intended to be confidential.

The effort to inform clients/patients about group therapy need not be considered an onerous burden for psychologists. Burlingame, Fuhriman, and Johnson (2001) reported that pregroup preparation and efforts to establish good group cohesion at the start of treatment tended to facilitate outcomes in group therapy.

10.04 Providing Therapy to Those Served by Others

In deciding whether to offer or provide services to those already receiving mental health services elsewhere, psychologists carefully consider the treatment issues and the potential client's/patient's welfare. Psychologists discuss these issues with the client/patient or another legally authorized person on behalf of the client/patient in order to minimize the risk of confusion and conflict, consult with the other service providers when appropriate, and proceed with caution and sensitivity to the therapeutic issues. [This standard is similar to Standard 4.04 of the 1992 Ethics Code.]

Psychologists could respond with one of two extreme solutions when approached by prospective clients/patients who are currently seeing someone else in treatment. On the one hand, the psychologist could simply accept the client/patient without asking questions or only commenting that the client/patient needs to discontinue treatment with the old therapist. On the other hand, the psychologist could refuse to accept any client/patient currently seeing anyone else regardless of the circumstances.

A middle approach is usually the best. It may be appropriate to accept clients/patients who are currently seeing another therapist if it is understood why the previous therapy is being terminated and whether the change appears to be in the best interest of the clients/patients. The reason for a change may be thoughtful and reasonable. For example, the prior therapist could have been, through no fault of her or his own, dropped from a provider panel and the client/patient can no longer afford the cost of treatment or has determined that the client/patient has problems that would best be treated by another therapist. On the other hand, the reason for a change may be impulsive or ill-considered. At times it may be best for the potential new therapist to instruct the client/patient to go back to the prior therapist and try to work out or resolve whatever issues appear to be present.

**10.05 Sexual Intimacies With
Current Therapy Clients/Patients**

Psychologists do not engage in sexual intimacies with current therapy clients/patients. [This standard is similar to Standard 4.05 of the 1992 Ethics Code.]

Sexual contact can greatly harm individual clients/patients. The reported rate of lifetime sexual contact between psychiatrists, psychologists, and social workers and their clients/patients ranges between .02 and 3.0 percent for woman psychotherapists and .09 and 12.1 percent for male psychotherapists (Pope, 1994). Although these studies have their unique methodological limitations, some generalizations can be made. Typically older male psychotherapists have sexual relations with younger female clients/patients. Sexual contact with former clients/patients is more frequent than sexual contact with current clients/patients.

It appears that the frequency of client/patient/therapist sexual contact is decreasing in recent years. If the decline is indeed occurring, it may be because of the criminalization of this behavior in many states, because of an increase in the number of female psychologists (who have lower rates of exploitation), or because of educational and preventative efforts by psychological associations and licensing boards.

Research shows that sexual contact with clients/patients has a high potential for severe harm. For example, Bouhoutsos et al. (1983) reported on 704 respondents who had treated a total of 559 clients/patients who had been sexually involved with previous therapists. Ninety percent of the respondents reported ill effects, including 11% who were hospitalized and 1% who committed suicide. Taylor and Wagner (1976) surveyed 34 published accounts of sexual activity between psychotherapists and clients/patients. They concluded that 21% of the cases had positive effects, 32% had mixed effects, and 45% had negative effects for either the client/patient, therapist, or both. Similarly, Burgess (1981) reported that all of 16 women who had sexual relationships with their gynecologists reported feeling humiliated and embarrassed by the sexual contact.

Although each of these studies has its unique methodological limitations, the overall conclusion is the same: Sexual contact harms most clients/patients. In addition to harming the client/patient involved, sexual contact between psychologists and clients/patients harms the public image for psychologists in general and may deter some people from seeking the help they need.

Protecting Clients/Patients From Sexual Exploitation

Sexual exploitation occurs for many reasons. Sometimes the exploiting psychotherapists or supervisors have longstanding personality disorders, or have serious sexual disorders (e.g., pedophilia, sexual sadism). Other psychologists have impairment either through the abuse of substances or from a serious mental illness. Still others may have recently had a major loss, such as a divorce or career reversal, and feel particularly lonely and vulnerable. During this time they let their personal needs overshadow their normal judgment. Often they are "lovesick" (believe themselves in love) and block out the role of a psychologist. Finally, some psychologists are poorly trained and have not learned to recognize and handle transference, countertransference, or boundary issues in psychotherapy. Although it is very difficult, if not impossible, to prevent sexual exploitation by psychologists with longstanding personality or sexual disorders, the profession can do more to prevent misconduct by psychotherapists who are temporarily impaired or undertrained. One of the most important steps is for psychologists (and supervisors) to talk about their sexual feelings toward clients/patients and better ways to handle those feelings (Pope, Sonne, & Holroyd, 1993).

All humans, including psychologists, are sexual beings. It is normal to have sexual feelings about clients/patients and for clients/patients to have sexual feelings about their psychologists. The problem is not the presence of sexual feelings but the way that those feelings are handled.

As a profession we can do a better job of reducing sexual exploitation by focusing on sexual feelings in psychotherapy in general. Housman and Stake (1999) found that many graduate students in psychology did not have adequate training in the ethics surrounding sexual attraction to clients/patients. Paxton, Lovett, and Riggs (2001) found that few psychologists had specific learning experiences in their graduate training program dealing with the responsible management of sexual feelings in the therapeutic relationship. The minority who did reported that they felt better prepared to handle such sexual feelings.

Some of the characteristics associated with psychology trainees who committed sexual boundary violations are prior counseling or quasi-counseling experience, such as a volunteer, in which clear boundaries were not enforced; inexperience as a therapist; and loneliness. In addition, there may be inappropriate faculty models or lack of adequate supervision (Hamilton & Spruill, 1999).

The intensity of the treatment relationship commonly activates sexual needs and fantasies on the part of both the psychologist and the client/patient. Graduate programs can reduce the likelihood of sexual contact by focusing on the issues of transference and countertransference, educating students about the inevitability of sexual attraction between psychologists and clients/patients, and having supervisors who are willing to discuss sexual feelings openly (Hamilton & Spruill, 1999). Supervisors who openly discuss the reality of sexual attraction can help their trainees to gain or recover the objectivity needed to deal with these emotions constructively. Fortunately, more graduate training programs are beginning to address these issues (Samuel & Gorton, 1998). Model curricula have been developed including training exercises and vignettes (Bricklin et al., 2001; Samuel & Gorton, 1998; Schoener, 1999).

10.06 Sexual Intimacies With Relatives or Significant Others of Current Therapy Clients/Patients

Psychologists do not engage in sexual intimacies with individuals they know to be close relatives, guardians, or significant others of current clients/patients. Psychologists do not terminate therapy to circumvent this standard. [This standard is new.]

In addition to the problems that develop with sexual contact with clients/patients, students, and former clients/patients, problems can also occur if psychologists initiate romantic relationships with close relatives or friends of clients/patients. For example, what if a psychologist initiated a romantic relationship with the mother of a child/patient. Under the 1992 Ethics Code, this would usually be charged under the standard dealing with harmful multiple relationships. The 2002 Ethics Code explicitly prohibits it.

10.07 Therapy With Former Sexual Partners

Psychologists do not accept as therapy clients/patients persons with whom they have engaged in sexual intimacies. [This standard is similar to Standard 4.06 of the 1992 Ethics Code.]

It is believed that a prior sexual relationship would create too much potential for conflict for therapy to be conducted effectively.

10.08 Sexual Intimacies With
Former Therapy Clients/Patients

(a) [No Sexual Intimacies With Former Clients/Patients for Two Years.] *Psychologists do not engage in sexual intimacies with former clients/patients for at least two years after cessation or termination of therapy.* [This standard is similar to Standard 4.07a of the 1992 Ethics Code.]

(b) [Sexual Intimacies With Former Clients/Patients After Two Years.] *Psychologists do not engage in sexual intimacies with former clients/patients even after a two-year interval except in the most unusual circumstances. Psychologists who engage in such activity after the two years following cessation or termination of therapy and of having no sexual contact with the former client/patient bear the burden of demonstrating that there has been no exploitation, in light of all relevant factors, including (1) the amount of time that has passed since therapy terminated; (2) the nature, duration, and intensity of the therapy; (3) the circumstances of termination; (4) the client's/patient's personal history; (5) the client's/patient's current mental status; (6) the likelihood of adverse impact on the client/patient; and (7) any statements or actions made by the therapist during the course of therapy suggesting or inviting the possibility of a posttermination sexual or romantic relationship with the client/patient. (See also Standard 3.05, Multiple Relationships.)* [This standard is similar to Standard 4.07b of the 1992 Ethics Code.]

The 2002 APA Ethics Code always prohibits sexual relationships with clients/patients and almost always prohibits sexual relationships with former clients/patients. After 2 years a sexual relationship may occur in unusual circumstances after appropriate steps are taken to protect the former client/patient and maintain objectivity. The psychologist has the responsibility of demonstrating that there is no exploitation after considering relevant factors listed in the Ethics Code.

This principle does not mean "Two Years and a Green Light." It means "Two Years and a Flashing Red Light." The burden is on the psychologist to demonstrate that exploitation did not occur according to the standards listed earlier. Sexual contact with former clients/patients is viewed as a rare exception. It is an "almost never" standard.

Incidents have been reported where the therapist terminated treatment with the client/patient only for the purpose of initiating a romantic relationship. In one situation, the client/patient and psychologist talked about having a romantic relationship during psychotherapy. They terminated treatment on one day and literally started dating the next day. Although therapy had ended, the relationship still gave a disproportionate amount of power to the former psychologist who can use influence and information to keep the relationship going. Even before APA prohibited sexual relationships with former clients/patients (for at least 2 years), APA's and other ethics committees commonly disciplined psychologists who initiated romantic relationships with clients/patients shortly after termination.

Consideration was given to changing the 2 year rule to an "in perpetuity rule," but this did not occur for two reasons: First, the standard was still the subject of substantial debate within the profession. No consensus had emerged in the profession concerning the desirability of an in perpetuity rule. Second there was doubt whether an in perpetuity rule could have survived legal challenges in state courts even if it was adopted (*Caddy v. Florida*, 2000).

10.09 Interruption of Therapy

When entering into employment or contractual relationships, psychologists make reasonable efforts to provide for orderly and appropriate resolution of responsibility for client/patient care in the event that the employment or contractual relationship ends, with paramount consideration given to the welfare of the client/patient. (See also Standard 3.12, Interruption of Psychological Services.) [This standard is similar to Standard 4.08b of the 1992 Ethics Code.]

10.10 Terminating Therapy

(a) [General Rule on Terminating Therapy.] *Psychologists terminate therapy when it becomes reasonably clear that the client/patient no longer needs the service, is not likely to benefit, or is being harmed by continued service.* [This standard is similar to Standard 4.09b of the 1992 Ethics Code.]

(b) [Terminating Therapy When Threatened.] *Psychologists may terminate therapy when threatened or otherwise endangered by the client/patient or another person with whom the client/ patient has a relationship.* [This standard is new.]

(c) [Pretermination Counseling.] *Except where precluded by the actions of clients/patients or third-party payors, prior to termination psychologists provide pretermination counseling and suggest alternative service providers as appropriate.* [This standard is similar to Standard 4.09c of the 1992 Ethics Code.]

Usually clients/patients and their psychologists reach an agreement that treatment is no longer needed because the presenting problems of the clients/patients have been addressed. At other times clients/patients may decide unilaterally that they do not want to continue in treatment.

Sometimes psychologists should consider making a referral or terminating because therapy is not going well, such as when (a) clients/patients want to continue in treatment even though they are worsening despite the best efforts of the psychologist; (b) the psychologist may develop a strong antipathy toward a client/patient; (c) a psychologist may learn that the client/patient has problems outside of her or his area of competence after seeing the client/patient for several sessions; (d) a client/patient has developed an excessive and unhealthy dependence on the psychologist; (e) a client/patient spends time in therapy unproductively (such as engaging in chit chat about apparently mundane events and, despite assiduous efforts of the psychologist, refuses to address more substantive issues); (f) a client/patient refuses to pay for services; or (g) a managed care company terminates treatment abruptly without contacting the psychologist first.

Although not specifically addressed in the Ethics Code, psychologists should also consider their responsibilities for after-hour coverage or coverage when they go on vacations, if they become ill and must take extended leave from work, or when planning to retire (Finkelstein & Barnett, 2000).

In addition to a potential ethics violation, the premature termination of treatment may place the psychologist at risk of a malpractice suit based on the concept of legal abandonment, which means the professional terminated treatment when she or he knew or should have known that the client/patient needed and would have benefited from more treatment. The concept of abandonment has been applied primarily in medical malpractice cases although its extension to psychotherapy would seem logical (VandeCreek & Knapp, 2001).

Psychologists in independent practice may refuse to accept potential clients/patients into treatment for any reason, including the perceived ability of the client/patient to pay for services. However, they generally do not have the unqualified right to terminate an existing relationship unless the treatment is completed, the client/patient ends the relationship, or the psychotherapist recommends alternative services.

According to the 2002 APA Ethics Code, psychologists may terminate treatment, even without the consent of the clients/patients, if they no longer need treatment, are not likely to benefit from treatment, or may be harmed by the treatment. In addition, the psychologist may terminate if the client/patient threatens the safety of the psychologist. Generally speaking, psychologists are required to provide termination counseling to the clients/patients except when precluded by actions of third-party payors or clients/patients.

When Treatment Will Not Benefit or
May Harm the Client/Patient

Some patients may want to continue treatment when it would be meaningless or even harmful to them. It can be clinically indicated to restrict or refuse an appointment with some clients/patients at certain times. The duty to provide appointments only refers to the duty to provide clinically appropriate appointments. When refusing to schedule appointments with impulsive or manipulative clients/patients, psychologists should document their treatment decision carefully to avoid the appearance of neglect.

Some clients/patients with pervasive personality disorders may make manipulative threats. It is not in the interest of these clients/patients to allow them to continue a pattern of self-defeating behaviors. The Ethics Code is not intended to coerce psychologists into reinforcing disruptive or harmful behavior. Sometimes clients/patients engage in vague and manipulative suicide threats that appear more designed to engender reactions from others than to reflect a serious depression or suicidality. It is hardly in the best interest of these clients/patients to allow them to continue this self-defeating pattern of behaviors.

> The risk of ultimate successful suicide is increased . . . because (a) the more often a suicide gesture is made, the more likely death by mistake will occur (wrong pills, too many, the expected rescue being thwarted) [and] (b) the client may need to use increasingly dangerous methods to provide the same response. (Dawson & MacMillan, 1993, p. 121)

Psychologists should not misconstrue the doctrine of abandonment as requiring them to reinforce disruptive and self-defeating behaviors. Nonetheless, the decision to restrict appointments with these clients/patients should be done carefully. Even clients/patients who engage in manipulative gestures can seriously harm or even kill themselves.

Although the parameters of the abandonment theory are not always well defined, refusing to treat clients/patients while they are a serious threat to themselves or others would constitute abandonment. After the immediate crisis has passed, psychologists can then take measures to address the disruptive behavior or refer them elsewhere.

From a risk management perspective, it is advisable to document such decisions in detail. The duty to refer or consult arises when the therapist determines, or should have determined, that the current treatments are unlikely to help the client/patient. This duty may become apparent in the first interview with the client/patient, or it may not become apparent until therapy has been conducted for many sessions.

The issue of referrals was considered in the case of *Osheroff v. Chestnut Lodge* (1985), where a client/patient was diagnosed as having a personality disorder and received 7 months of intensive psychodynamic psychotherapy in a hospital. His family complained about the lack of improvement, and, after the hospital refused to change the treatment plan, he transferred to another hospital. There the client/patient responded well to medications and was discharged within 3 months. The court determined that the psychiatrists in the first hospital were negligent in their diagnosis and treatment of the client/patient. Expert witnesses opined that the treating psychiatrists should have modified the treatment plan when it became obvious that the client/patient was not responding to the intensive psychotherapy.

If, after doing all of these things, the psychologist is still unable to help the client/patient, then consideration should be given to discussing the prognosis candidly with the client/patient. This situation requires great clinical acumen. Of course, it is possible that the treatment may be preventing the client/patient from deteriorating further or that the client/patient otherwise places great value on the treatment. Anytime clients/patients show life endangering features, psychologists should err on the side of recommending continued treatment either from themselves or another competent professional.

A Client/Patient From Hell I

A psychologist received a request to resume treatment with a former client/patient. The psychologist, who had moved into an administrative position and was seeing no new clients, declined and referred her to another psychologist in her clinic. The former client/ patient made numerous phone calls pleading to be reinstated as a client/patient and she eventually called the psychologist at home stating that she had just ingested a large quantity of drugs and was "saying good-bye." The psychologist arranged for the involuntary hospitalization of the client/patient but refused again to provide any treatment.

A Client/Patient From Hell II

A female client/patient developed an extreme transference to her psychologist, also a woman. She spent time in therapy asking if the psychologist loved her. She made little or no progress in therapy and refused to sign a release so that the psychologist could talk to the physician handling her medications. She repeatedly called the psychologist during the night and then hung-up immediately before the psychologist could answer the phone. When the psychologist pressed the call-back feature on the phone and her client/patient answered, she denied making the phone call.

In both of these cases the client/patient had developed extreme transference reactions which eliminated the possibility of therapeutic success. Unless these transference reactions are dealt with successfully, it is unlikely that clients/patients will benefit from continuing in psychotherapy with their psychologists.

The duty to refer arises when the psychologist determines or should have determined that she or he lacks the ability or expertise to help the client/patient. Although the need to refer may sometimes become apparent in the first phone conversation or interview with the client/patient, at other times it may not become apparent until therapy has been conducted for a while. For some disorders, such as schizophrenia, organic brain disorders, or manic-depressive disorders, verbal psychotherapy alone will not produce sufficient benefits, and nonmedical psychotherapists have a duty to refer to a physician, preferably a psychiatrist. Other disorders, such as depression or anxiety, may respond either to psychotherapy or psychopharmacology. Referral or consultation in these cases would be indicated when the client/patient has no reasonable likelihood of deriving therapeutically meaningful benefit from working with the current psychologist.

When the Psychologist Is Not Available

Clients/patients may feel abandoned any time that the psychologist is not reasonably available. This may occur if the psychologist takes an extended vacation and provides no professional back-up. Or it may occur if a treatment relationship ends abruptly such as when a psychologist suddenly moves to another city or leaves an internship setting and no efforts were made to prepare the client/patient for the change.

One client/patient wrote advice to psychiatrists from a client's/ patient's point of view.

> Many times therapists underestimate their importance to their clients/patients. Cold-turkey termination can be destructive. Consideration may be given, if the therapist is moving away, to reduced visits to make up for distance. . . . Try cushioning the trauma by weaning your former patients from you by allowing telephone calls and/or correspondence with you. . . . I do not exaggerate when I state that the pain you may be diminishing could be lifesaving. (Crabtree, 1993, p. 23)

Chapter 6
SUMMARIES OF
SPECIFIC TOPICS

The entire Ethics Code applies to all psychologists. Consequently, a situation can seldom be viewed from the standpoint of one single standard or even the ethical standards from one single section of the Code. For example, a psychologist who provides psychotherapy would be held accountable to all of the standards of the Ethics Code, not just those contained in Section 10 on therapy.

Nonetheless, it may be useful to review what the Ethics Code says about some specific themes, activities, or roles. This section briefly summarizes the ethical standards according to content. These are not identical to specific sections of the Ethics Code. For example, Section 10 contains the ethical standards dealing with therapy, although other standards throughout the Code of Conduct also specifically reference therapy.

The standards are grouped into general themes (responsibilities to others, competence, informed consent, accuracy [honesty], and confidentiality), roles of psychologists (therapy, assessment, supervision, consulting, organizational consulting, forensic roles, research, and teaching), and other issues (conflicts of interest, electronic transmissions, dealing with diverse groups, fees, and documentation).

GENERAL THEMES

The general themes of the Code of Conduct reviewed here include responsibilities to others, competence (including competence using experimental treatments, and impairment), informed consent (including informed consent in therapy, assessment, teaching and supervision, and research), accuracy (honesty), and confidentiality (including confidentiality in informed consent, storing confidential information, disclosure of confidential information, and confidentiality in research). For each of the general themes, we also identify the moral principles that appear to underlie them.

Responsibilities to Others

The moral principle that best approximates the theme of responsibilities to others is Principle B, Fidelity and Responsibility. This moral standard specifically instructs psychologists to be "concerned about the ethical compliance of their colleagues' scientific and professional conduct." It also states that psychologists should be "aware of their professional and scientific responsibilities to society and to the specific communities in which they work."

When organizations place demands on psychologists which conflict with the Ethics Code, psychologists should attempt to resolve the conflict in a manner consistent with the Ethics Code (1.02).* When psychologists learn of ethical violations by other psychologists, they attempt to reach an informal resolution, but if an informal resolution does not seem possible, then further action may be required (1.03, 1.04). Psychologists cooperate with ethics committees (1.05) and do not recklessly file complaints (1.06).

However, the obligations to uphold professional standards are not absolute and must be balanced by General Principle D, Justice. Psychologists do not discriminate against other professionals on the basis of ethics complaints that are unresolved (1.08) and must respect confidentiality rights before taking actions against an apparent ethical violation by a psychologist (1.04, 1.05).

The responsibilities to others can also be considered under Principle E, Respect for People's Rights and Dignity. Psychologists to not engage in unfair discrimination (3.01), sexual harassment (3.02), or knowingly demean others (3.03). When approached by those requesting services who are being served by others, psychologists proceed with caution considering the best interests of the client/patient (10.04).

Competence

The concept of competence appears to be based primarily on General Principle A, Beneficence and Nonmaleficence. That is, psychologists "strive to benefit those with whom they work and take care to do no harm." Special considerations need to be taken when developing innovative or

---

*These brief summaries cannot do justice to the details or nuances found in the specific standards. Readers should look to the standards referenced to obtain a full understanding of their intent, meaning, and potential application.

experimental treatments. Competence requires not only the skills to perform the work competently, but it also requires emotional competence. General Principle A states that "psychologists strive to be aware of the possible effect of their own physical and mental health on their ability to help those with whom they work."

In addition, concepts of competence are found in General Principle D, Justice. According to that principle, psychologists "take precautions to ensure that . . . the boundaries of their competence, and the limitations of their expertise do not lead to or condone unjust practices."

Psychologists must be competent in their services, teaching, and research (2.01a), take efforts to maintain their expertise (2.03), and base their decisions on the scientific or professional knowledge base of the discipline (2.04). Psychologists must be competent when treating specific populations where age, gender, culture, and so forth significantly impact the quality of treatment (2.01b); moving into new areas of work (2.01c); providing services to underserved populations (2.01d); implementing innovative treatments (2.01e); assuming forensic roles (2.01f); or dealing with emergencies (2.02). Psychologists should only delegate services to supervisees or others who are competent to perform them (2.05). Psychologists should refrain from undertaking professional activities if personal problems will prevent them from performing competently (2.06a) and they should withdraw from professional activities when their emotional problems threaten the quality of services (2.06b). Statements to the media are based on appropriate psychological knowledge and practice (5.04).

Issues of competence are addressed in sections on research and assessments. Research must be conducted in compliance with the approved protocol (8.01). The results of assessments must be based on information sufficient to justify it (9.01a) and psychologists may give opinions on individuals whom they have not personally evaluated, as long as the limitations of the data are acknowledged (9.01b). Psychologists do not use obsolete tests (9.08a) nor do they base decisions on obsolete test results (9.08b). Psychologists use appropriate procedures when developing (9.05) and interpreting tests (9.06). They do not promote the use of tests by unqualified persons (9.07).

Experimental Treatments. When entering into new areas of practice in which generally acceptable preparatory standards do not exist, psychologists nonetheless take steps to protect their clients/patients (2.01e). They are required to inform potential clients/patients of the experimental nature of these treatments, potential risks, alternative treatments, and the voluntary nature of their participation (10.01b). Psychologists who are conducting research on experimental treatments clarify to participants ahead of time that the services are experimental and explain the procedures for assignment into control groups, and available treatment alternatives (8.02).

Impairment. Psychologists must refrain from professional activities when they know or should know that they are impaired (2.06a) and, if they appear to be impaired, seek consultation as to whether to withdraw from such work activities (2.06b). Educators may require students to discuss personal problems if it appears that the students are impaired (7.04).

Informed Consent

Informed consent is based primarily on General Principle E, Respect for People's Rights and Dignity. That principle states that psychologists respect the "self-determination and autonomy" of the recipients of their services. In addition, Principle C, Integrity, also appears relevant in that psychologists need to give accurate information to the recipients of their services.

The Ethics Code contains general statements about informed consent (primarily in 3.10) and more specific statements about informed consent throughout the Code depending on the services being provided (therapy, assessment, teaching, supervision, or research).

Informed consent (3.10a) requires the person (a) has the ability to give consent; (b) has been given information relevant to the decision to participate; (c) knows that participation is voluntary; and (d) has the opportunity to ask questions. If persons are not legally able to give consent, then psychologists seek to obtain their approval, consider (but not necessarily honor) their preferences, and get approval from those who can give legal consent. Psychologists document consent (3.10d). When dealing with persons who are not legally able to give consent, psychologists nonetheless strive to get assent (3.10b).

The information given in the consent process includes information about uses of information or limits of confidentiality (4.02a) and especially the limits of confidentiality in the use of electronic transmissions (4.02c). These discussions should occur as early as possible in the relationship (4.02b). Visual or audio recordings should not be done without the consent of the person being recorded (4.03; however, see exceptions in 8.03). Except in unusual circumstances, psychologists may not disclose confidential information about clients/patients without their consent (4.05) including in their writings or public presentations with personally identifiable information (4.07). Nor do psychologists put identifying information into databases without the consent of clients/patients (6.02b) (they may enter information into those databases if they code it or delete personal identifiers).

See also Confidentiality and Informed Consent (p. 169).

Informed Consent in Therapy. Before providing therapy, psychologists inform participants about the nature of therapy, including fees and limits of confidentiality (10.01). If providing experimental treatments, psychologists must inform prospective participants of the experimental nature of the treatment, potential risks, and treatment alternatives (10.01b). Supervisors must ensure that their supervisees inform clients/patients of the supervisory relationship (10.01c). When providing couples or family therapy, psychologists inform parties ahead of time concerning their roles and probable relationship with each person (10.02a). When providing group therapy, psychologists must describe the roles and responsibilities of parties ahead of time (10.03). When deciding whether to offer services to those who are being treated by others, psychologists discuss these issues with involved persons (10.04). When psychological services are court ordered, psychologists inform the recipient of the nature of the anticipated services (3.10c).

Psychologists inform clients/patients about fees before beginning services or as soon as feasible (6.04a), discuss anticipated limits in financing of services (6.04d), and give clients/patients an opportunity to settle their debts before turning them over to collection agencies or courts for nonpayment of delinquent fees (6.04e). Informed consent is acquired before recording the voices or images of persons (4.03).

Informed Consent in Assessments. Psychologists obtain informed consent for assessments (9.03a) and obtain consent when using the services of an interpreter (9.03c). When courts order individuals to be assessed, psychologists nonetheless explain the nature and purpose of the assessment (9.03b). However, informed consent for assessments is waived if it is court ordered, if it is part of a routine educational or organizational activity, or if the decisional capacity of the individual is being assessed (9.03a). Psychologists who offer assessment or testing services must describe the purposes, norms, and applications of their procedures accurately (9.09).

Informed Consent in Teaching and Supervision. Psychologists responsible for education or training programs describe the programs accurately (7.02), and inform students ahead of time of any requirement for mandatory therapy (7.05a). Psychologists who are supervisors inform supervisees of the procedures for evaluation at the outset of their work together (7.06a).

Informed Consent in Research. Psychologists inform research participants of (a) the purposes, expected duration, and procedures for the research; (b) their right not to participate or withdraw; (c) the foreseeable consequences of withdrawing and foreseeable factors that may influence their decision to withdraw; (d) prospective benefits from the research; (e) limits on confidentiality; (f) incentives for participation; and (g) whom to contact with questions (8.02a).

Psychologists who are conducting research on experimental treatments clarify to participants ahead of time about the procedures for assignment into control groups, available treatment alternatives, and the fact that the treatments are experimental (8.02b). Psychologists obtain informed consent before recording the voice or image of participants (unless these are naturalistic observations; 8.03).

In some circumstances, researchers can dispense with informed consent for research if it involves (a) normal educational practices; (b) anonymous questionnaires or archival records where participation would not place individuals at risk for adverse consequences; or (c) organizational research related to job functioning (8.05).

Researchers may use deception if (a) the use of deception is justified and alternative methods of getting the same information are not feasible; (b) there is no deceit about physical pain or emotional distress; and (c) psychologists debrief participants as soon as possible, preferably at the end of the treatment (8.07).

Accuracy (Honesty)

General Principle C, Integrity, encourages psychologists to "promote accuracy, honesty, and truthfulness in the science, teaching, and practice of psychology" and not to "engage in fraud, subterfuge, or intentional misrepresentation of fact."

Psychologists have a responsibility to correct the misuse or misrepresentations of their work when they become aware of it (1.01). They do not file ethics complaints recklessly or with disregard for the truth (1.07). Psychologists do not knowingly make false or deceptive public statements (5.01a) and do not misrepresent their credentials (5.01b) or degrees (5.01c). When they hire others, they retain responsibility for the accuracy of the statements made (5.02a), do not compensate media persons for news items (5.02b), and clearly identify paid advertisements as such (5.02c). Psychologists take reasonable efforts to report the nature of health care services accurately to funding sources (6.06).

Psychologists describe nondegree workshops accurately (5.03) and when they are in charge of degree granting programs, they ensure the accuracy of the representations of the program (7.02), including the disclosure of any requirement for mandatory therapy (7.05). As teachers, they present information accurately (7.03). They explain the limits of their conclusions based on record reviews, consultations, or supervision (9.01c).

As researchers, psychologists do not fabricate data (8.10a) and, if they learn of significant errors, take steps to correct them (8.10b). Psychologists do not plagiarize (8.11) and only take publication credit for work they have actually performed (8.12).

See also the section on Informed Consent (pp. 166-168).

Confidentiality

The principle of confidentiality is based on General Principle A, Beneficence and Nonmaleficence, because the unwarranted disclosure of information could harm the recipients of services. In addition, it is based on General Principle B, Fidelity and Responsibility, because confidentiality is essential to preserve an atmosphere of trust. Finally, it is based on General Principle E, Respect for People's Rights and Dignity, which states that psychologists respect "the rights of individuals to privacy, confidentiality, and self-determination."

Psychologists take reasonable precautions to protect confidentiality rights (4.01). Special precautions are taken when giving informed consent, storing records, disclosing confidential information, and conducting research.

Confidentiality and Informed Consent. One of the components of informed consent is to review confidentiality interests which is especially important for therapy (10.01a) or court-ordered services (3.10c). At the beginning of therapy, or as soon as it is feasible, psychologists discuss the relevant limitations on confidentiality and the foreseeable uses of the information generated through their psychological activities (4.02a). The discussion of confidentiality occurs thereafter as new circumstances may warrant (4.02b). Also, psychologists inform individuals of the limitations on confidentiality before embarking on couples (10.02a) or group therapy (10.03), when there are conflicting roles in forensic work (3.05c), before providing services at the request of a third party (3.07), or before offering services via electronic transmission (4.02c).

Storing Confidential Information. Psychologists maintain appropriate confidentiality in creating, storing, accessing, transferring, and disposing of records under their control (6.02a), and code or otherwise disguise confidential data stored in databases (6.02b), and plan for the transfer of confidential records in the event of their death or disability (6.02c).

Disclosure of Confidential Information. Psychologists may disclose confidential information with the appropriate consent of organizational clients, the individual client/patient, or of another legally authorized person on behalf of the client/patient unless prohibited by law (4.05b). Psychologists may not disclose confidential information without the consent of clients/patients in order to address or report an ethical violation (1.04, 1.05). They attempt to protect confidentiality interests when responding to an ethics complaint (1.06). Test data are released only with a client's/patient's written consent or in response to a court order (9.04).

Psychologists discuss confidential information obtained in their work only for appropriate scientific or professional purposes and only with persons clearly concerned with such matters (4.04b). In written reports and consultations, psychologists only include germane information (4.04a). Even when getting consultations, psychologists try to avoid disclosing confidential information that reasonably could lead to the identification of clients/patients, and they disclose only enough to the extent necessary to achieve the purposes of the consultation (4.06). For didactic or writing purposes, psychologists do not disclose personally identifiable information concerning their clients/patients unless they disguise the information or have the client's/patient's consent (4.07). Psychologists are obligated to keep information private and may only disclose it without consent in rare circumstances such as when getting a professional consultation or protecting the client/patient, psychologist, or others from harm (4.05b).

Confidentiality in Research. Psychologists consult about confidential matters only with persons clearly concerned with the issue at hand (4.04b), and they protect the confidentiality of research participants in their writings or didactic presentations (4.07). When conducting research, psychologists inform clients/patients of the probable limitations on confidentiality (8.02a) and obtain consent if there is a voice or image recording that could identify the research participant (8.03). If sharing research data with other researchers, psychologists may need to take steps to protect the confidentiality rights of the subjects (8.14).

ROLES OF PSYCHOLOGISTS

The roles of psychologists include those of conducting therapy (including sexual contact, emergencies, termination, and group therapy), assessment, supervision, consultation, organizational consultation, forensic work, research, and teaching.

Therapists

Psychologists do not exploit those over whom they have control (3.08) and they cooperate with other professionals to help their clients/patients (3.09). They seek permission before recording the voices or images of those to whom they provide services (4.03). Psychologists may not use testimonials from clients/patients in therapy or those who would be vulnerable to exploitation (5.05). Psychologists delivering mental health services may only represent degrees that were earned from regionally accredited universities or which were the basis of their license (5.01c). They may not solicit testimonials from current therapy clients/patients or others who are vulnerable to undue influence (5.05). Psychologists show appropriate concern when dealing with persons who are currently receiving services from others (10.04). Psychologists clarify roles ahead of time when providing services at the request of third parties (3.07).

See also Informed Consent in Therapy (p. 167).

See also Competence (including Experimental Treatments; pp. 164-166).

See also Fees (p. 178).

Sexual Contact. Psychologists may not have sexual intimacies with current therapy clients/patients (10.05), with significant others or close relatives of current clients/patients (10.06), or with former clients/patients except under highly restricted circumstances (10.08). In addition, psychologists should not conduct therapy with former sexual partners (10.07).

Emergency Services. Psychologists may work outside of their usual areas of competence to provide mental health services in emergencies (2.02). They may waive confidentiality if necessary to protect the safety of a client/patient or others (4.05). Psychologists may engage in in-person solicitation while providing disaster relief services (5.06). They may withhold records for nonpayment of services except in an emergency (6.03). Psychologists may terminate clients/patients who threaten them (10.10b).

Termination. Psychologists should terminate therapy if they have personal problems that will impair their ability to provide the necessary services (2.06b). Informed consent procedures require telling clients/patients of the anticipated course of treatment (10.01). Psychologists make plans in advance for the handling of records in the event that treatment is terminated (6.02c). They make plans to facilitate the continuation of services in the event that psychological services are interrupted (3.12). They discuss the termination or transfer of clients/patients early in treatment especially if limitations in services due to financing can be anticipated (6.04d). Psychologists make arrangements for the orderly transition of clients/patients when entering into employment contracts (10.09).

Psychologists must terminate therapy when it becomes reasonably clear that the client/patient is not benefiting or is not likely to benefit (10.10a). Except when precluded by third-party payors, psychologists provide pretermination counseling and make referrals (10.10c).

Group Therapy. Prospective students must be informed ahead of time when group therapy is required as part of a course or program (7.02), and faculty with evaluative authority should not provide that group therapy (7.05b). Psychologists providing group therapy describe the responsibilities of all parties and the limits of confidentiality (10.03).

Assessment

Psychologists use reasonable skill in reaching their conclusions (9.01) and in using tests, especially when it involves the assessment of diverse populations (9.02). They obtain informed consent for assessments, although there are some exceptions (9.03). Psychologists may release raw test data to certain individuals with a client/patient release (9.04). Psychologists must use appropriate procedures when constructing (9.05) and interpreting tests (9.06). They do not promote the use of tests by unqualified persons, except trainees (9.07). Psychologists do not base their recommendations on outdated test results (9.08a) or use obsolete tests (9.08b). They use automated testing services appropriately (9.09). Psychologists take steps to ensure that explanations of the results are given to the individual tested (or a designated representative), except in certain situations (9.10).

See also Informed Consent in Assessments (p. 167).

See also Forensic Experts (pp. 174).

Supervision

Psychologists delegate work to supervisees only if they are competent to perform the assigned tasks and if their performance is monitored

(2.05). Psychologists inform supervisees of the standards for feedback (7.06a) and evaluate them based on their actual performance (7.06b). Their supervisees must inform clients/patients of the supervised nature of the relationship (10.01c). Psychologists take reasonable steps to protect their supervisees from harm (3.04) and exploitation (3.08) and do not have sex with them (7.07). Psychologists avoid delegating responsibilities to supervisees when a multiple relationship risks the loss of objectivity or exploitation (2.05). Psychologists do not promote the use of assessment by unqualified persons, except trainees (9.07).

General Consultation

General Principle B, Fidelity and Responsibility, notes that "psychologists consult with, refer to, or cooperate with other professionals and institutions to the extent needed to serve the best interests of those with whom they work." Consultation is one of the ways that psychologists can ensure the competence of their work (2.01a, 2.01b, 2.01c). Psychologists who are impaired should seek consultation or terminate services (2.06b).

Other standards deal with psychologists who serve as consultants to other psychologists. Psychologists who are asked to review the work of another psychologist are not required to report ethics violations (1.04). Consulting psychologists may receive confidential information without the consent of clients/patients (4.06) if the information is restricted to that which is germane to the consultation and does not include identifying information. Psychologists who offer assessment or scoring services to others must describe their services accurately (9.09a).

Organizational Consultation

Organizational psychologists, like other psychologists, avoid harmful conflicts of interests (3.06), inform clients about the nature of services ahead of time if services are requested by a third party (3.07), describe the nature of services accurately (3.10, 3.11), inform clients of the limits of confidentiality (4.02), and, except in unusual circumstances, disclose information only with client consent (4.05a, 4.05b). Psychologists may consult with others as long as identifying information is not disclosed (4.06) and may present information in a didactic forum as long as identifying information is not included (4.07). Psychologists make plans for facilitating services in the event that they are interrupted (3.12).

In some situations, such as when doing organizational consulting or preemployment or security testing, third-party arrangements may prevent psychologists from explaining the test results directly to the person being assessed (9.10). Consulting psychologists may dispense with informed consent for research related to job or organizational effectiveness if there is no risk to the employability of the person being tested and confidentiality is protected (8.05). Psychologists do not need to obtain informed consent for testing as a routine organizational activity (9.03a).

Organizational consultants do not accept referral fees (6.07).

Forensic Experts

When assuming forensic roles, psychologists become reasonably familiar with the court rules governing their participation (2.01f). They create or maintain the documentation needed for the forensic purposes (6.01b).

When forensic psychologists are required by law, institutional policies, or extraordinary circumstances to serve in more than one role in judicial or administrative proceedings, they clarify role expectations and confidentiality limits (3.05c). They clarify roles if services are requested by a third party (3.07). When psychological services are court ordered, psychologists nonetheless inform the individual of the nature of the services ordered (3.10c). Psychologists do not need to get the informed consent of participants for court-ordered tests but should explain the nature and purpose of the evaluation (9.03a). Psychologists may refuse to turn over raw test data to attorneys, others, or clients/patients with a client/patient release if the release is likely to harm the client/patient (9.04).

Typically psychologists give opinions only on people they have evaluated, but they may conduct a record review or otherwise give an opinion under some circumstances (9.01c).

Research

Psychologists should conduct research only in areas in which they are competent (2.01, 8.01) or they become competent if they are moving into new areas (2.01c). Psychologists have or acquire competence when an understanding of age, gender, race, and so forth is essential for effective research (2.01b).

Psychologists must follow acceptable standards when doing research with psychological tests (9.05). They ensure the quality of services delegated to research assistants (2.05).

The informed consent procedures in Standard 3.10 apply to research. Psychologists inform their host institutions about research (8.01) and obtain informed consent from research participants (8.02) except when it is conducted as part of a routine educational or consulting activity (8.05, 9.03a). Psychologists must obtain informed consent when recording voices or images in research, except in some unusual circumstances (8.03).

Psychologists must protect subordinates or students from feeling co-erced into participating in research (8.04), and the inducements should not be such that they are likely to be considered coercive (8.06). Decep-tion in research is to be avoided whenever possible (8.07). Participants should be debriefed (8.08). Animal subjects in research should be treated humanely (8.09). Research results are not falsified (8.10) and are not pub-lished as original data if they have been published elsewhere (8.11). Psy-chologists should share their research data with others under some cir-cumstances (8.14). Psychologists may not plagiarize (8.11) and review-ers should protect the confidentiality of the manuscripts they review (8.15). Standard 8.12 describes the criteria for determining authorship. They do not publish as original, data that has been published elsewhere (8.13).

Psychologists who conduct research use assessment instruments com-petently (9.05). They do not misrepresent their research findings (5.01b). Psychologists keep records to allow for the replication of the research design and analyses (6.01).

See also Informed Consent in Research (p. 168).

See also Confidentiality in Research (p. 170).

Teaching

Psychologists must be competent in those areas in which they teach (2.01a) or they must undertake steps to gain that competence (2.01c). Psychologists ensure that teaching assistants can perform their assigned duties (2.05).

The standards dealing with teachers focus mainly on protection for students. Psychologists responsible for educational programs must take reasonable steps to ensure that they will provide the experiences neces-sary for students to obtain the credentials advertised by the program (7.01). The descriptions of programs (7.02), individual classes (7.03a), and con-tinuing education programs (5.03) should be accurate.

Teachers present psychological information accurately (7.03b). They may not require students to disclose personal information unless the re-quirements for such disclosures are clearly identified in advance or it is necessary to evaluate a student who appears to be impaired (7.04). Fac-ulty may not provide mandatory group or individual therapy to students whom they also may be required to evaluate (7.05b). Psychologists give students timely and specific feedback (7.06a). They evaluate students on the basis of objective performance measures that have been presented to the students ahead of time (7.06b). Faculty may not have sexual relation-ships with students in their department (7.07). Students may conduct as-sessments for training purposes under appropriate supervision (9.07).

Students are to be protected from the adverse consequences of failing to participate in research and are offered alternative methods to gain course credit if research participation is part of a class requirement (8.04b). Teachers may conduct research without consent of the participants if it is part of the normal educational practices or involves studies of instructional strategies (8.05).

Students usually get primary authorship on studies based on their dissertations (although this exception may not occur in unusual circumstances). Psychologists should discuss potential publication credits with students as early as feasible (8.12c).

Teachers must protect students from harm (3.04), especially when using innovative techniques (2.01e) and do not exploit students (3.08). They disguise confidential information when using it for didactic purposes (4.07).

See also Informed Consent in Teaching and Supervision (p. 167-168).

OTHER ISSUES

Other issues that may warrant special categorization include conflicts of interests (multiple relationships), electronic transmissions, the protection of diverse groups, fees, and documentation.

Conflicts of Interests

A conflict of interest can occur when the personal goals of psychologists conflict with their obligations to clients/patients, students, supervisees, or research participants, or when the professional obligations of psychologists conflict with each other. Indeed concerns about conflicts were mentioned in the General Principle A, Beneficence and Nonmaleficence ("When conflicts occur among psychologists' obligations or concerns, they attempt to resolve these conflicts in a responsible fashion that avoids or minimizes harm") and General Principle B, Fidelity and Responsibility (psychologists "manage conflicts of interest that could lead to exploitation or harm").

One of the more obvious potential conflicts of interests could occur when multiple relationships arise. Psychologists refrain from entering into multiple relationships that could lead to harm or exploitation (3.05a). When multiple relationships are unavoidable, psychologists attempt to resolve them with regard for the best interests of the affected persons (3.05b), and they attempt to clarify roles when asked to serve in more than one role in a judicial or administrative hearing (3.05c). Psychologists refrain from taking on roles that would create a harmful conflict of interest (3.06) and avoid exploiting those over whom they have administrative authority (3.08). Faculty who are responsible for evaluating student performance do not conduct therapy with those students (7.05b). Psychologists avoid delegating responsibilities to supervisees when there is a risk of a multiple relationship that could lead to the loss of objectivity or exploitation (2.05). When conducting research with subordinates, psychologists protect them from adverse consequences of refusing to participate in that research (8.04).

Psychologists refrain from sexual intimacies with students and supervisees (7.07); clarify roles in couples therapy (10.02); avoid sexual intimacies with current clients/patients (10.05), relatives of current clients/patients (10.06), and former therapy clients/patients (10.08); and do not conduct therapy with former sexual partners (10.07).

Electronic Transmissions

All of the ethical standards relating to informed consent, competence, and confidentiality apply to electronic transmissions to the same extent that they apply to other forms of communication or information storage. In addition, psychologists who offer services via electronic means must inform clients/patients and others of the limitations of confidentiality (4.02c). Representations made via electronic means must be accurate (5.01). Psychologists are responsible for the confidentiality of all records, including those transferred through electronic means (6.02).

Protecting Diverse Groups

Psychologists need to acquire the necessary competence when dealing with certain populations, such as cultural or linguistic minorities, if it is necessary for the effective implementation of the services or research (2.01b). Psychologists do not engage in unfair discrimination (3.01) or knowingly engage in demeaning behavior (3.03).

When working with diverse populations, psychologists use assessment instruments that are appropriate for the population tested, and, if such tests are not available, they interpret the results with appropriate reservations (9.02b), make adaptations only if they are derived from a sound knowledge base (9.02c), and make their interpretations with consideration for the situational, personal, linguistic, and cultural differences that may affect the results (9.06). When using interpreters, psychologists obtain consent and ensure the confidentiality of information obtained (9.03c).

Fees

Informing recipients of services about fees should occur as part of the informed consent process (10.01) whereby psychologists make financial arrangements clear at the beginning of the relationship or as soon as feasible thereafter (see also 6.04a). Psychologists do not misrepresent their fees (5.01b, 6.04c), take reasonable steps to ensure the accuracy of their reports to third-party payors (6.06), and may not take fees for referrals (6.07). Fees are consistent with the law (6.04b) and psychologists discuss anticipated limits on services as soon as feasible (6.04d). Bartering is permitted unless it is clinically contraindicated or exploitative (6.05). The fees of nondegree educational programs must be represented accurately by those who create or present them (5.03).

Documentation

The standards on record keeping require psychologists to maintain confidentiality in creating, storing, and disposing of records (6.02a), protect confidential information in databases (6.02b), and facilitate the transfer of records in the event of their death, disability, or retirement (6.02c). They may not withhold records for nonpayment of services during emergencies (6.03). Psychologists are required to document informed consent (3.10d).

Psychologists obtain informed consent before recording the voices or images of others (4.03) although there are a few exceptions when research is being conducted (8.03).

REFERENCES

Ackerman, S., & Hilsenroth, M. (2001). A review of therapist character-istics and techniques negatively impacting the therapeutic alliance. *Psychotherapy: Theory, Research, Practice, Training, 38,* 171-185.

Allison, K., Echemendia, R., Crawford, I., & Robinson, W. L. (1996). Predicting cultural competence: Implications for practice and train-ing. *Professional Psychology: Research and Practice, 27,* 386-393.

American Psychological Association. (1992). *Ethical Principles of Psy-chologists and Code of Conduct.* Washington, DC: Author.

American Psychological Association. (1993). *Guidelines for Ethical Con-duct in the Care and Use of Animals in Research.* Washington, DC: Author.

American Psychological Association. (1994). Guidelines for child cus-tody evaluations in divorce proceedings. *American Psychologist, 49,* 677-680.

American Psychological Association. (2001). *Publication Manual of the American Psychological Association* (5th ed.). Washington, DC: Au-thor.

Anderson, S. K., & Kitchener, K. S. (1996). Nonromantic, nonsexual post therapy relationships between psychologists and former clients: An exploratory study of critical incidents. *Professional Psychology: Re-search and Practice, 27,* 59-66.

Anderson, S. K., & Kitchener, K. S. (1998). Nonsexual posttherapy rela-tionships: A conceptual framework to assess ethical risks. *Profes-sional Psychology: Research and Practice, 29,* 91-99.

Appelbaum, P. (1985). *Tarasoff* and the clinician: Problems in fulfilling the duty to protect. *American Journal of Psychiatry, 142,* 429.

Barnett, J. (1999, November/December). My life as a small town psy-chologist. *The Maryland Psychologist,* pp. 20-21.

Barnett, J. E., & Hillard, D. (2001). Psychologist distress and impairment: The availability, nature and use of colleague assistance programs for psychologists. *Professional Psychology: Research and Practice, 32*, 205-210.

Barrett, M., & Berman, J. (2001). Is psychotherapy more effective when therapists disclose information about themselves? *Journal of Consulting and Clinical Psychology, 69*, 597-603.

Bateman, Y. (1992). Liability of doctor or other health practitioner to third party contracting contagious disease from doctor's patient. *American Law Reports, 5*, 370-393.

Beauchamp, T., & Childress, J. (2001). *Principles of Biomedical Ethics* (5th ed.). New York: Oxford University Press.

Belar, C., Brown, R., Hersch, L., Hornyak, L., Rozensky, R., Sheridan, E., Brown, R., & Reed, G. (2001). Self-assessment in clinical health psychology: A model for ethical expansion of practice. *Professional Psychology: Research and Practice, 32*, 135-141.

Bersoff, D., & Koeppl, P. M. (1993). The relation between ethical codes and moral principles. *Ethics and Behavior, 3*, 345-357.

Binder, R., & McNiel, D. (1996). Application of the *Tarasoff* ruling and its effect on the victim and the therapeutic relationship. *Psychiatric Services, 47*, 1212-1215.

Borkovec, T., Echemendia, R., Ragusea, S., & Ruiz, M. (2001). The Pennsylvania Practice Research Network and future possibilities for clinically meaningful and scientifically rigorous psychotherapy effectiveness research. *Clinical Psychology: Science and Practice, 8*, 155-167.

Borum, R. (2000). Assessing violence risk among youths. *Journal of Clinical Psychology, 58*, 1263-1286.

Bouhoutsos, J., Holroyd, J., Lerman, H., Forer, B. R., & Greenberg, M. (1983). Sexual intimacies between therapists and their former clients. *Psychotherapy, 25*, 249-257.

Bricklin, P., Knapp, S., & VandeCreek, L. (2001). *Educational Modules on Ethics.* Washington DC: APA Insurance Trust.

Bridges, N. (2001). Therapist's self-disclosure: Expanding the comfort zone. *Psychotherapy: Theory, Research, Practice, Training, 38*, 21-30.

Burgess, A. (1981). Physician sexual misconduct and patients' responses. *American Journal of Psychiatry, 136*, 1335-1342.

Burlingame, G., Fuhriman, A., & Johnson, J. (2001). Cohesion in group therapy. *Psychotherapy: Theory, Research, Practice, Training, 38*, 373-379.

Butcher, J. (1996, January). Of errors and questionable advice: A clarifying response to Gordon's evaluation of MMPI/MMPI-2. *Bulletin of the Colorado Psychological Association, 19*, 3, 8-9.

Caddy v. Florida, 764 So.2nd 625 (Fla.App. 1 Dist. 2000).

California Psychological Association AIDS Committee. (1994, December). Confidentiality and prevention of HIV transmission. *California Psychologist*, pp. 17, 21.

Canadian Psychological Association. (1991). *Canadian Code of Ethics for Psychologists, Revised.* Ottawa, Ontario, Canada: Author.

Canter, M., Bennett, B., Jones, S., & Nagy, T. (1994). *Ethics for Psychologists.* Washington, DC: American Psychological Association.

Canterbury v. Spence, 464 F. Supp. 772 (D.C. Cir. 1972).

Cirigliano, M., & Sun, A. (1998). Advising patients about herbal therapies. *Journal of the American Medical Association, 280*, 1565-1566.

Clay, R. (2000, July/August). APA Task Force considers changes to proposed ethics code. *APA Monitor*, pp. 86-87.

Cobb v. Grant, 502 P. 2d 1 (1972).

Committee on Ethical Guidelines for Forensic Psychologists. (1991). Specialty guidelines for forensic psychologists. *Law and Human Behavior, 15*, 655-665.

Crabtree, P. (1993, April 21). Premature termination: Observations from both sides: Patient's view. *Psychatric News*, pp. 23, 30.

Dawson, D., & MacMillan, H. (1993). *Relationship Management of the Borderline Patient.* New York: Brunner/Mazel.

Druss, B., Rohrbaugh, R., Kosten, T., Hoff, R., & Rosenheck, R. (1998). Use of alternative medicine in major depression. *Psychiatric Services, 49*, 1397.

Finkelstein, J., & Barnett, J. (2000, January/February). The A B Cs of termination. *The Maryland Psychologist*, pp. 14-15.

Fisher, C. (2000). Relationship ethics in psychological research: One feminist's journey. In M. Brabek (Ed.), *Practicing Feminist Ethics in Psychology* (pp. 125-142). Washington, DC: American Psychological Association.

Fly, B., van Bark, W., Weinman, L., Kitchener, K. S., & Lang, P. (1997). Ethical transgressions of psychology graduate students: Critical incidents with implications for training. *Professional Psychology: Research and Practice, 28*, 542-546.

Fortuny, L. A., & Mullaney, H. (1998). Assessing patients whose language you do not know: Can the absurd be ethical? *The Clinical Neuropsychologist, 12*, 113-126.

Gavey, N., & Braun, V. (1997). Ethics and the publication of clinical case material. *Professional Psychology: Research and Practice, 28*, 399-404.

Gilmer, W. (1973). *Cochran's Law Lexicon* (5th ed.). Cincinnati, OH: Anderson.

Gordon, R. (1993). Ethics based on protection of the transference. *Issues in Psychoanalytic Psychology, 15*, 95-105.

Gordon, R. (1995, October). Common mistakes made with the MMPI/MMPI-2. *Bulletin of the Colorado Psychological Association*, pp. 4-7.

Grisso, T., & Appelbaum, P. (1998). *MacArthur Competence Assessment Tool for Treatment (MacCAT-T)*. Sarasota, FL: Professional Resource Press.

Guthiel, T., & Gabbard, G. (1993). The concept of boundaries in clinical practice: Theoretical and risk management dimensions. *American Journal of Psychiatry, 150*, 188-196.

Guthiel, T., & Gabbard, G. (1998). Misuses and misunderstandings of boundary theory in clinical and regulatory settings. *American Journal of Psychiatry, 155*, 409-414.

Haas, L., Benedict, J. G., & Kobos, J. (1998). Psychotherapy by telephone: Risks and benefits for psychologists and consumers. *Professional Psychology: Research and Practice, 29*, 154-160.

Haas, L., & Malouf, J. (2002). *Keeping Up the Good Work: A Practitioner's Guide to Mental Health Ethics* (3rd ed.). Sarasota, FL: Professional Resource Press.

Haas, L., Malouf, J., & Mayerson, N. (1986). Ethical dilemmas in psychological practice: Results of a national survey. *Professional Psychology: Research and Practice, 17*, 316-321.

Hall, G. C. N. (2001). Psychotherapy research with ethnic minorities: Empirical, ethical, and conceptual issues. *Journal of Consulting and Clinical Psychology, 69*, 502-510.

Hamilton, J., & Spruill, J. (1999). Identifying and reducing risk factors related to trainee-client sexual misconduct. *Professional Psychology: Research and Practice, 30*, 318-327.

Handelsman, M., Knapp, S., & Gottlieb, M. (2002). Positive ethics. In R. Snyder & S. Lopez (Eds.), *Handbook of Positive Psychology* (pp. 731-744). New York: Oxford University Press.

Handelsman, M., Martinez, A., Geisendorger, S., Jordan, L., Wagner, L., Daniel, P., & Davis, S. (1995). Does legally mandated consent to psychotherapy ensure ethical appropriateness?: The Colorado experience. *Ethics and Behavior, 5*, 119-129.

Health and Human Services. (2002, August 14). Standards for the privacy of individuality identifiable health information: Final rule. *Federal Register, 67,* 53181-53273.

Herman, J. (1992). *Trauma and Recovery.* New York: Basic Books.

Hill, C., & Knox, S. (2001). Self-disclosure. *Psychotherapy: Theory, Research, Practice, Training, 38,* 413-422.

Horvath, A. (2001). The alliance. *Psychotherapy: Theory, Research, Practice, Training, 38,* 365-372.

Housman, L., & Stake, J. (1999). The current state of sexual ethics training in clinical psychology: Issues of quantity, quality, and effectiveness. *Professional Psychology: Research and Practice, 30,* 302-311.

Jacob-Timm, S. (1999). Ethically challenging situations encountered by school psychologists. *Psychology in the Schools, 36,* 205-217.

Johnson, W. B., & Campbell, C. (2002). Character and fitness requirements for professional psychologists: Are there any? *Professional Psychology: Research and Practice, 33,* 46-53.

Johnston, S., & Farber, B. (1996). The maintenance of boundaries in psychotherapeutic practice. *Psychotherapy: Theory, Research, Practice, Training, 33,* 391-402.

Kanner, A. (2000, February). Stuffing our kids: Should psychologists help advertisers manipulate children? *The California Psychologist,* pp. 24-25.

Kearney, E. (1998). Ethical dilemmas in the treatment of adolescent gang members. *Ethics and Behavior, 8,* 49-57.

Kimmel, A. (1998). In defense of deception. *American Psychologist, 53,* 803-804.

Kitchener, K. S. (1984). Intuition, critical evaluation, and ethical principles: The foundation for ethical decisions in counseling psychology. *The Counseling Psychologist, 12,* 43-55.

Kitchener, K. S. (2000). *Foundations of Ethical Practice, Research, and Teaching.* Mahwah, NJ: Erlbaum.

Knapp, S., VandeCreek, L., & Tepper, L. (2000). *Pennsylvania Law and Psychology* (3rd ed.). Harrisburg, PA: Pennsylvania Psychological Association.

Koocher, G., & Keith-Spiegel, P. (1998). *Ethics in Psychology* (2nd ed.). New York: Oxford University Press.

Kozlowski, N., Rupert, P., & Crawford, I. (1998). Psychotherapy with HIV-infected clients: Factors influencing notification of third parties. *Psychotherapy: Theory, Research, Practice, Training, 35,* 105-115.

Lam, A., & Sue, S. (2001). Client diversity. *Psychotherapy: Theory, Research, Practice, Training, 38,* 479-486.

Lamb, D., & Catanzaro, S. (1998). Sexual and nonsexual boundary violations involving psychologists, clients, supervisees, and students: Implications for professional practice. *Professional Psychology: Research and Practice, 29*, 498-503.

Lambert, M., & Barley, D. (2001). Research summary on the therapeutic relationship and psychotherapy outcome. *Psychotherapy: Theory, Research, Practice, Training, 38*, 357-361.

Lees-Haley, P., & Courtney, J. (2000). Disclosure of tests and raw data to the courts: A need for reform. *Neuropsychology Review, 10*, 169-174.

Martin, M. (2000). *Meaningful Work.* New York: Oxford University Press.

Martin, S. (1999, July/August). Revision of Ethics Committee calls for stronger former client sex roles. *APA Monitor*, p. 44.

Monahan, J., & Steadman, H. (1996). Violent storms and violent people: How meteorology can inform risk communication in mental health law. *American Psychologist, 51*, 931-938.

Monahan, J., Steadman, H., Appelbaum, P., Robins, P., Mulvey, E., Silver, E., Roth, L., & Grisso, T. (2000). Developing a clinically useful actuarial tool for assessing risk. *British Journal of Psychiatry, 176*, 312-319.

Nagy, T. (2000). *Ethics in Plain English.* Washington, DC: American Psychological Association.

National Computer Systems. (1995). Frequency of use for the MMPI/MMPI-2. Personal communication. Cited in Butcher, J. (1996, January). Of errors and questionable advice: A clarifying response to Gordon's evaluation of MMPI/MMPI-2. *Bulletin of the Colorado Psychological Association*, pp. 8-9.

Orne, D. R., & Doarman, A. L. (2001). Ethical dilemmas and U.S. Air Force clinical psychologists: A survey. *Professional Psychology: Research and Practice, 32*, 305-311.

Osheroff v. Chestnut Lodge, 490 A. 2d 720 (Md. App. 1985).

Otto, R. (2000). Assessing and managing violence risk in outpatient settings. *Journal of Clinical Psychology, 56*, 1239-1262.

Paxton, C., Lovett, J., & Riggs, M. (2001). The nature of professional training and perceptions of adequacy in dealing with sexual feelings in psychotherapy: Experiences of clinical faculty. *Ethics and Behavior, 11*, 175-189.

Pipes, R. (1997). Nonsexual relationships between psychotherapists and their former clients: Obligations of psychologists. *Ethics and Behavior, 7*, 27-41.

Pope, K. (1990). Ethical and malpractice issues in hospital practice. *American Psychologist, 45,* 1066-1070.

Pope, K. (1994). *Sexual Involvement With Therapists.* Washington, DC: American Psychological Association.

Pope, K., & Brown, L. (1996). *Recovered Memories of Abuse: Assessment, Therapy, Forensics.* Washington, DC: American Psychological Association.

Pope, K., Levenson, H., & Schover, L. (1979). Sexual intimacy in psychology training: Results and implications of a national survey. *American Psychologist, 34,* 682-689.

Pope, K., Sonne, J., & Holroyd, J. (1993). *Sexual Feelings in Psychotherapy.* Washington, DC: American Psychological Association.

Pope, K., Tabachnick, B., & Keith-Spiegel, P. (1987). Ethics of practice: The beliefs and behaviors of psychologists as therapists. *American Psychologist, 42,* 993-1006.

Pope, K. S., & Vetter, V. A. (1992). Ethical dilemmas encountered by members of the American Psychological Association. *American Psychologist, 47,* 397-411.

Procidano, M., Busch-Rossnagel, N., Reznikoff, M., & Geisinger, K. (1995). Responding to a graduate students' professional deficiencies: A national survey. *Journal of Clinical Psychology, 51,* 416-433.

Ragusea, S. A. (2002). A professional living will for psychologists and other mental health professionals. In L. VandeCreek & T. L. Jackson (Eds.), *Innovations in Clinical Practice: A Source Book* (Vol. 20, pp. 301-305). Sarasota, FL: Professional Resource Press.

Reaves, R. (2000, August 6). *Destroying Myths About Psychology Regulatory Boards.* Unpublished manuscript.

Report of the Ethics Committee, 1996. (1997). *American Psychologist, 52,* 897-905.

Report of the Ethics Committee, 1997. (1998). *American Psychologist, 53,* 969-980.

Report of the Ethics Committee, 1998. (1999). *American Psychologist, 54,* 701-710.

Report of the Ethics Committee, 1999. (2000). *American Psychologist, 55,* 207-214.

Report of the Ethics Committee, 2000. (2001). *American Psychologist, 56,* 680-688.

Richards, P. S., & Potts, R. (1995). Using spiritual interventions in psychotherapy: Practices, successes, failures, and ethical concerns of Mormon psychotherapists. *Professional Psychology: Research and Practice, 26,* 163-170.

Roberts, L. W., Battaglia, J., & Epstein, R. (1999). Frontier ethics: Mental health care needs and ethical dilemmas in rural communities, *Psychiatric Services, 50*, 497-503.

Robinson, W., & Reid, P. (1985). Sexual intimacies in psychotherapy revisited. *Professional Psychology: Research and Practice, 16*, 512-520.

Samuel, S., & Gorton, G. (1998). National survey of psychology internship directors regarding education for prevention of psychologist-patient sexual exploitation. *Professional Psychology: Research and Practice, 29*, 86-90.

Sandifer, B. (1989, September). Dual relationships: Ethical hazards in small-town practice. *Mississippi Psychologist*, p. 7.

Santiago-Rivera, A., & Altarriba, J. (2002). The role of language in therapy with the Spanish-English bilingual client. *Professional Psychology: Research and Practice, 33*, 30-38.

Schank, J., & Skovholt, T. (1997). Dual-relationship dilemmas of rural and small-community psychologists. *Professional Psychology: Research and Practice, 28*, 44-49.

Schoener, G. R. (1999). Preventive and remedial boundaries training for helping professionals and clergy: Successful approaches and useful tools. *Journal of Sex Education and Therapy, 24*, 209-217.

Shadish, W. (1994). APA Ethics and student authorship in master's theses. *The American Psychologist, 49*, 1096.

Simon, R. (1992). *Clinical Psychiatry and the Law* (2nd ed.). Washington, DC: American Psychiatric Press.

Somer, E., & Saadon, M. (1999). Therapist-client sex: Retrospective reports. *Professional Psychology: Theory and Practice, 30*, 504-509.

Steering Committee. (2001). Empirically supported therapy relationships: Conclusions and recommendations of the Division 29 Task Force. *Psychotherapy: Theory, Research, Practice, Training, 38*, 495-497.

Stromberg, D., Stone, G., & Claiborn, C. (1993). Informed consent: Therapists' beliefs and practices. *Professional Psychology: Research and Practice, 24*, 153-159.

Sullivan, L., & Ogloff, J. (1998). Appropriate supervisor-graduate student relationships. *Ethics and Behavior, 8*, 229-248.

Sullivan, T., Martin, W., & Handelsman, M. (1993). Practical benefits of an informed-consent procedure: An empirical investigation. *Professional Psychology: Research and Practice, 24*, 160-163.

Tarasoff v. Regents of the University of California et al., 551 P. 2d 334 (Cal. S. Ct. 1976).

Taylor, B. J., & Wagner, N. W. (1976). Sex between therapists and clients: A review and analysis. *Professional Psychology, 7*, 593-601.

Templeman, T. (1992, Summer). Dual relationships and extra therapy contacts between Oregon psychologists and their clients. *Oregon Psychologist,* pp. 16-19.

Thoreson, R., Miller, M., & Krauskopf, C. (1989). The distressed psychologists: Prevalence and treatment considerations. *Professional Psychology: Research and Practice, 20*, 153-158.

Tryon, G. (2001). School psychology students' beliefs about their preparation and concern with ethical issues. *Ethics and Behavior, 11*, 375-394.

Tubbs, P., & Pomerantz, A. (2001). Ethical behaviors of psychologists: Changes since 1987. *Journal of Clinical Psychology, 57*, 395-399.

Turner, S., DeMers, S., Fox, H. R., & Reed, G. (2001). APA Guidelines for Test User Qualifications: An Executive Summary. *American Psychologist, 56*, 1099-1113.

VandeCreek, L., & Knapp, S. (2001). *Tarasoff and Beyond* (3rd ed.). Sarasota, FL: Professional Resources Press.

Vasquez, M. (1994). Implications of the 1992 Ethics Code for the practice of individual psychotherapy. *Professional Psychology: Research and Practice, 25*, 321-328.

Weinberger, L., & Sreenivasan, S. (1994). Ethical and professional conflicts in correctional psychology. *Professional Psychology: Research and Practice, 25*, 161-167.

White v. North Carolina, 388 S. E. 2d 148 (1990), *review denied,* 393 S. E. 2d 891 (1990).

Woody, R. H. (1998). Bartering for psychological services. *Professional Psychology: Research and Practice, 29*, 174-178.

Woody, R. H. (2000, April). Risk management and office personnel. *The Louisiana Psychologist, 13*, 15.

 **APPENDICES**

Appendix A

APA Guidelines*

- APA's General Guidelines for Providers of Psychological Services (1987)

- Guidelines for Providers of Psychological Services to Ethnic, Linguistic, and Culturally Diverse Populations (1990)

- Record Keeping Guidelines (1993)

- Guidelines for Child Custody Evaluations in Divorce Proceedings (1994)

- Guidelines for Ethical Conduct in the Care and Use of Animals (1996)

- Guidelines for the Evaluation of Dementia and Age-Related Cognitive Decline (1998)

- Guidelines for Psychological Evaluations in Child Protection Matters (1998)

- Guidelines for Psychotherapy With Lesbian, Gay, and Bisexual Clients (2000)

- Guidelines on Multicultural Education, Training, Research, Practice, and Organizational Change for Psychologists (2002)

---

*APA Division 41 (Forensic Psychology/American Psychology-Law Society) Specialty Guidelines for Forensic Psychologists (1991) were referenced in the 1992 Ethics Code but were never formally adopted by the APA Council of Representatives.

Appendix B

Policy Statements From the
APA Ethics Committee*

Policy	American Psychologist
"Take Home" Tests	July 1994, p. 665
Advertisements and Canned Columns	July 1994, p. 664
Internship Applications and Confidential Materials	July 1994, p. 664
Military Psychologists and Confidentiality	July 1994, p. 665
Limitations on Testing	August 1995, p. 713
Referrals and Fees	August 1995, p. 713
Services by Telephone, Teleconferencing, and Internet	August 1998, p. 979
Policy on Barring Resignations During Ethics Investigations	November 1997, p. 1253; and December 1997, p. 1388

*From Report of the Ethics Committee, 2000. *American Psychologist, 56*, 680-688 (2001). Copies of these policy statements can be found at the Ethics Office page of the APA Website, http://www.apa.org/ethics/

Appendix C

Definitions in the Ethics Code

Barter: *"The acceptance of goods, services, or other nonmonetary remuneration from clients/patients in return for psychological services."* (6.05)

Multiple Relationships: *"When a psychologist is in a professional role with a person and (1) at the same time is in another role with the same person, (2) at the same time is in a relationship with a person closely associated with or related to the person with whom they have the professional relationship, or (3) promises to enter into another relationship in the future with the person or a person closely associated with or related to the person."* (3.05a)

Public Statements: *"Include but are not limited to paid or unpaid advertising, product endorsements, grant applications, licensing applications, other credentialing applications, brochures, printed matter, directory listings, personal resumes or curriculum vitae, or comments for use in media such as print or electronic transmission, statements in legal proceedings, lectures and public oral presentations, and published materials."* (5.01a)

Reasonable: *"The prevailing professional judgment of psychologists engaged in similar activities in similar circumstances, given the knowledge the psychologist had or should have had at the time."* (Introduction and Applicability)

Sexual Harassment: *"Sexual solicitation, physical advances, or verbal or nonverbal conduct that is sexual in nature, that occurs in connection with the psychologist's activities or roles as a psychologist, and that either (1) is unwelcome, is offensive, or creates a hostile workplace or educational environment, and the psychologist knows or is told this or (2) is sufficiently severe or intense to be abusive to a reasonable person in the context. Sexual harassment can consist of a single intense or severe act or of multiple persistent or pervasive acts."* (3.02)

Test Data: *"Refers to raw and scaled scores, client/patient responses to test questions or stimuli, and psychologists' notes and recordings concerning client/patient statements and behavior during an examination. Those portions of test materials that include client/patient responses are included in the definition of 'test data'."* (9.04a)

Test Materials: *"Refers to manuals, instruments, protocols, and test questions or stimuli and does not include 'test data' as defined in Standard 9.04, Release of Test Data."* (9.11)

Appendix D

Ethical Principles of Psychologists and Code of Conduct 2002*

History and Effective Date. This version of the APA Ethics Code was adopted by the American Psychological Association's Council of Representatives during its meeting, August 21, 2002, and is effective beginning June 1, 2003. Inquiries concerning the substance or interpretation of the APA Ethics Code should be addressed to the Director, Office of Ethics, American Psychological Association, 750 First Street, NE, Washington, DC 20002-4242. The Ethics Code and information regarding the Code can be found on the APA web site, http://www.apa.org/ethics. The standards in this Ethics Code will be used to adjudicate complaints brought concerning alleged conduct occurring on or after the effective date. Complaints regarding conduct occurring prior to the effective date will be adjudicated on the basis of the version of the Ethics Code that was in effect at the time the conduct occurred.

The APA has previously published its Ethics Code as follows:

American Psychological Association. (1953). *Ethical Standards of Psychologists.* Washington, DC: Author.

American Psychological Association. (1959). Ethical standards of psychologists. *American Psychologist, 14,* 279-282.

American Psychological Association. (1963). Ethical standards of psychologists. *American Psychologist, 18,* 56-60.

American Psychological Association. (1968). Ethical standards of psychologists. *American Psychologist, 23,* 357-361.

American Psychological Association. (1977, March). Ethical standards of psychologists. *APA Monitor,* pp. 22-23.

American Psychological Association. (1979). *Ethical Standards of Psychologists.* Washington, DC: Author.

American Psychological Association. (1981). Ethical principles of psychologists. *American Psychologist, 36,* 633-638.

American Psychological Association. (1990). Ethical principles of psychologists (Amended June 2, 1989). *American Psychologist, 45,* 390-395.

American Psychological Association. (1992). Ethical principles of psychologists and code of conduct. *American Psychologist, 47,* 1597-1611.

Request copies of the APA's *Ethical Principles of Psychologists and Code of Conduct* from the APA Order Department, 750 First Street, NE, Washington, DC 20002-4242, or phone (202) 336-5510.

INTRODUCTION AND APPLICABILITY

The American Psychological Association's (APA's) Ethical Principles of Psychologists and Code of Conduct (hereinafter referred to as the Ethics Code) consists of an Introduction, a Preamble, five General Principles (A–E), and specific Ethical Standards. The Introduction discusses the intent, organization, procedural considerations, and scope of application of the Ethics Code. The Preamble and General Principles are aspirational goals to guide psychologists toward the highest ideals of psychology. Although the Preamble and General Principles are not themselves enforceable rules, they should be considered by psychologists in arriving at an ethical course

---

*Note. From "Ethical Principles of Psychologists and Code of Conduct" by the American Psychological Association. Copyright © 2002 by the American Psychological Association. Reprinted with permission.

of action. The Ethical Standards set forth enforceable rules for conduct as psychologists. Most of the Ethical Standards are written broadly, in order to apply to psychologists in varied roles, although the application of an Ethical Standard may vary depending on the context. The Ethical Standards are not exhaustive. The fact that a given conduct is not specifically addressed by an Ethical Standard does not mean that it is necessarily either ethical or unethical.

This Ethics Code applies only to psychologists' activities that are part of their scientific, educational, or professional roles as psychologists. Areas covered include but are not limited to the clinical, counseling, and school practice of psychology; research; teaching; supervision of trainees; public service; policy development; social intervention; development of assessment instruments; conducting assessments; educational counseling; organizational consulting; forensic activities; program design and evaluation; and administration. This Ethics Code applies to these activities across a variety of contexts, such as in person, postal, telephone, internet, and other electronic transmissions. These activities shall be distinguished from the purely private conduct of psychologists, which is not within the purview of the Ethics Code.

Membership in the APA commits members and student affiliates to comply with the standards of the APA Ethics Code and to the rules and procedures used to enforce them. Lack of awareness or misunderstanding of an Ethical Standard is not itself a defense to a charge of unethical conduct.

The procedures for filing, investigating, and resolving complaints of unethical conduct are described in the current Rules and Procedures of the APA Ethics Committee. APA may impose sanctions on its members for violations of the standards of the Ethics Code, including termination of APA membership, and may notify other bodies and individuals of its actions. Actions that violate the standards of the Ethics Code may also lead to the imposition of sanctions on psychologists or students whether or not they are APA members by bodies other than APA, including state psychological associations, other professional groups, psychology boards, other state or federal agencies, and payors for health services. In addition, APA may take action against a member after his or her conviction of a felony, expulsion or suspension from an affiliated state psychological association, or suspension or loss of licensure. When the sanction to be imposed by APA is less than expulsion, the 2001 Rules and Procedures do not guarantee an opportunity for an in-person hearing, but generally provide that complaints will be resolved only on the basis of a submitted record.

The Ethics Code is intended to provide guidance for psychologists and standards of professional conduct that can be applied by the APA and by other bodies that choose to adopt them. The Ethics Code is not intended to be a basis of civil liability. Whether a psychologist has violated the Ethics Code standards does not by itself determine whether the psychologist is legally liable in a court action, whether a contract is enforceable, or whether other legal consequences occur.

The modifiers used in some of the standards of this Ethics Code (e.g., *reasonably, appropriate, potentially*) are included in the standards when they would (1) allow professional judgment on the part of psychologists, (2) eliminate injustice or inequality that would occur without the modifier, (3) ensure applicability across the broad range of activities conducted by psychologists, or (4) guard against a set of rigid rules that might be quickly outdated. As used in this Ethics Code, the term *reasonable* means the prevailing professional judgment of psychologists engaged in similar activities in similar circumstances, given the knowledge the psychologist had or should have had at the time.

In the process of making decisions regarding their professional behavior, psychologists must consider this Ethics Code in addition to applicable laws and psychology board regulations. In applying the Ethics Code to their professional work, psychologists may consider other materials and guidelines that have been adopted or endorsed by scientific and professional psychological organizations and the dictates of their own conscience, as well as consult with others within the field. If this Ethics Code establishes a higher standard of conduct than is required by law, psychologists must meet the higher ethical standard. If psychologists' ethical responsibilities conflict with law, regulations, or other governing legal authority, psychologists make known their commitment to this Ethics Code and take steps to resolve the conflict in a responsible manner. If the conflict is unresolvable via such means, psychologists may adhere to the requirements of the law, regulations, or other governing authority in keeping with basic principles of human rights.

PREAMBLE

Psychologists are committed to increasing scientific and professional knowledge of behavior and people's understanding of themselves and others and to the use of such knowledge to improve the condition of individuals, organizations, and society. Psychologists respect and protect civil and human rights and the central importance of freedom of inquiry and expression in research, teaching, and publication. They strive to help the public in developing informed judgments and choices concerning human behavior. In doing so, they perform many roles, such as researcher, educator, diagnostician, therapist, supervisor, consultant, administrator, social interventionist, and expert witness. This Ethics Code provides a common set of principles and standards upon which psychologists build their professional and scientific work.

This Ethics Code is intended to provide specific standards to cover most situations encountered by psychologists. It has as its goals the welfare and protection of the individuals and groups with whom psychologists work and the education of members, students, and the public regarding ethical standards of the discipline.

The development of a dynamic set of ethical standards for psychologists' work-related conduct requires a personal commitment and lifelong effort to act ethically; to encourage ethical behavior by students, supervisees, employees, and colleagues; and to consult with others concerning ethical problems.

GENERAL PRINCIPLES

This section consists of General Principles. General Principles, as opposed to Ethical Standards, are aspirational in nature. Their intent is to guide and inspire psychologists toward the very highest ethical ideals of the profession. General Principles, in contrast to Ethical Standards, do not represent obligations and should not form the basis for imposing sanctions. Relying upon General Principles for either of these reasons distorts both their meaning and purpose.

Principle A: Beneficence and Nonmaleficence

Psychologists strive to benefit those with whom they work and take care to do no harm. In their professional actions, psychologists seek to safeguard the welfare and rights of those with whom they interact professionally and other affected persons, and the welfare of animal subjects of research. When conflicts occur among psychologists' obligations or concerns, they attempt to resolve these conflicts in a responsible fashion that avoids or minimizes harm. Because psychologists' scientific and professional judgments and actions may affect the lives of others, they are alert to and guard against personal, financial, social, organizational, or political factors that might lead to misuse of their influence. Psychologists strive to be aware of the possible effect of their own physical and mental health on their ability to help those with whom they work.

Principle B: Fidelity and Responsibility

Psychologists establish relationships of trust with those with whom they work. They are aware of their professional and scientific responsibilities to society and to the specific communities in which they work. Psychologists uphold professional standards of conduct, clarify their professional roles and obligations, accept appropriate responsibility for their behavior, and seek to manage conflicts of interest that could lead to exploitation or harm. Psychologists consult with, refer to, or cooperate with other professionals and institutions to the extent needed to serve the best interests of those with whom they work. They are concerned about the ethical compliance of their colleagues' scientific and professional conduct. Psychologists strive to contribute a portion of their professional time for little or no compensation or personal advantage.

Principle C: Integrity

Psychologists seek to promote accuracy, honesty, and truthfulness in the science, teaching, and practice of psychology. In these activities psychologists do not steal, cheat, or engage in fraud, subterfuge, or intentional misrepresentation of fact. Psychologists strive to keep their promises and to avoid unwise or unclear commitments. In situations in which deception may be ethically justifiable to maximize benefits and minimize harm, psychologists have a serious obligation to consider the need for, the possible consequences of, and their responsibility to correct any resulting mistrust or other harmful effects that arise from the use of such techniques.

Principle D: Justice

Psychologists recognize that fairness and justice entitle all persons to access to and benefit from the contributions of psychology and to equal quality in the processes, procedures, and services being conducted by psychologists. Psychologists exercise reasonable judgment and take precautions to ensure that their potential biases, the boundaries of their competence, and the limitations of their expertise do not lead to or condone unjust practices.

Principle E: Respect for People's Rights and Dignity

Psychologists respect the dignity and worth of all people, and the rights of individuals to privacy, confidentiality, and self-determination. Psychologists are aware that special safeguards may be necessary to protect the rights and welfare of persons or communities whose vulnerabilities impair autonomous decision making. Psychologists are aware of and respect cultural, individual, and role differences, including those based on age, gender, gender identity, race, ethnicity, culture, national origin, religion, sexual orientation, disability, language, and socioeconomic status and consider these factors when working with members of such groups. Psychologists try to eliminate the effect on their work of biases based on those factors, and they do not knowingly participate in or condone activities of others based upon such prejudices.

ETHICAL STANDARDS

1. Resolving Ethical Issues

1.01   Misuse of Psychologists' Work

If psychologists learn of misuse or misrepresentation of their work, they take reasonable steps to correct or minimize the misuse or misrepresentation.

1.02   Conflicts Between Ethics and Law, Regulations, or Other Governing Legal Authority

If psychologists' ethical responsibilities conflict with law, regulations, or other governing legal authority, psychologists make known their commitment to the Ethics Code and take steps to resolve the conflict. If the conflict is unresolvable via such means, psychologists may adhere to the requirements of the law, regulations, or other governing legal authority.

1.03   Conflicts Between Ethics and Organizational Demands

If the demands of an organization with which psychologists are affiliated or for whom they are working conflict with this Ethics Code, psychologists clarify the nature of the conflict, make known their commitment to the Ethics Code, and to the extent feasible, resolve the conflict in a way that permits adherence to the Ethics Code.

1.04   Informal Resolution of Ethical Violations

When psychologists believe that there may have been an ethical violation by another psychologist, they attempt to resolve the issue by bringing it to the attention of that individual, if an informal resolution appears appropriate and the intervention does not violate any confidentiality rights that may be involved. (See also Standards 1.02, Conflicts Between Ethics and Law, Regulations, or Other Governing Legal Authority, and 1.03, Conflicts Between Ethics and Organizational Demands.)

1.05   Reporting Ethical Violations

If an apparent ethical violation has substantially harmed or is likely to substantially harm a person or organization and is not appropriate for informal resolution under Standard 1.04, Informal Resolution of Ethical Violations, or is not resolved properly in that fashion, psychologists take further action appropriate to the situation. Such action might include referral to state or national committees on professional ethics, to state licensing boards, or to the appropriate institutional authorities. This standard does not apply when an intervention would violate confidentiality rights or when psychologists have been retained to review the work of another psychologist whose professional conduct is in question. (See also Standard 1.02, Conflicts Between Ethics and Law, Regulations, or Other Governing Legal Authority.)

1.06   Cooperating With Ethics Committees

Psychologists cooperate in ethics investigations, proceedings, and resulting requirements of the APA or any affiliated state psychological association to which they belong. In doing so, they address any confidentiality issues. Failure to cooperate is itself an ethics violation. However, making a request for deferment of adjudication of an ethics complaint pending the outcome of litigation does not alone constitute noncooperation.

1.07   Improper Complaints

Psychologists do not file or encourage the filing of ethics complaints that are made with reckless disregard for or willful ignorance of facts that would disprove the allegation.

1.08   Unfair Discrimination Against Complainants and Respondents

Psychologists do not deny persons employment, advancement, admissions to academic or other programs, tenure, or promotion, based solely upon their having made or their being the subject of an ethics complaint. This does not preclude taking action based upon the outcome of such proceedings or considering other appropriate information.

2. Competence

2.01   Boundaries of Competence

(a) Psychologists provide services, teach, and conduct research with populations and in areas only within the boundaries of their competence, based on their education, training, supervised experience, consultation, study, or professional experience.

(b) Where scientific or professional knowledge in the discipline of psychology establishes that an understanding of factors associated with age, gender, gender identity, race, ethnicity, culture, national origin, religion, sexual orientation, disability, language, or socioeconomic status is essential for effective implementation of their services or research, psychologists have or obtain the training, experience, consultation, or supervision necessary to ensure the competence of their services, or they make appropriate referrals, except as provided in Standard 2.02, Providing Services in Emergencies.

(c) Psychologists planning to provide services, teach, or conduct research involving populations, areas, techniques, or technologies new to them undertake relevant education, training, supervised experience, consultation, or study.

(d) When psychologists are asked to provide services to individuals for whom appropriate mental health services are not available and for which psychologists have not obtained the competence necessary, psychologists with closely related prior training or experience may provide such services in order to ensure that services are not denied if they make a reasonable effort to obtain the competence required by using relevant research, training, consultation, or study.

(e) In those emerging areas in which generally recognized standards for preparatory training do not yet exist, psychologists nevertheless take reasonable steps to ensure the competence of their work and to protect clients/patients, students, supervisees, research participants, organizational clients, and others from harm.

(f) When assuming forensic roles, psychologists are or become reasonably familiar with the judicial or administrative rules governing their roles.

2.02 Providing Services in Emergencies

In emergencies, when psychologists provide services to individuals for whom other mental health services are not available and for which psychologists have not obtained the necessary training, psychologists may provide such services in order to ensure that services are not denied. The services are discontinued as soon as the emergency has ended or appropriate services are available.

2.03 Maintaining Competence

Psychologists undertake ongoing efforts to develop and maintain their competence.

2.04 Bases for Scientific and Professional Judgments

Psychologists' work is based upon established scientific and professional knowledge of the discipline. (See also Standards 2.01e, Boundaries of Competence, and 10.01b, Informed Consent to Therapy.)

2.05 Delegation of Work to Others

Psychologists who delegate work to employees, supervisees, or research or teaching assistants or who use the services of others, such as interpreters, take reasonable steps to (1) avoid delegating such work to persons who have a multiple relationship with those being served that would likely lead to exploitation or loss of objectivity; (2) authorize only those responsibilities that such persons can be expected to perform competently on the basis of their education, training, or experience, either independently or with the level of supervision being provided; and (3) see that such persons perform these services competently. (See also Standards 2.02, Providing Services in Emergencies; 3.05, Multiple Relationships; 4.01, Maintaining Confidentiality; 9.01, Bases for Assessments; 9.02, Use of Assessments; 9.03, Informed Consent in Assessments; and 9.07, Assessment by Unqualified Persons.)

2.06   **Personal Problems and Conflicts**

(a) Psychologists refrain from initiating an activity when they know or should know that there is a substantial likelihood that their personal problems will prevent them from performing their work-related activities in a competent manner.

(b) When psychologists become aware of personal problems that may interfere with their performing work-related duties adequately, they take appropriate measures, such as obtaining professional consultation or assistance, and determine whether they should limit, suspend, or terminate their work-related duties. (See also Standard 10.10, Terminating Therapy.)

3. Human Relations

3.01   **Unfair Discrimination**

In their work-related activities, psychologists do not engage in unfair discrimination based on age, gender, gender identity, race, ethnicity, culture, national origin, religion, sexual orientation, disability, socioeconomic status, or any basis proscribed by law.

3.02   **Sexual Harassment**

Psychologists do not engage in sexual harassment. Sexual harassment is sexual solicitation, physical advances, or verbal or nonverbal conduct that is sexual in nature, that occurs in connection with the psychologist's activities or roles as a psychologist, and that either (1) is unwelcome, is offensive, or creates a hostile workplace or educational environment, and the psychologist knows or is told this or (2) is sufficiently severe or intense to be abusive to a reasonable person in the context. Sexual harassment can consist of a single intense or severe act or of multiple persistent or pervasive acts. (See also Standard 1.08, Unfair Discrimination Against Complainants and Respondents.)

3.03   **Other Harassment**

Psychologists do not knowingly engage in behavior that is harassing or demeaning to persons with whom they interact in their work based on factors such as those persons' age, gender, gender identity, race, ethnicity, culture, national origin, religion, sexual orientation, disability, language, or socioeconomic status.

3.04   **Avoiding Harm**

Psychologists take reasonable steps to avoid harming their clients/patients, students, supervisees, research participants, organizational clients, and others with whom they work, and to minimize harm where it is foreseeable and unavoidable.

3.05   Multiple Relationships

(a)   A multiple relationship occurs when a psychologist is in a professional role with a person and (1) at the same time is in another role with the same person, (2) at the same time is in a relationship with a person closely associated with or related to the person with whom the psychologist has the professional relationship, or (3) promises to enter into another relationship in the future with the person or a person closely associated with or related to the person.

A psychologist refrains from entering into a multiple relationship if the multiple relationship could reasonably be expected to impair the psychologist's objectivity, competence, or effectiveness in performing his or her functions as a psychologist, or otherwise risks exploitation or harm to the person with whom the professional relationship exists.

Multiple relationships that would not reasonably be expected to cause impairment or risk exploitation or harm are not unethical.

(b)   If a psychologist finds that, due to unforeseen factors, a potentially harmful multiple relationship has arisen, the psychologist takes reasonable steps to resolve it with due regard for the best interests of the affected person and maximal compliance with the Ethics Code.

(c)   When psychologists are required by law, institutional policy, or extraordinary circumstances to serve in more than one role in judicial or administrative proceedings, at the outset they clarify role expectations and the extent of confidentiality and thereafter as changes occur. (See also Standards 3.04, Avoiding Harm, and 3.07, Third-Party Requests for Services.)

3.06   Conflict of Interest

Psychologists refrain from taking on a professional role when personal, scientific, professional, legal, financial, or other interests or relationships could reasonably be expected to (1) impair their objectivity, competence, or effectiveness in performing their functions as psychologists or (2) expose the person or organization with whom the professional relationship exists to harm or exploitation.

3.07   Third-Party Requests for Services

When psychologists agree to provide services to a person or entity at the request of a third party, psychologists attempt to clarify at the outset of the service the nature of the relationship with all individuals or organizations involved. This clarification includes the role of the psychologist (e.g., therapist, consultant, diagnostician, or expert witness), an identification of who is the client, the probable uses of the services provided or the information obtained, and the fact that there may be limits to confidentiality. (See also Standards 3.05, Multiple Relationships, and 4.02, Discussing the Limits of Confidentiality.)

3.08   Exploitative Relationships

Psychologists do not exploit persons over whom they have supervisory, evaluative, or other authority such as clients/patients, students, supervisees, research participants, and employees. (See also Standards 3.05, Multiple Relationships; 6.04, Fees and Financial Arrangements; 6.05, Barter With Clients/Patients; 7.07, Sexual Relationships With Students and Supervisees; 10.05, Sexual Intimacies With Current Therapy Clients/Patients; 10.06, Sexual Intimacies With Relatives or Significant Others of Current Therapy Clients/Patients; 10.07, Therapy With Former Sexual Partners; and 10.08, Sexual Intimacies With Former Therapy Clients/Patients.)

3.09   Cooperation With Other Professionals

When indicated and professionally appropriate, psychologists cooperate with other professionals in order to serve their clients/patients effectively and appropriately. (See also Standard 4.05, Disclosures.)

3.10   Informed Consent

(a)   When psychologists conduct research or provide assessment, therapy, counseling, or consulting services in person or via electronic transmission or other forms of communication, they obtain the informed consent of the individual or individuals using language that is reasonably understandable to that person or persons except when conducting such activities without consent is mandated by law or governmental regulation or as otherwise provided in this Ethics Code. (See also Standards 8.02, Informed Consent to Research; 9.03, Informed Consent in Assessments; and 10.01, Informed Consent to Therapy.)

(b)   For persons who are legally incapable of giving informed consent, psychologists nevertheless (1) provide an appropriate explanation, (2) seek the individual's assent, (3) consider such persons' preferences and best interests, and (4) obtain appropriate permission from a legally authorized person, if such substitute consent is permitted or required by law. When consent by a legally authorized person is not permitted or required by law, psychologists take reasonable steps to protect the individual's rights and welfare.

(c)   When psychological services are court ordered or otherwise mandated, psychologists inform the individual of the nature of the anticipated services, including whether the services are court ordered or mandated and any limits of confidentiality, before proceeding.

(d)   Psychologists appropriately document written or oral consent, permission, and assent. (See also Standards 8.02, Informed Consent to Research; 9.03, Informed Consent in Assessments; and 10.01, Informed Consent to Therapy.)

3.11   Psychological Services Delivered To or Through Organizations

(a)   Psychologists delivering services to or through organizations provide information beforehand to clients and when appropriate those directly affected by the services about (1) the nature and objectives of the services, (2) the intended recipients, (3) which of the individuals are clients, (4) the relationship the psychologist will have with each person and the organization, (5) the probable uses of services provided and information obtained, (6) who will have access to the information, and (7) limits of confidentiality. As soon as feasible, they provide information about the results and conclusions of such services to appropriate persons.

(b) If psychologists will be precluded by law or by organizational roles from providing such information to particular individuals or groups, they so inform those individuals or groups at the outset of the service.

3.12   Interruption of Psychological Services

Unless otherwise covered by contract, psychologists make reasonable efforts to plan for facilitating services in the event that psychological services are interrupted by factors such as the psychologist's illness, death, unavailability, relocation, or retirement or by the client's/patient's relocation or financial limitations. (See also Standard 6.02c, Maintenance, Dissemination, and Disposal of Confidential Records of Professional and Scientific Work.)

4. Privacy And Confidentiality

4.01   Maintaining Confidentiality

Psychologists have a primary obligation and take reasonable precautions to protect confidential information obtained through or stored in any medium, recognizing that the extent and limits of confidentiality may be regulated by law or established by institutional rules or professional or scientific relationship. (See also Standard 2.05, Delegation of Work to Others.)

4.02   Discussing the Limits of Confidentiality

(a) Psychologists discuss with persons (including, to the extent feasible, persons who are legally incapable of giving informed consent and their legal representatives) and organizations with whom they establish a scientific or professional relationship (1) the relevant limits of confidentiality and (2) the foreseeable uses of the information generated through their psychological activities. (See also Standard 3.10, Informed Consent.)

(b) Unless it is not feasible or is contraindicated, the discussion of confidentiality occurs at the outset of the relationship and thereafter as new circumstances may warrant.

(c) Psychologists who offer services, products, or information via electronic transmission inform clients/patients of the risks to privacy and limits of confidentiality.

4.03   Recording

Before recording the voices or images of individuals to whom they provide services, psychologists obtain permission from all such persons or their legal representatives. (See also Standards 8.03, Informed Consent for Recording Voices and Images in Research; 8.05, Dispensing With Informed Consent for Research; and 8.07, Deception in Research.)

4.04   Minimizing Intrusions on Privacy

(a)   Psychologists include in written and oral reports and consultations, only information germane to the purpose for which the communication is made.

(b)   Psychologists discuss confidential information obtained in their work only for appropriate scientific or professional purposes and only with persons clearly concerned with such matters.

4.05   Disclosures

(a)   Psychologists may disclose confidential information with the appropriate consent of the organizational client, the individual client/patient, or another legally authorized person on behalf of the client/patient unless prohibited by law.

(b)   Psychologists disclose confidential information without the consent of the individual only as mandated by law, or where permitted by law for a valid purpose such as to (1) provide needed professional services; (2) obtain appropriate professional consultations; (3) protect the client/patient, psychologist, or others from harm; or (4) obtain payment for services from a client/patient, in which instance disclosure is limited to the minimum that is necessary to achieve the purpose. (See also Standard 6.04e, Fees and Financial Arrangements.)

4.06   Consultations

When consulting with colleagues, (1) psychologists do not disclose confidential information that reasonably could lead to the identification of a client/patient, research participant, or other person or organization with whom they have a confidential relationship unless they have obtained the prior consent of the person or organization or the disclosure cannot be avoided, and (2) they disclose information only to the extent necessary to achieve the purposes of the consultation. (See also Standard 4.01, Maintaining Confidentiality.)

4.07   Use of Confidential Information for Didactic or Other Purposes

Psychologists do not disclose in their writings, lectures, or other public media, confidential, personally identifiable information concerning their clients/patients, students, research participants, organizational clients, or other recipients of their services that they obtained during the course of their work, unless (1) they take reasonable steps to disguise the person or organization, (2) the person or organization has consented in writing, or (3) there is legal authorization for doing so.

5. Advertising and Other Public Statements

5.01   Avoidance of False or Deceptive Statements

(a)   Public statements include but are not limited to paid or unpaid advertising, product endorsements, grant applications, licensing applications, other credentialing applications, brochures, printed matter, directory listings, personal resumes or curricula vitae, or comments for use in media such as print or electronic transmission, statements in legal proceedings, lectures and public oral presentations, and published materials. Psychologists do not knowingly make public statements that are false, deceptive, or fraudulent concerning their research, practice, or other work activities or those of persons or organizations with which they are affiliated.

(b) Psychologists do not make false, deceptive, or fraudulent statements concerning (1) their training, experience, or competence; (2) their academic degrees; (3) their credentials; (4) their institutional or association affiliations; (5) their services; (6) the scientific or clinical basis for, or results or degree of success of, their services; (7) their fees; or (8) their publications or research findings.

(c) Psychologists claim degrees as credentials for their health services only if those degrees (1) were earned from a regionally accredited educational institution or (2) were the basis for psychology licensure by the state in which they practice.

5.02 Statements by Others

(a) Psychologists who engage others to create or place public statements that promote their professional practice, products, or activities retain professional responsibility for such statements.

(b) Psychologists do not compensate employees of press, radio, television, or other communication media in return for publicity in a news item. (See also Standard 1.01, Misuse of Psychologists' Work.)

(c) A paid advertisement relating to psychologists' activities must be identified or clearly recognizable as such.

5.03 Descriptions of Workshops and Non-Degree-Granting Educational Programs

To the degree to which they exercise control, psychologists responsible for announcements, catalogs, brochures, or advertisements describing workshops, seminars, or other non-degree-granting educational programs ensure that they accurately describe the audience for which the program is intended, the educational objectives, the presenters, and the fees involved.

5.04 Media Presentations

When psychologists provide public advice or comment via print, internet, or other electronic transmission, they take precautions to ensure that statements (1) are based on their professional knowledge, training, or experience in accord with appropriate psychological literature and practice; (2) are otherwise consistent with this Ethics Code; and (3) do not indicate that a professional relationship has been established with the recipient. (See also Standard 2.04, Bases for Scientific and Professional Judgments.)

5.05   Testimonials

Psychologists do not solicit testimonials from current therapy clients/patients or other persons who because of their particular circumstances are vulnerable to undue influence.

5.06   In-Person Solicitation

Psychologists do not engage, directly or through agents, in uninvited in-person solicitation of business from actual or potential therapy clients/patients or other persons who because of their particular circumstances are vulnerable to undue influence. However, this prohibition does not preclude (1) attempting to implement appropriate collateral contacts for the purpose of benefiting an already engaged therapy client/patient or (2) providing disaster or community outreach services.

6. Record Keeping and Fees

6.01   Documentation of Professional and Scientific Work and Maintenance of Records

Psychologists create, and to the extent the records are under their control, maintain, disseminate, store, retain, and dispose of records and data relating to their professional and scientific work in order to (1) facilitate provision of services later by them or by other professionals, (2) allow for replication of research design and analyses, (3) meet institutional requirements, (4) ensure accuracy of billing and payments, and (5) ensure compliance with law. (See also Standard 4.01, Maintaining Confidentiality.)

6.02   Maintenance, Dissemination, and Disposal of Confidential Records of Professional and Scientific Work

(a) Psychologists maintain confidentiality in creating, storing, accessing, transferring, and disposing of records under their control, whether these are written, automated, or in any other medium. (See also Standards 4.01, Maintaining Confidentiality, and 6.01, Documentation of Professional and Scientific Work and Maintenance of Records.)

(b) If confidential information concerning recipients of psychological services is entered into databases or systems of records available to persons whose access has not been consented to by the recipient, psychologists use coding or other techniques to avoid the inclusion of personal identifiers.

(c) Psychologists make plans in advance to facilitate the appropriate transfer and to protect the confidentiality of records and data in the event of psychologists' withdrawal from positions or practice. (See also Standards 3.12, Interruption of Psychological Services, and 10.09, Interruption of Therapy.)

6.03   Withholding Records for Nonpayment

Psychologists may not withhold records under their control that are requested and needed for a client's/patient's emergency treatment solely because payment has not been received.

6.04   Fees and Financial Arrangements

(a)   As early as is feasible in a professional or scientific relationship, psychologists and recipients of psychological services reach an agreement specifying compensation and billing arrangements.
(b)   Psychologists' fee practices are consistent with law.
(c)   Psychologists do not misrepresent their fees.
(d)   If limitations to services can be anticipated because of limitations in financing, this is discussed with the recipient of services as early as is feasible. (See also Standards 10.09, Interruption of Therapy, and 10.10, Terminating Therapy.)
(e)   If the recipient of services does not pay for services as agreed, and if psychologists intend to use collection agencies or legal measures to collect the fees, psychologists first inform the person that such measures will be taken and provide that person an opportunity to make prompt payment. (See also Standards 4.05, Disclosures; 6.03, Withholding Records for Nonpayment; and 10.01, Informed Consent to Therapy.)

6.05   Barter With Clients/Patients

Barter is the acceptance of goods, services, or other nonmonetary remuneration from clients/patients in return for psychological services. Psychologists may barter only if (1) it is not clinically contraindicated, and (2) the resulting arrangement is not exploitative. (See also Standards 3.05, Multiple Relationships, and 6.04, Fees and Financial Arrangements.)

6.06   Accuracy in Reports to Payors and Funding Sources

In their reports to payors for services or sources of research funding, psychologists take reasonable steps to ensure the accurate reporting of the nature of the service provided or research conducted, the fees, charges, or payments, and where applicable, the identity of the provider, the findings, and the diagnosis. (See also Standards 4.01, Maintaining Confidentiality; 4.04, Minimizing Intrusions on Privacy; and 4.05, Disclosures.)

6.07   Referrals and Fees

When psychologists pay, receive payment from, or divide fees with another professional, other than in an employer-employee relationship, the payment to each is based on the services provided (clinical, consultative, administrative, or other) and is not based on the referral itself. (See also Standard 3.09, Cooperation With Other Professionals.)

7. Education and Training

7.01 Design of Education and Training Programs

Psychologists responsible for education and training programs take reasonable steps to ensure that the programs are designed to provide the appropriate knowledge and proper experiences, and to meet the requirements for licensure, certification, or other goals for which claims are made by the program. (See also Standard 5.03, Descriptions of Workshops and Non-Degree-Granting Educational Programs.)

7.02 Descriptions of Education and Training Programs

Psychologists responsible for education and training programs take reasonable steps to ensure that there is a current and accurate description of the program content (including participation in required course- or program-related counseling, psychotherapy, experiential groups, consulting projects, or community service), training goals and objectives, stipends and benefits, and requirements that must be met for satisfactory completion of the program. This information must be made readily available to all interested parties.

7.03 Accuracy in Teaching

(a) Psychologists take reasonable steps to ensure that course syllabi are accurate regarding the subject matter to be covered, bases for evaluating progress, and the nature of course experiences. This standard does not preclude an instructor from modifying course content or requirements when the instructor considers it pedagogically necessary or desirable, so long as students are made aware of these modifications in a manner that enables them to fulfill course requirements. (See also Standard 5.01, Avoidance of False or Deceptive Statements.)

(b) When engaged in teaching or training, psychologists present psychological information accurately. (See also Standard 2.03, Maintaining Competence.)

7.04 Student Disclosure of Personal Information

Psychologists do not require students or supervisees to disclose personal information in course- or program-related activities, either orally or in writing, regarding sexual history, history of abuse and neglect, psychological treatment, and relationships with parents, peers, and spouses or significant others except if (1) the program or training facility has clearly identified this requirement in its admissions and program materials or (2) the information is necessary to evaluate or obtain assistance for students whose personal problems could reasonably be judged to be preventing them from performing their training- or professionally related activities in a competent manner or posing a threat to the students or others.

7.05 Mandatory Individual or Group Therapy

(a) When individual or group therapy is a program or course requirement, psychologists responsible for that program allow students in undergraduate and graduate programs the option of selecting such therapy from practitioners unaffiliated with the program. (See also Standard 7.02, Descriptions of Education and Training Programs.)

(b) Faculty who are or are likely to be responsible for evaluating students' academic performance do not themselves provide that therapy. (See also Standard 3.05, Multiple Relationships.)

7.06 Assessing Student and Supervisee Performance

(a) In academic and supervisory relationships, psychologists establish a timely and specific process for providing feedback to students and supervisees. Information regarding the process is provided to the student at the beginning of supervision.

(b) Psychologists evaluate students and supervisees on the basis of their actual performance on relevant and established program requirements.

7.07   Sexual Relationships With Students and Supervisees

Psychologists do not engage in sexual relationships with students or supervisees who are in their department, agency, or training center or over whom psychologists have or are likely to have evaluative authority. (See also Standard 3.05, Multiple Relationships.)

8. Research and Publication

8.01   Institutional Approval

When institutional approval is required, psychologists provide accurate information about their research proposals and obtain approval prior to conducting the research. They conduct the research in accordance with the approved research protocol.

8.02   Informed Consent to Research

(a) When obtaining informed consent as required in Standard 3.10, Informed Consent, psychologists inform participants about (1) the purpose of the research, expected duration, and procedures; (2) their right to decline to participate and to withdraw from the research once participation has begun; (3) the foreseeable consequences of declining or withdrawing; (4) reasonably foreseeable factors that may be expected to influence their willingness to participate such as potential risks, discomfort, or adverse effects; (5) any prospective research benefits; (6) limits of confidentiality; (7) incentives for participation; and (8) whom to contact for questions about the research and research participants' rights. They provide opportunity for the prospective participants to ask questions and receive answers. (See also Standards 8.03, Informed Consent for Recording Voices and Images in Research; 8.05, Dispensing With Informed Consent for Research; and 8.07, Deception in Research.)

(b) Psychologists conducting intervention research involving the use of experimental treatments clarify to participants at the outset of the research (1) the experimental nature of the treatment; (2) the services that will or will not be available to the control group(s) if appropriate; (3) the means by which assignment to treatment and control groups will be made; (4) available treatment alternatives if an individual does not wish to participate in the research or wishes to withdraw once a study has begun; and (5) compensation for or monetary costs of participating including, if appropriate, whether reimbursement from the participant or a third-party payor will be sought. (See also Standard 8.02a, Informed Consent to Research.)

8.03 Informed Consent for Recording Voices and Images in Research

Psychologists obtain informed consent from research participants prior to recording their voices or images for data collection unless (1) the research consists solely of naturalistic observations in public places, and it is not anticipated that the recording will be used in a manner that could cause personal identification or harm, or (2) the research design includes deception, and consent for the use of the recording is obtained during debriefing. (See also Standard 8.07, Deception in Research.)

8.04 Client/Patient, Student, and Subordinate Research Participants

(a) When psychologists conduct research with clients/patients, students, or subordinates as participants, psychologists take steps to protect the prospective participants from adverse consequences of declining or withdrawing from participation.
(b) When research participation is a course requirement or an opportunity for extra credit, the prospective participant is given the choice of equitable alternative activities.

8.05 Dispensing With Informed Consent for Research

Psychologists may dispense with informed consent only (1) where research would not reasonably be assumed to create distress or harm and involves (a) the study of normal educational practices, curricula, or classroom management methods conducted in educational settings; (b) only anonymous questionnaires, naturalistic observations, or archival research for which disclosure of responses would not place participants at risk of criminal or civil liability or damage their financial standing, employability, or reputation, and confidentiality is protected; or (c) the study of factors related to job or organization effectiveness conducted in organizational settings for which there is no risk to participants' employability, and confidentiality is protected or (2) where otherwise permitted by law or federal or institutional regulations.

8.06 Offering Inducements for Research Participation

(a) Psychologists make reasonable efforts to avoid offering excessive or inappropriate financial or other inducements for research participation when such inducements are likely to coerce participation.

(b) When offering professional services as an inducement for research participation, psychologists clarify the nature of the services, as well as the risks, obligations, and limitations. (See also Standard 6.05, Barter With Clients/Patients.)

8.07 Deception in Research

(a) Psychologists do not conduct a study involving deception unless they have determined that the use of deceptive techniques is justified by the study's significant prospective scientific, educational, or applied value and that effective nondeceptive alternative procedures are not feasible.

(b) Psychologists do not deceive prospective participants about research that is reasonably expected to cause physical pain or severe emotional distress.

(c) Psychologists explain any deception that is an integral feature of the design and conduct of an experiment to participants as early as is feasible, preferably at the conclusion of their participation, but no later than at the conclusion of the data collection, and permit participants to withdraw their data. (See also Standard 8.08, Debriefing.)

8.08 Debriefing

(a) Psychologists provide a prompt opportunity for participants to obtain appropriate information about the nature, results, and conclusions of the research, and they take reasonable steps to correct any misconceptions that participants may have of which the psychologists are aware.

(b) If scientific or humane values justify delaying or withholding this information, psychologists take reasonable measures to reduce the risk of harm.

(c) When psychologists become aware that research procedures have harmed a participant, they take reasonable steps to minimize the harm.

8.09 Humane Care and Use of Animals in Research

(a) Psychologists acquire, care for, use, and dispose of animals in compliance with current federal, state, and local laws and regulations, and with professional standards.

(b) Psychologists trained in research methods and experienced in the care of laboratory animals supervise all procedures involving animals and are responsible for ensuring appropriate consideration of their comfort, health, and humane treatment.

(c) Psychologists ensure that all individuals under their supervision who are using animals have received instruction in research methods and in the care, maintenance, and handling of the species being used, to the extent appropriate to their role. (See also Standard 2.05, Delegation of Work to Others.)

(d) Psychologists make reasonable efforts to minimize the discomfort, infection, illness, and pain of animal subjects.

(e) Psychologists use a procedure subjecting animals to pain, stress, or privation only when an alternative procedure is unavailable and the goal is justified by its prospective scientific, educational, or applied value.

(f)   Psychologists perform surgical procedures under appropriate anesthesia and follow techniques to avoid infection and minimize pain during and after surgery.

(g)   When it is appropriate that an animal's life be terminated, psychologists proceed rapidly, with an effort to minimize pain and in accordance with accepted procedures.

8.10   Reporting Research Results

(a)   Psychologists do not fabricate data. (See also Standard 5.01a, Avoidance of False or Deceptive Statements.)

(b)   If psychologists discover significant errors in their published data, they take reasonable steps to correct such errors in a correction, retraction, erratum, or other appropriate publication means.

8.11   Plagiarism

Psychologists do not present portions of another's work or data as their own, even if the other work or data source is cited occasionally.

8.12   Publication Credit

(a)   Psychologists take responsibility and credit, including authorship credit, only for work they have actually performed or to which they have substantially contributed. (See also Standard 8.12b, Publication Credit.)

(b)   Principal authorship and other publication credits accurately reflect the relative scientific or professional contributions of the individuals involved, regardless of their relative status. Mere possession of an institutional position, such as department chair, does not justify authorship credit. Minor contributions to the research or to the writing for publications are acknowledged appropriately, such as in footnotes or in an introductory statement.

(c)   Except under exceptional circumstances, a student is listed as principal author on any multiple-authored article that is substantially based on the student's doctoral dissertation. Faculty advisors discuss publication credit with students as early as feasible and throughout the research and publication process as appropriate. (See also Standard 8.12b, Publication Credit.)

8.13   Duplicate Publication of Data

Psychologists do not publish, as original data, data that have been previously published. This does not preclude republishing data when they are accompanied by proper acknowledgment.

8.14   Sharing Research Data for Verification

(a)   After research results are published, psychologists do not withhold the data on which their conclusions are based from other competent professionals who seek to verify the substantive claims through reanalysis and who intend to use such data only for that purpose, provided that the confidentiality of the participants can be protected and unless legal rights concerning proprietary data preclude their release. This does not preclude psychologists from requiring that such individuals or groups be responsible for costs associated with the provision of such information.

(b) Psychologists who request data from other psychologists to verify the substantive claims through reanalysis may use shared data only for the declared purpose. Requesting psychologists obtain prior written agreement for all other uses of the data.

8.15 Reviewers

Psychologists who review material submitted for presentation, publication, grant, or research proposal review respect the confidentiality of and the proprietary rights in such information of those who submitted it.

9. Assessment

9.01 Bases for Assessments

(a) Psychologists base the opinions contained in their recommendations, reports, and diagnostic or evaluative statements, including forensic testimony, on information and techniques sufficient to substantiate their findings. (See also Standard 2.04, Bases for Scientific and Professional Judgments.)

(b) Except as noted in 9.01c, psychologists provide opinions of the psychological characteristics of individuals only after they have conducted an examination of the individuals adequate to support their statements or conclusions. When, despite reasonable efforts, such an examination is not practical, psychologists document the efforts they made and the result of those efforts, clarify the probable impact of their limited information on the reliability and validity of their opinions, and appropriately limit the nature and extent of their conclusions or recommendations. (See also Standards 2.01, Boundaries of Competence, and 9.06, Interpreting Assessment Results.)

(c) When psychologists conduct a record review or provide consultation or supervision and an individual examination is not warranted or necessary for the opinion, psychologists explain this and the sources of information on which they based their conclusions and recommendations.

9.02 Use of Assessments

(a) Psychologists administer, adapt, score, interpret, or use assessment techniques, interviews, tests, or instruments in a manner and for purposes that are appropriate in light of the research on or evidence of the usefulness and proper application of the techniques.

(b) Psychologists use assessment instruments whose validity and reliability have been established for use with members of the population tested. When such validity or reliability has not been established, psychologists describe the strengths and limitations of test results and interpretation.

(c) Psychologists use assessment methods that are appropriate to an individual's language preference and competence, unless the use of an alternative language is relevant to the assessment issues.

9.03   Informed Consent in Assessments

(a) Psychologists obtain informed consent for assessments, evaluations, or diagnostic services, as described in Standard 3.10, Informed Consent, except when (1) testing is mandated by law or governmental regulations; (2) informed consent is implied because testing is conducted as a routine educational, institutional, or organizational activity (e.g., when participants voluntarily agree to assessment when applying for a job); or (3) one purpose of the testing is to evaluate decisional capacity. Informed consent includes an explanation of the nature and purpose of the assessment, fees, involvement of third parties, and limits of confidentiality and sufficient opportunity for the client/patient to ask questions and receive answers.

(b) Psychologists inform persons with questionable capacity to consent or for whom testing is mandated by law or governmental regulations about the nature and purpose of the proposed assessment services, using language that is reasonably understandable to the person being assessed.

(c) Psychologists using the services of an interpreter obtain informed consent from the client/patient to use that interpreter, ensure that confidentiality of test results and test security are maintained, and include in their recommendations, reports, and diagnostic or evaluative statements, including forensic testimony, discussion of any limitations on the data obtained. (See also Standards 2.05, Delegation of Work to Others; 4.01, Maintaining Confidentiality; 9.01, Bases for Assessments; 9.06, Interpreting Assessment Results; and 9.07, Assessment by Unqualified Persons.)

9.04   Release of Test Data

(a) The term *test data* refers to raw and scaled scores, client/patient responses to test questions or stimuli, and psychologists' notes and recordings concerning client/patient statements and behavior during an examination. Those portions of test materials that include client/patient responses are included in the definition of *test data*. Pursuant to a client/patient release, psychologists provide test data to the client/patient or other persons identified in the release. Psychologists may refrain from releasing test data to protect a client/patient or others from substantial harm or misuse or misrepresentation of the data or the test, recognizing that in many instances release of confidential information under these circumstances is regulated by law. (See also Standard 9.11, Maintaining Test Security.)

(b) In the absence of a client/patient release, psychologists provide test data only as required by law or court order.

9.05   Test Construction

Psychologists who develop tests and other assessment techniques use appropriate psychometric procedures and current scientific or professional knowledge for test design, standardization, validation, reduction or elimination of bias, and recommendations for use.

9.06   Interpreting Assessment Results

When interpreting assessment results, including automated interpretations, psychologists take into account the purpose of the assessment as well as the various test factors, test-taking abilities, and other characteristics of the person being assessed, such as situational, personal, linguistic, and cultural differences, that might affect psychologists' judgments or reduce the accuracy of their interpretations. They indicate any significant limitations of their interpretations. (See also Standards 2.01b and c, Boundaries of Competence, and 3.01, Unfair Discrimination.)

9.07   Assessment by Unqualified Persons

Psychologists do not promote the use of psychological assessment techniques by unqualified persons, except when such use is conducted for training purposes with appropriate supervision. (See also Standard 2.05, Delegation of Work to Others.)

9.08   Obsolete Tests and Outdated Test Results

(a)   Psychologists do not base their assessment or intervention decisions or recommendations on data or test results that are outdated for the current purpose.

(b)   Psychologists do not base such decisions or recommendations on tests and measures that are obsolete and not useful for the current purpose.

9.09   Test Scoring and Interpretation Services

(a)   Psychologists who offer assessment or scoring services to other professionals accurately describe the purpose, norms, validity, reliability, and applications of the procedures and any special qualifications applicable to their use.

(b)   Psychologists select scoring and interpretation services (including automated services) on the basis of evidence of the validity of the program and procedures as well as on other appropriate considerations. (See also Standard 2.01b and c, Boundaries of Competence.)

(c)   Psychologists retain responsibility for the appropriate application, interpretation, and use of assessment instruments, whether they score and interpret such tests themselves or use automated or other services.

9.10   Explaining Assessment Results

Regardless of whether the scoring and interpretation are done by psychologists, by employees or assistants, or by automated or other outside services, psychologists take reasonable steps to ensure that explanations of results are given to the individual or designated representative unless the nature of the relationship precludes provision of an explanation of results (such as in some organizational consulting, preemployment or security screenings, and forensic evaluations), and this fact has been clearly explained to the person being assessed in advance.

9.11   Maintaining Test Security

The term *test materials* refers to manuals, instruments, protocols, and test questions or stimuli and does not include *test data* as defined in Standard 9.04, Release of Test Data. Psychologists make reasonable efforts to maintain the integrity and security of test materials and other assessment techniques consistent with law and contractual obligations, and in a manner that permits adherence to this Ethics Code.

10. Therapy

10.01   Informed Consent to Therapy

(a)   When obtaining informed consent to therapy as required in Standard 3.10, Informed Consent, psychologists inform clients/patients as early as is feasible in the therapeutic relationship about the nature and anticipated course of therapy, fees, involvement of third parties, and limits of confidentiality and provide sufficient opportunity for the client/patient to ask questions and receive answers. (See also Standards 4.02, Discussing the Limits of Confidentiality, and 6.04, Fees and Financial Arrangements.)

(b)   When obtaining informed consent for treatment for which generally recognized techniques and procedures have not been established, psychologists inform their clients/patients of the developing nature of the treatment, the potential risks involved, alternative treatments that may be available, and the voluntary nature of their participation. (See also Standards 2.01e, Boundaries of Competence, and 3.10, Informed Consent.)

(c)   When the therapist is a trainee and the legal responsibility for the treatment provided resides with the supervisor, the client/patient, as part of the informed consent procedure, is informed that the therapist is in training and is being supervised and is given the name of the supervisor.

10.02   Therapy Involving Couples or Families

(a)   When psychologists agree to provide services to several persons who have a relationship (such as spouses, significant others, or parents and children), they take reasonable steps to clarify at the outset (1) which of the individuals are clients/patients and (2) the relationship the psychologist will have with each person. This clarification includes the psychologist's role and the probable uses of the services provided or the information obtained. (See also Standard 4.02, Discussing the Limits of Confidentiality.)

(b)   If it becomes apparent that psychologists may be called on to perform potentially conflicting roles (such as family therapist and then witness for one party in divorce proceedings), psychologists take reasonable steps to clarify and modify, or withdraw from, roles appropriately. (See also Standard 3.05c, Multiple Relationships.)

10.03 Group Therapy

When psychologists provide services to several persons in a group setting, they describe at the outset the roles and responsibilities of all parties and the limits of confidentiality.

10.04 Providing Therapy to Those Served by Others

In deciding whether to offer or provide services to those already receiving mental health services elsewhere, psychologists carefully consider the treatment issues and the potential client's/patient's welfare. Psychologists discuss these issues with the client/patient or another legally authorized person on behalf of the client/patient in order to minimize the risk of confusion and conflict, consult with the other service providers when appropriate, and proceed with caution and sensitivity to the therapeutic issues.

10.05 Sexual Intimacies With Current Therapy Clients/Patients

Psychologists do not engage in sexual intimacies with current therapy clients/patients.

10.06 Sexual Intimacies With Relatives or Significant Others of Current Therapy Clients/Patients

Psychologists do not engage in sexual intimacies with individuals they know to be close relatives, guardians, or significant others of current clients/patients. Psychologists do not terminate therapy to circumvent this standard.

10.07 Therapy With Former Sexual Partners

Psychologists do not accept as therapy clients/patients persons with whom they have engaged in sexual intimacies.

10.08 Sexual Intimacies With Former Therapy Clients/Patients

(a) Psychologists do not engage in sexual intimacies with former clients/patients for at least two years after cessation or termination of therapy.

(b) Psychologists do not engage in sexual intimacies with former clients/patients even after a two-year interval except in the most unusual circumstances. Psychologists who engage in such activity after the two years following cessation or termination of therapy and of having no sexual contact with the former client/patient bear the burden of demonstrating that there has been no exploitation, in light of all relevant factors, including (1) the amount of time that has passed since therapy terminated; (2) the nature, duration, and intensity of the therapy; (3) the circumstances of termination; (4) the client's/patient's personal history; (5) the client's/patient's current mental status; (6) the likelihood of adverse impact on the client/patient; and (7) any statements or actions made by the therapist during the course of therapy suggesting or inviting the possibility of a posttermination sexual or romantic relationship with the client/patient. (See also Standard 3.05, Multiple Relationships.)

10.09 Interruption of Therapy

When entering into employment or contractual relationships, psychologists make reasonable efforts to provide for orderly and appropriate resolution of responsibility for client/patient care in the event that the employment or contractual relationship ends, with paramount consideration given to the welfare of the client/patient. (See also Standard 3.12, Interruption of Psychological Services.)

10.10 Terminating Therapy

(a) Psychologists terminate therapy when it becomes reasonably clear that the client/patient no longer needs the service, is not likely to benefit, or is being harmed by continued service.

(b) Psychologists may terminate therapy when threatened or otherwise endangered by the client/patient or another person with whom the client/patient has a relationship.

(c) Except where precluded by the actions of clients/patients or third-party payors, prior to termination psychologists provide pretermination counseling and suggest alternative service providers as appropriate.

SUBJECT INDEX